BLOOMSBURY CURRICULUM BASICS

Teaching Primary History

By Matthew Howorth

Online resources accompany this book at: www.bloomsbury.com/BCB-Teaching-History

Please type the URL into your web browser and follow the instructions to access the resources. If you experience any problems, please contact Bloomsbury at: companionwebsite@bloomsbury.com

BLOOMSBURY

LONDON · OXFORD · NEW YORK · NEW DELHI · SYDNEY

BLOOMSBURY EDUCATION
An imprint of Bloomsbury Publishing Plc
50 Bedford Square, London, WC1B 3DP, UK
1385 Broadway, New York, NY 10018, USA
29 Earlsfort Terrace, Dublin 2, Ireland

www.bloomsbury.com

Bloomsbury is a registered trademark of Bloomsbury Publishing Plc

British Library Cataloguing-in-Publication Data
A catalogue record for this book is available from the British Library.

ISBN:
PB 978-1-4729-2062-1
ePub 978-1-4729-2064-5
ePDF 978-1-4729-2063-8

Library of Congress Cataloging-in-Publication Data
A catalog record for this book is available from the Library of Congress.

10 9 8 7 6 5

Typeset by NewGen Knowledge Works (P) Ltd., Chennai, India
Printed and bound in Great Britain by CPI Group (UK) Ltd, Croydon CR0 4YY

This book is produced using paper that is made from wood grown in managed, sustainable
forests. It is natural, renewable and recyclable. The logging and manufacturing processes
conform to the environmental regulations of the country of origin.

To view more of our titles please visit www.bloomsbury.com

Table of Contents

Part 3: Upper Key Stage 2

Introduction

Tackling the new curriculum

The national history curriculum changed in 2013 and there are some exciting new features. Look at it as *exciting* rather than daunting: a challenge for some teachers, who will need to change parts of their schemes of work, but ultimately better for pupils. Much of KS1 has remained as it was, with just a few tweaks and additions, and most KS1 planning can stay relatively the same.

KS2 has a number of changes – mainly, to encourage pupils to learn how to interpret different historical events. People see things from different angles and in different ways; we do now, and we always have done! So rather than filling pupils' heads with dates and facts, encourage them to consider what happened from different points of view: why and how might people see things differently? Encourage them to be inquisitive and to ask questions. Why might somebody think one way, yet somebody else think another? This is where you can use everyday examples and events that happen on a daily basis to reinforce the point.

The Romans, Anglo-Saxons and Vikings all have to be taught in the new curriculum at KS2, giving pupils a chronological grasp of what happened pre-1066. There is still plenty of scope to look at some tasty topics after that, ensuring that there is plenty for pupils to get excited about.

To get a better grasp of what has changed and what has essentially stayed the same, refer to **Bloomsbury Online Resource i.**

Teaching of the new curriculum is split between overview and depth studies, giving teachers some freedom; it also doesn't have to be taught in chronological order, although it may make sense to at least do some of it that way. Also, the local history study can be combined with one of the other topics and made into a depth study. The Tudors have gone from the new curriculum, although they could be looked at in the local history study, or one aspect of Tudor history (for instance the Armada) could be taken on in the 'study of an aspect or theme in British history that extends pupils' chronological knowledge beyond 1066'.

Ideas for medium-term plans and schemes of work

The National Curriculum lists the historical periods that have to be studied, but the suggested topics within each period are just that: *suggestions*. They are non-statutory, so it is possible to have a fair amount of choice in what you teach. If you don't want to teach the suggestion that is made in the National Curriculum, you don't have to, as long as what you do teach satisfies the main period of study.

In terms of what you teach, think about who you are teaching it to; some topics are better grasped and understood in Year 5 or 6 rather than Year 3 or 4, for instance. Think about the subject matter: is it appropriate for the pupils, both in terms of subject matter and level? Would they get more out of it if they were in Year 5 or 6, or is it a topic they can enjoy in Years 3 and 4?

This book will give you plenty of ideas of how to teach the topics, so you can choose how much depth you want to go into. Each one at KS2 will have activities that you can simplify and do with Years 3 and 4, but also plenty of more complicated activities and extension work should you choose to study it with Years 5 and 6. There are also lots of samples of schemes of work and medium-term plans on the internet.

The chapters in this book will provide information and teaching ideas for the vast majority of the topics listed, and those not included in this book are available online at www.bloomsbury.com/BCB-Teaching-History. Also listed online are other topics of study, ideas and resources.

How this book works

This book is split into three main parts: KS1, Lower KS2 and Upper KS2. Each chapter within these sections focuses on the curricular units of study and includes an overview of each topic listed followed by three lesson plans, and also identifies areas for further research for both teachers and pupils including books, films/TV programmes and iPad apps. The lesson plans themselves include starter and plenary activities and extension tasks; there are ideas for school trips, lists of online resources and sample questions. Each chapter concludes with a list of cross-curricular links and a summary of learning and progression.

It is important to challenge pupils to think for themselves, to form their own opinions on events and to interpret them in different ways, rather than blindly following and believing facts that they are told. It is vital that they question motives and reasons behind the decisions and actions people made, looking at the past with an inquisitive nature. Do not recite endless dates for them to learn; of course, some dates are important to remember, but it is much better for pupils to be excited by the past rather than bored by it. The more they realise that people were just like we are today, the more they will understand how and why people behaved in the ways they did.

Make sure pupils understand some basic historical terms:

BC: *Before Christ*; the number of years before Jesus was born. 33 BC would mean 33 years before Christ was born.

AD: *Anno Domini*, Latin for Year of our Lord. AD 45 would be 45 years after the birth of Christ.

Chronology: Arranging dates or events in the order that they happened. So the dates 1914, 1066, 1588, 1939 and 1666 in chronological order would be 1066, 1588, 1666, 1914, 1939.

Sources: In looking at historical evidence, we look at sources. There are different types of sources:

  Primary: Primary sources are from the time of the event in question. They are direct evidence from eye witnesses who were there at the time of the event. A primary source can be in many forms, such as a letter, report, diary, memoir, artefact or work of art. Primary sources can be very useful in understanding how people felt at the time of an event.

Secondary: A secondary source is one that is *not* from the time of the event in question. These sources may be compiled after the writer has studied primary sources, and completed with the benefit of hindsight. However, they may be written after the writer has just studied other secondary sources. A secondary source can be a textbook, painting or any written evidence done after the event. Secondary sources can be very useful and may be well balanced, but it does depend where they got their information. When looking at historical evidence, it is important to consider the *provenance* of the source.

Provenance: The provenance of a source tells us who wrote a source, when they wrote it and for what purpose. We have to look at the provenance of a source to get a better understanding of how useful and reliable it is. A source written by an eyewitness may be biased, depending on what their personal objectives and opinions were at the time.

Example 1: A Royalist who supported Charles I during the Civil War would have a different opinion about the king than a Parliamentarian who fought against him.

Example 2: A painting done in the 1800s showing the murder of the two princes in the Tower would probably be based on the account of their murder written during Tudor times by Thomas More. But Thomas More was a Tudor man, with a high position under Henry VIII's reign. Henry's father, Henry VII (the first of the Tudor monarchs), seized the crown from Richard III, the man generally held responsible for the murder of the two princes. Thomas More would have been about five years old when the two princes disappeared without trace, and More was raised by John Moreton, a man who had fallen out bitterly with Richard III. So would More's account of the disappearance of the two princes be an eyewitness account? No, as he wasn't there when the boys disappeared. Would it be a contemporary account, done at the time? Again, no, because More was a young child in 1483–1485, the period in which the princes probably disappeared. Would it be a reliable account? Maybe, maybe not; as mentioned earlier, More was Lord Chancellor under Henry VIII and his account was written in Tudor times – to write anything different would be akin to writing one's own death warrant. Is it an accurate account? Maybe, we don't know for sure. Is it a useful account? Very, as it is what many people would have thought at the time, and have done since. However, this just shows that caution with which some sources have to be considered. Looking at the provenance will help you decide how useful and reliable a source is.

At the start of each topic, the relevant section from the National Curriculum for Primary History is quoted under the heading 'What does the curriculum say?'. The extract is from DfE, *The National Curriculum in England: Key Stages 1 and 2 Framework documents* (September 2013), pp 188-192. The full document can be found here: www.gov.uk/government/publications/national-curriculum-in-england-primary-curriculum

Part 1:
Key Stage 1

1 Changes within living memory

What does the curriculum say?

- *Pupils should be taught about changes in living memory. Where appropriate, these should be used to reveal aspects of change in national life.*

How homes have changed

In 30 seconds. . .

Homes have changed drastically over the last 500 years – from Tudor times, with wooden houses with no glass or proper chimney; to Victorian houses, with many people living and sleeping in a room; to the modern houses of today. Objects have changed as time has gone on, as has sanitation. The location of homes has also changed, as transport has enabled people to travel further to work each day.

What do I need to know?

Different materials

Many Tudor houses were built of wood; only the rich could afford stone. After the Great Fire of London in 1666, a law was passed that said houses had to be built mainly with stone or bricks. Only the rich had glass in the windows, so draughty holes supplied the ventilation and acted as makeshift chimneys.

Tudor houses

Tudor houses were usually made with wood and wattle and daub, often creating a black-and-white effect that can still be seen today. The timber was bare, and wattle and daub was a mixture of clay, mud or dung smeared over interwoven sticks. Tudor houses can often be recognised by the wooden beams. Although modern houses may copy the Tudor style, they can be easily spotted by looking carefully at how straight the wood is: if it is perfectly straight, it has been cut by a machine and is not Tudor. Some Tudor houses would overhang the street; if the house opposite also overhung, it was possible for the two neighbours to shake hands! The close proximity and material of the houses were both factors that quickened the spread of the Great Fire in 1666. Richer Tudors could afford to have houses made of stone or brick, like Hampton Court Palace, originally built for Thomas Wolsey but generally known for its more famous resident, Henry VIII.

Victorian houses

Victorian times saw the creation of back-to-back houses in long terraces, often in close proximity to the factories where people worked. Bricks were mostly used, with the new railways transporting materials across the country. Heating was provided by a fireplace, with a chimney to get rid of the smoke. Some houses would have an outside toilet, but many shared a communal toilet at the end of each street. Richer people lived in larger villas and had rooms for servants. They would normally have one room, the drawing room, which was kept and used only on special occasions and for entertaining.

Modern houses

Houses are made of all sorts of materials these days and there are lots of different types: detached, semi-detached, terraced, flats, maisonettes, bungalows. They all contain features we take for granted but which would have been unimaginable to our ancestors – glass windows, heating at the touch of a button and more than one bathroom.

Sanitation

Tudor residents threw their rubbish out onto the street, which resulted in filthy towns and cities, full of human waste and festering rubbish. In Victorian terraces the communal toilet at the end of the street caused a health problem if it overflowed into the well that provided the water supply; cholera was a killer and it took a long time, with thousands of deaths, before John Snow made the link between the disease and polluted water. Waste was channelled into the river, which would then be used for drinking water: not a good idea! The Thames used to get very smelly and in 1858 Parliament closed because of the incredible stench from it, known as the Big Stink.

Location, location

In Tudor times, people either walked or, if rich enough, rode a horse; it was not uncommon for people to live their whole life without venturing too far from their village. Horse-drawn carriages in the 1800s enabled people to travel further afield and the transport revolution saw the arrival of the train. In the early 1900s the car was invented, and, as this mode of transport became more affordable over the years, so garages started appearing with houses.

Useful links

http://resources.woodlands-junior.kent.sch.uk/homework/houses.html
www.schoolsnet.com/pls/hot_school/sn_primary.page_pls_unit_detail?x=16180339&p_unit_id=70
www.theschoolrun.com/homework-help/houses-and-homes

Lesson 1 What sorts of homes do people live in today?

Getting started
Ask pupils to get into groups and list all the different types of house they can think of. Then take feedback as a class and see what answers there are.

Class activities
- Following on from the starter activity, explain that people live in different sorts of homes.
- Show some pictures of houses that are different sizes and shapes. Ask pupils to write down how many people they think live in each house and whether the occupants are rich, poor or average in terms of wealth.
- Pupils write a sentence or two explaining their choices.
- Looking at examples, discuss as a group why it is that people live in different sorts of homes.
- Identify things that are of importance to people in choosing somewhere to live: top priorities may include cost, proximity to work, amount of space, the local neighbourhood, whether it has a garden or outside space, nearby schools, etc.
- Why do the pupils live in the homes that they live in? Ask pupils to describe where they live and what is in their local area.

Plenary material
Pupils imagine that they are about to choose their first home. What features are most important to them?

Lesson 2 What can we find out from the outside of homes?

Getting started
Ask pupils to describe what they see as they approach their home. What features are visible?

Class activities
- Recap that in the last lesson the class learnt that there were different sorts of homes, with different features, rooms and surroundings.
- Ask the pupils if all homes look the same from the outside. What differences are there?
- Show pictures of different external features of domestic dwellings.
- Ask the pupils to list the different features they see. What does it tell us about the people who live there?

Plenary material
Pupils match a selection of different people with a list of different houses. They are given basic information about the person or family living in the houses and have to match them up with the correct home.

Lesson 3 How were homes long ago different from homes today?

Getting started

Ask the pupils how old their homes are. What parts or rooms in their home would they not have used or needed 100 years ago?

Class activities

- Show pupils pictures of a Tudor house, a Victorian house and a modern house. Ask them to put the houses in the order in which they were built. How did they make their decision?
- Explain that materials for building houses have changed; show the class a Tudor house and ask the pupils to describe the materials used to build it. Correct answers if necessary.
- Ask pupils if they can think of any problems with using wood. (Wood rots and burns.)
- Hand pupils a picture of a Tudor house. Ask them to label the main features and colour it.

Plenary material

Pupils imagine they live in a Tudor house. How would it differ from a modern house?

Further activities for pupils

- How were homes long ago different from homes today? Compare modern houses with Victorian houses. Look at features of Victorian houses. Identify key features. Identify two or more homes built at different times.
- What would we find inside people's homes a long time ago? Recognise different rooms and household objects. Describe characteristics of objects from long ago.
- How have some objects changed from long ago? Identify the same object but pictured at different times.

Further research for pupils

Show pupils clips from programmes such as *A Man For All Seasons* (Tudor); *Oliver Twist* (Victorian) and *Location, Location, Location* (modern) to contrast and compare houses from different periods.

Cross-curricular links

Art and design: Pupils design an estate agent's brochure to sell a Tudor, Victorian or modern house.
English: Pupils write a series of short diary entries, imagining they are visiting a house in Tudor or Victorian times (or another period). They should describe objects as well as the house itself.
Geography: Pupils research areas in their locality or further afield that have different period properties.
Computing: Pupils prepare a fact file about a house from a particular period.
Science: Pupils investigate objects that symbolise the period of history that they were made in.

Progression

1. Pupils recognise that people live in different styles of houses.
2. Pupils can place houses from different times in chronological order.
3. Pupils can identify different building materials used to build houses.
4. Pupils can identify and name key features from different houses.
5. Pupils can explain why people live in different houses.
6. Pupils can deduce aspects of people's lives from the houses they lived in, across different times.

How seaside holidays have changed

In 30 seconds. . .

Lack of both opportunity and transport severely limited those looking to travel years ago. However, the Industrial Revolution brought first stagecoaches, then trains, which enabled people to get away for a holiday on the beach. The seaside resorts were very popular, with Victorians enjoying musical entertainment, donkey rides and Punch and Judy shows. Most people bathed as they couldn't swim. Today the attraction of a holiday by the sea still remains.

What do I need to know?

Holiday? What holiday?

Holidays as we know them are a relatively recent luxury; it wasn't until 1936 that the Annual Holiday Bill made an annual holiday from work statutory. Before that, the Bank Holiday Act of 1871 added various religious festivals such as Boxing Day and Easter Monday to the days free from work. This came about partly because people would skip the Monday after pay day anyway to have some time off.

Getting out and about

In Tudor times, people rarely travelled for a holiday; rich young men would sometimes go for an adventure overseas, but this was certainly not the norm. Steamers used to transport people in the early 1800s to the seaside, but the Industrial Revolution and trains changed everything. Now, people could afford to travel greater distances to visit the coast. These days, we still use the train, or drive to the seaside.

Things to do

Victorians enjoyed bathing in the sea, although many people could not swim in those days. Other attractions included donkey rides, Punch and Judy shows, various entertainment acts (musical, theatrical, comedy), fish and chips, and ice cream. Rich Victorians would use a bathing machine to provide privacy while getting changed, and bathing costumes looked very different to those today. Piers were built out to sea, to enable tourists to walk further out over the water and breathe in the sea air.

Popular places to go

With trains transporting workers from the cities to the seaside at weekends and on bank holidays, places like Blackpool, Brighton, Southend and Bournemouth became huge attractions.

Useful links

www.everyschool.co.uk/history-key-stage-1-seaside-holidays.html

Lesson 1 What key holidays do we have?

Getting started
In groups, pupils talk about a recent holiday that they have had.

Class activities
- Ask pupils when they have holidays. What period of the year do their holidays tend to be?
- Explain that this was not always the case; people did not always get time away from work each year.
- Ask pupils what days are holidays for everyone. Can they name any religious festivals?
- Investigate what sorts of holidays pupils have and the activities they do. Pupils record their answers.

Plenary material
Show a number of popular holiday destinations. Pupils comment on what they can do there.

Lesson 2 How have seaside holidays changed?

Getting started
Pupils imagine they are going to the seaside for the day. What would they pack?

Class activities
- Look at photographs of modern seaside holidays. What activities are there?
- Show seaside activities from Victorian times and today. Ask pupils to sort them.
- Explain what Victorians used to do at the seaside.

Plenary material
Pupils discuss what they would like to have done in Victorian times at the seaside, and why.

Lesson 3 Similarities and differences

Getting started
Pupils imagine they are going on a Victorian seaside holiday. What would they pack?

Class activities
- Look at various aspects of Victorian seaside holidays (travelling to the beach by train, different activities on the beach, getting changed, type of dress/costume, entertainment) and compare them with what we do today.

Plenary material
Show pictures of various features of seaside holidays, from Victorian times and the present. Pupils hold up a sign saying *past* or *present* to indicate which era the feature is from.

Further activities for pupils

- Watch a presentation (e.g. PowerPoint) of seaside holidays – now and then.

Further research for pupils

www.crickweb.co.uk/ks1history.html
Comparing seaside holidays.
www.britishpathe.com Lots of great clips from years ago, including one from 1898!
Orlando the Marmalade Cat: A Seaside Holiday by Kathleen Hale.

Cross-curricular links

Art and design: Pupils design a poster advertising a Victorian seaside holiday resort.
English: Pupils write a creative account of visiting a Victorian seaside resort for the first time. Describe the day from when you wake up to when you head back from the resort.
Music: Listen to the song 'I do like to be beside the seaside' by John A. Glover-Kind. Print out the lyrics and have a sing along. Encourage pupils to try to write another verse, or their own version.
Drama: Watch a Punch and Judy show. Pupils act it out or write a short script in the same style in a group.
Geography: Get a map of Britain and plot where the major seaside resorts were in Victorian times. On a world map, plot where the major seaside resorts are today.

Progression

1. Pupils understand which parts of the year key holidays take place.
2. Pupils can identify main holiday times in the year and place them in chronological order.
3. Pupils can identify features associated with seaside holidays today.
4. Pupils can identify features associated with seaside holidays in the past.
5. Pupils can distinguish between holidays in the more recent and more distant past.
6. Pupils can sort information into categories that distinguish the present from the past.

Schools in Victorian times

In 30 seconds. . .

In Victorian times not every child went to school, as many could not afford it. The rich would be taught at home by a governess and then the boys would be sent to boarding schools like Eton, Rugby and Harrow, or a grammar school. Poorer families expected their children to work in factories or down mines; the money this work brought back to the household was seen as more important than getting an education. Eventually, schools were set up for poorer children – dame schools, ragged schools and board schools. Later, all children had to go to school and it was made freely available to all.

What do I need to know?

Important dates

1844: Parliament passes a law stating that children have to attend school for six half-days a week.
1870: Education Act sets up school boards to provide and run schools in areas where they are needed.
1880: An Act makes it compulsory for children aged 5–10 to go to school.
1891: Some schools become free and thus available to all.

Types of school

Boarding schools: Schools for rich boys, where they would board (remain all term).
Grammar schools: Day schools.
Dame schools: So called because they were run by women and were free.
Ragged schools: Schools set up in poor areas, so called because of the ragged clothes of those who attended.
Sunday schools: Schools run by churches, where pupils would be taught Bible stories and reading.
Workhouse schools: Some factories provided schools to provide their child workers with a basic education.

Lessons and learning

Children were taught the three Rs (**r**eading, **w**riting and a**r**ithmetic), and religion was also important. Instead of physical education they did 'drill', which involved stretches, running and jumping. Classes could be very big in some schools, and teachers could be helped by monitors, older children who assisted in the teaching.

Equipment

Children would write on a slate, which would be wiped clean when full; this gave rise to the saying 'a clean slate', meaning a fresh start. An abacus was used for counting, and older children used a pen and inkwell in their copybook. Rules were strict when using the copybook, and from this came the phrase 'blot your copybook', referring to a serious error.

Punishments

Punishments in Victorian schools were very different to those today, although parents and especially grandparents may find some of the stories familiar. Any slight indiscretion could be punished with a cane, and those who complained to parents would often get the same punishment at home for misbehaving at school. Lines were also given, as well as detentions, but perhaps the most famous Victorian punishment was wearing a dunce's hat and sitting in the corner, given for slow learners; there was no recognition of learning difficulties.

The teachers

Teachers were generally very strict and they often taught by repetition; work was chanted back and copied down over and over again until it had been memorised. Teaching was a profession often carried out by unmarried women, which is why we still generally refer to female teachers as 'Miss', even if they are married.

Useful links

www.theschoolrun.com/homework-help/victorian-era Contains a short video about being in a Victorian school.
www.bbc.co.uk/schools/primaryhistory/victorian_britain/children_at_school/ Information, photos and videos.
www.victorianschool.co.uk/school.html A company that visits to put on a 'Victorian experience' day at your school, plus a list of Victorian schools to visit if you prefer. They're based in Somerset but will travel nationwide.

Lesson 1 How school has changed

Getting started
Pupils look around the room and discuss what would have existed in Victorian times.

Class activities
- Following on from the starter, pupils fill in a sheet showing various objects from Victorian times and the present day, sorting them into the correct time.
- Explain that many of the features we have now were also represented in Victorian times, but in different ways: heating (fireplace/radiator), counting (abacus/calculator), books (slate/paper), pens (dip pen/fountain pen), board (chalkboard/whiteboard).

Plenary material
Ask how the pupils get to school each day. How many would have been close enough to walk in Victorian times?

Lesson 2 Different types of Victorian schools

Getting started
In groups, pupils discuss and feed back on how many different types of schools they can think of today.

Class activities
- Ask pupils at what age they start school these days. Do they know at what age they are allowed to leave school? Explain how things were different in Victorian times, with children from poorer families expected to work.
- Explain the different types of schools in Victorian times. Do any of these schools still exist today? (Big boarding schools, Sunday schools, etc.)
- Look at how various laws and Acts changed education during Victorian times. Pupils plot on a timeline the most significant ones.

Plenary material
In groups, pupils write down one type of school in Victorian times; other groups take turns asking one question about it, to which the answer is yes or no. After three questions, can they guess the type of school the group was thinking of?

Lesson 3 Life as a Victorian schoolchild

Getting started
Pupils wait outside the classroom and then enter as if they were in a Victorian school. You must keep a straight face and pretend to be as strict as a Victorian teacher. Tell the pupils to all stand behind their chair, say 'Good morning' in unison and then sit down. Throughout the lesson, they must put their hand up and wait to be asked before speaking.

Class activities
- Explain that teachers were very strict in Victorian times. List some of the punishments available to them.
- Use either a slate or a dipping pen and ink pot to give pupils an idea of how a Victorian child worked. Pupils copy out phrases in a Victorian style.

Plenary material
Discuss how the pupils have behaved in the lesson. How would they have fared if they were in a Victorian classroom?

Further activities for pupils

- Compile a list of rules for your school or classroom from Victorian times.
- Watch a presentation (e.g. PowerPoint) that shows the features of a Victorian classroom.
- Make sure the children understand that some subjects taught during Victorian times were the same as today, and some were different.
- Look at your school timetable and compare it to a Victorian timetable.

Further research for pupils

http://resources.woodlands-junior.kent.sch.uk/homework/victorians/children/schools.htm
www.bbc.co.uk/schools/primaryhistory/victorian_britain/victorian_schools/ Contains some key points, photos and video clips.
https://vimeo.com/14694475 First in a series of five video clips on the life of Maggie Johnson. The whole series is worth a look, but this episode shows life in the schoolroom.

Cross-curricular links

Art and design: Make a poster of Victorian rules for the class.
English: Imagine you are a pupil in a Victorian school. Describe what happens to you and your classmates as you go through the day.
Computing: Research the different types of Victorian schools and design a poster describing some of the features of one or more of them.
Geography: Look on a map to see where the big boarding schools were in Victorian times, and find out whether they still exist today.
PE: Perform some Victorian drill exercises in class or the playground: try stretches, jumps and running.

Progression

1. Pupils recognise objects within a school from the present day and Victorian times.
2. Pupils can identify different types of Victorian schools.
3. Pupils understand and can explain reasons why not all children went to school in Victorian times.
4. Pupils can identify features of a Victorian classroom and the subjects they did.
5. Pupils recognise that rules about education changed during the Victorian era.
6. Pupils can compare and contrast their own day at school with that of a Victorian child.

Man's first Moon landing

In 30 seconds. . .

For many many years, people used to gaze up at the stars, wondering what was up there. In the 1960s, there was a race between East and West (the Soviet Union as it was at the time, which we now know as Russia, and the USA) to see who would be the first to go into space. The Soviet Union got there first with Yuri Gagarin in 1961, but it was the USA who landed the first men on the Moon. On 20 July 1969, Neil Armstrong took the first steps by humankind on the Moon's surface, closely followed by Buzz Aldrin.

What do I need to know?

'We choose to go to the Moon in this decade and do the other things, not because they are easy, but because they are hard, because that goal will serve to organise and measure the best of our energies and skills, because that challenge is one that we are willing to accept, one we are unwilling to postpone, and one which we intend to win.'

John F. Kennedy, from a speech delivered on 12 September 1962

Important dates

4 October 1957: The first artificial satellite, *Sputnik 1*, is launched into space by the Soviet Union.
12 April 1961: Yuri Gagarin becomes the first human in outer space.
20 July 1969: Neil Armstrong becomes the first man on the Moon, followed by Buzz Aldrin.

Important people

Yuri Gagarin: First man in space.
Neil Armstrong: First man to step on the Moon.
Buzz Aldrin: Part of Apollo 11 mission and second man on the Moon, after Armstrong.
Michael Collins: Third man in the Apollo 11 crew, who stayed on the ship.
John F. Kennedy: US president who was committed to the Space Race but was assassinated in 1963.
Richard Nixon: US president at the time of Armstrong setting foot on the Moon.

The race for space

There was a race to get the first human into space. The Soviet Union won the race, sending Yuri Gagarin into space, where he also became the first person to orbit the Earth. Both the Soviet Union and the USA worked hard to be the first to send a man to the Moon. US president John F. Kennedy had said, 'I believe that this nation should commit itself to achieving the goal, before this decade is out, of landing a man on the Moon and returning him safely to the Earth.' Neil Armstrong had trained as a pilot in the US Navy and flew in the Korean War before joining the NASA Astronaut Corps in 1962. He first flew into space in 1966 on the *Gemini 8*, and he joined fellow astronauts Buzz Aldrin and Michael Collins on the Apollo 11 mission for the historic trip. But while Armstrong and Aldrin got ready to step onto the Moon, Collins had to stay on board the Command Module (called *Columbia*) to make sure everything ran smoothly.

First steps

The Lunar Module (named *Eagle*), containing Armstrong and Aldrin, landed on the Moon at 4.17pm on 20 July. After reporting back to NASA headquarters, the two astronauts spent the next few hours resting and preparing to take their historic walk. Finally, at 10.56pm, Neil Armstrong climbed down a ladder and took the first steps on the Moon. Video cameras captured the incredible moment, beaming it back to Earth. Armstrong remarked, 'That's one small step for man, one giant leap for mankind.'

Things to do on the Moon

Armstrong and Aldrin spent over two hours exploring the surface of the Moon. During this time, they collected samples, took photos and planted the American flag. They also received a call from the US president, Richard Nixon. On their return to Earth, the three astronauts were kept in quarantine for 17 days in case they had picked up any harmful germs from the Moon.

Useful links

www.activityvillage.co.uk/neil-armstrong Contains lots of printable resources.

Lesson 1 Why go to the Moon?

Getting started
Hand pupils a drawing of Armstrong descending the ladder to take the first step on the Moon. What do they think he might say? Ask them to fill in a speech bubble.

Class activities
- Introduce the topic, and explain the Space Race between the Soviet Union and the USA. Why was the Space Race so important? Pupils should plot on a timeline the important dates in the Space Race.
- Discuss why people wanted to go to the Moon, and the dangers. What is the most exciting thing that pupils can imagine doing in their lifetime if they have the opportunity?
- Show pupils the front pages of newspapers reporting the Moon landing. Using a newspaper template, pupils make their own headlines. **(Bloomsbury Online Resource 1A)**

Plenary material
In groups, one pupil assumes the role of Neil Armstrong and the others ask questions about why he wants to go to the Moon.

Lesson 2 How did they get to the Moon?

Getting started
Split the class into groups and give them a number of different destinations of varying distances (for instance their home, the shops, the beach, another country, another planet). How would they get to each one?

Class activities
- Explain that different people with different jobs were needed within Apollo 11. In small groups of three or four, pupils imagine they are part of Apollo 11 and have to organise themselves to do the jobs needed.
- What problems would they encounter if any of them were unable to do their job?
- How might Michael Collins have felt about having to stay on board *Columbia* to monitor the situation? Encourage pupils to look at it from both sides. **(Bloomsbury Online Resource 1B)**

Plenary material
In groups, pupils have ten seconds to explain why they should be the first to step on a new planet ahead of the rest of their group.

Lesson 3 What happened on the Moon?

Getting started
Pupils imagine landing on a new planet. What might they find or hope to find?

Class activities
- Show the class pictures of footage of Armstrong setting foot on the Moon. How might he be feeling? List the emotions.
- What would the pupils do on the Moon? Hand them a list of objects. Pupils think about and discuss what each would be used for.

Plenary material
If pupils could take one object back from a new planet, what would it be and why?

Further activities for pupils

- Watch a presentation (e.g. PowerPoint) of the landing.
- Put a muddled sequence of events associated with the landing in the correct order.
- Write a newspaper front page describing the Moon landing.
- Debate whether it is right to explore other planets. What do we hope to find?

Further research for pupils

www.youtube.com/ watch?v=RMINSD7MmT4 Footage of the first Moon landing.
www.sciencemuseum.org.uk Lots of space-themed activities.
Moon Landing (pop up) by Richard Platt.
Apollo 11 – Another Great Children's Story Book by Pickatale. An interactive book app that tells the story of the Moon landing from the perspective of Neil Armstrong's imaginary dog.

Cross-curricular links

- **Art and design:** Create a picture or painting of the Moon landing and label it.
- **English:** Write a series of diary entries from various people involved in the Apollo 11 mission.
- **Science:** Research the technology and spacecraft needed to send people to the Moon.
- **Computing:** Create a poster advertising for new astronauts to go on a mission to a new planet.
- **Drama:** In small groups, either write a short script or improvise the Moon landing.

Progression

1. Pupils can say who the first human in space was and where he was from.
2. Pupils can plot on a timeline important events in the Space Race.
3. Pupils can explain what the Space Race was and why it was important.
4. Pupils can identify the crew members of Apollo 11.
5. Pupils can explain the different jobs the astronauts did.
6. Pupils can identify and explain the possible emotions felt by the astronauts.

---

2 Events beyond living memory

What does the curriculum say?

- *Pupils should be taught about events that are that are significant nationally or globally (for example, the Great Fire of London, the first aeroplane flight or events commemorated through festivals or anniversaries).*

Tutankhamun and the discovery of the tomb

In 30 seconds. . .

In 1922, English archaeologist Howard Carter uncovered the tomb of Tutankhamun while digging in the Valley of the Kings in Luxor, Egypt. Tutankhamun was a boy king (pharaoh) who had died as a teenager, and his tomb was very well preserved, full of thousands of objects from the time of his reign. Various theories were put forward explaining Tutankhamun's early death, although experts now think he may have suffered a leg injury, leading to infection, or that he died after contracting malaria. The man responsible for financially supporting the excavation work, Lord Carnarvon, died a year after funding the tomb's discovery and this – along with other mishaps to some people involved in the discovery of the tomb – led to the idea of the curse of the mummy.

What do I need to know?

Death of kings

In Ancient Egypt, pharaohs were buried in pyramids during the Old and Middle Kingdoms (2628–1638 BC), but in the New Kingdom (1504–1069 BC) they were buried in the Valley of the Kings, in tunnels underneath the ground. Many of these tunnels had been found by grave robbers, keen to plunder the treasure that was traditionally buried with a pharaoh. By the time that Howard Carter was digging, it was thought most, if not all, of the tombs in the area of the Valley of the Kings had already been discovered.

Digging deeper

In November 1922, Egyptologist Howard Carter was in his final season digging in Egypt. He had been looking for the tomb of Tutankhamun for years and his sponsor, Lord Carnarvon, had decided that this was to be the last year of searching. Continuing his search in the Valley of the Kings, Carter dug beneath some ancient workmen's huts and found a step cut into the rock. Further digging revealed 16 steps leading to a sealed doorway.

Opening the tomb

After breaking through the doorway, they discovered the unopened tomb of Tutankhamun. There were hundreds of objects in the antechamber and all of them were carefully removed, photographed and sketched. They were then shipped to Cairo. Carter and his team then broke into the burial chamber, where they found a number of shrines. After the fourth, they found the king's sarcophagus. The team did not raise the lid of the coffin for over a year, as they had to preserve all the objects they had removed thus far. When they did, they found a second coffin within and then a third, made of gold. Finally, inside the third coffin, they found the mummified remains of Tutankhamun. He had been found over 3,000 years after his death; the first time that a royal Egyptian mummy had been found untouched since burial.

A boy king

Tutankhamun was around 18 or 19 years old when he died; opinions about his height vary but he was probably between 5 feet 9 inches (175 cm) and 5 feet 11 inches (180 cm) tall. He was the son of Akhenaten and although it is not certain who his mother was, it is generally thought to have been Kira, a lesser wife of Akhenaten. Tutankhamun reigned from when he was around nine years old to when he died. Debates have raged over the years over his death: early reports suggested he was murdered by a blow to his skull; more recent opinions have cited an infection from a broken leg, or malaria. As Tutankhamun had died suddenly, his tomb was prepared in a hurry. Although grave robbers had broken in and taken some smaller objects, most of his tomb had lain untouched for over 3,000 years. After the discovery of the tomb, public interest in Egypt soared and some of the treasures from the tomb went on a world tour. The discovery of his intact tomb eventually made Tutankhamun the most famous pharaoh of all.

Key words

Pharaoh: King or queen of Ancient Egypt.
Pyramid: Stone structures in which Ancient Egyptians buried their pharaohs.
Valley of the Kings: Area in Egypt where many of the pharaohs were buried in underground chambers.
Antechamber: A small room that leads to a bigger one.
Sarcophagus: A stone coffin.

Important dates

c.1342 BC: Tutankhamun born.
c.1333–1324 BC: Tutankhamun reigns.
c.1324 BC: Tutankhamun dies.
AD 1922: The tomb of Tutankhamun is discovered.

Important people

Tutankhamun: Egyptian boy pharaoh.
Howard Carter: English archaeologist who discovered the tomb of Tutankhamun.
Lord Carnarvon: Financially backed the excavation of the tomb.

Useful links

http://history1900s.about.com/od/1920s/a/kingtut.htm
www.eyewitnesstohistory.com/tut.htm Primary account of Carter's discovery.
www.ancientegypt.co.uk/home.html Also suitable for pupils.
www.kingtutone.com

Lesson 1 The burial of kings

Getting started

Place a box or container upside down on your desk. Ask pupils to guess what might be underneath it. Tell them it is something amazing and exciting. All pupils write down what they think it might be.

Class activities

- To prepare, write each of the following words on a scrap of paper, one word per piece of paper: *curse, empty, caught, treasure*. Place each word within an envelope before sealing the envelopes and numbering them from 1–4. Place the set of four envelopes on a desk for one group of pupils. Repeat so you end up with as many sets of words as there are groups (use the same four words for each group).
- In their small groups, pupils assume the role of explorers and have to decide which envelope out of the four their group should open.
- Once they have chosen, explain that grave robbers used to look for the tombs of pharaohs, as they were filled with treasure. Describe how Tutankhamun's tomb had been partially raided and some objects taken, but the main burial chamber was intact until its discovery in 1922.
- Pupils open their chosen envelope and discover their fate as grave robbers!
- Pupils design their own simple board game version of the envelope game. Provide each group with a template that shows six boxes numbered 1–6, and ask them to draw the following in each of the boxes: a piece of treasure in two of the boxes; a bolt of lightning to symbolise a curse; some handcuffs to symbolise being caught. Leave two boxes blank to symbolise that nothing has been found. Pupils play the game by rolling a dice and seeing which square it lands on. Each player can only withstand three curses before they are out of the game. If the dice lands on the picture of the handcuffs, they have to roll again: if they roll an odd number, they have been caught and are out of the game, but if they roll an even number they get away! Players keep a written tally of how many pieces of treasure they have collected, and the player with the most treasure at the end of the game is the winner.

Plenary material

After fielding some guesses from pupils, lift the box used in the starter. Open the scrap of paper and read the words *imagination* and *anticipation*, two great reasons to inspire wonder and learning. Explain what the words mean and tell pupils they will be following this up next lesson.

Lesson 2 What's behind the door?

Getting started

Remind pupils about the plenary of the last lesson. Can they think of a time when they have used their imagination? Write ideas on the board. Then explain again what 'anticipation' means. When have pupils anticipated something (probably something exciting)? Write ideas on the board until they say 'a present', perhaps on a birthday or at Christmas. How did they feel before the surprise was revealed? Did they look at the parcel and wonder what it could be? What characteristics may give a hint as to what the present is? Write answers on the board: 'size', 'shape', 'weight', 'smell', 'feel' and 'sound'.

Class activities

• Tell the pupils to imagine they are in Howard Carter's position as he discovers the tomb in 1922. Explain that no tomb had been found intact before. Show them a picture of Carter next to the door. What is behind it? What is he thinking? Pupils fill in thought bubbles.
• Explain why pharaohs used to be buried along with treasure. Was it just the treasure that excited Carter? What else could he discover by examining the objects he found?

Plenary material

Pupils imagine they are modern archaeologists. If they could discover or dig anything up, what would excite them the most?

Lesson 3 What happened to Tutankhamun?

Getting started

Get pupils thinking with an investigative mindset by giving them a number of images, each showing a different scenario, and asking them to decide what has happened. Draw a grid on the board and write the words *heat, wind, water* and *cold* in the sections. Ask pupils to stick each image on the board in the section they think it should go in, according to the weather type they think was responsible. Suggested scenarios include washing in a crumpled heap below a clothes line, a frozen river, a flooded house, a bush fire, a snowman, and a tornado.

Class activities

• Following on from the starter, pupils are going to investigate what happened to Tutankhamun and how he died. With the pupils in groups or pairs, hand out pieces of paper giving a number of different things found from examining Tutankhamun's remains.
• Ask pupils what they can deduce from the clues. Once the answers have been given, ask pupils individually to fill in a box saying how they think Tutankhamun died.

Plenary material

Groups feed back to the class. One pupil from each group is the spokesperson for the group, explaining how they think Tutankhamun died.

Further activities for pupils

- Watch a presentation (e.g. PowerPoint) of Howard Carter and the discovery of the tomb.
- Watch a short clip on why scarab beetles were buried with pharaohs: www.bbc.co.uk/programmes/p0113lxp
- Investigate what happened to all the objects found in the tomb and where they are now.
- Look at the work of an archaeologist: why is their work so important in finding out about the past?
- Draw a comic strip of Tutankhamun's life, death and discovery. **(Bloomsbury Online Resource 2A)**

Further research for pupils

http://discoveringegypt.com/egyptian-hieroglyphic-writing/hieroglyphic-typewriter/ Pupils can write their own name in hieroglyphics!

www.dkfindout.com/uk/history/ancient-egypt/valley-kings/ Shows the discovery of the tomb and the layout.

www.mummytombs.com/market/books/egyptancient.children.htm A list of books for children on Ancient Egypt.

www.eyewitnesstohistory.com/tut.htm Includes quotes from Howard Carter.

Cross-curricular links

Art and design: Draw the coffin of Tutankhamun.
English: Write a series of diary entries as Howard Carter in 1922.
Religious studies: Investigate the religious beliefs of the Egyptians at the time of Tutankhamun, and discuss why they buried pharaohs with so many objects.
Computing: In groups or pairs, design a presentation (e.g. PowerPoint) of the discovery of the tomb.
Geography: Investigate Ancient Egypt and make a fact file on the region.
Science: Investigate how and why the Egyptians mummified their dead.
Drama: Re-enact the moment when Carter finds the tomb. Write a short script to be recorded for a radio show.

Progression

1. Pupils can explain where the Ancient Egyptians buried their pharaohs.
2. Pupils can identify objects placed in burial tombs with the pharaohs.
3. Pupils can explain the significance of these buried objects.
4. Pupils can explain different reasons why people wanted to discover these tombs.
5. Pupils can identify aspects of Tutankhamun's life from objects found in the tomb.

Mount Vesuvius and the destruction of Pompeii

In 30 seconds. . .

Mount Vesuvius erupted near Pompeii in AD 79, sending tonnes of volcanic ash and gas into the atmosphere. The towns of Pompeii, Herculaneum and Stabiae were most at risk, and although some people fled the area, others did not realise the danger they were in. Pliny the Younger provided an eyewitness account, describing the disaster as it unfolded. The next morning, the pyroclastic flow from Vesuvius destroyed everything in its path and around 16,000 people were killed. Pompeii remained buried until 1748 when archaeologists found it and made casts of the bodies that had been preserved by the volcanic ash.

What do I need to know?

Eruption

Before the eruption, Pompeii was a flourishing Roman city port with a favourable climate, with around 20,000 people living there. There had been an earthquake a few years before in AD 62, with a number of buildings destroyed. There had been signs of activity from the volcano in the days preceding the eruption, but these warnings had gone unheeded as the people didn't realise the danger they were in. Around 1pm on 24 August, AD 79, Mount Vesuvius erupted violently, sending volcanic ash, gas and stones high into the air. The ash fell upon Pompeii and some people tried to flee the area, whereas others stayed where they were.

Who was Pliny the Elder?

There were *two* men called Pliny: Pliny the Elder and Pliny the Younger. Pliny the Elder, a Roman official and poet, was in charge of the fleet at Misenum on the Bay of Naples. When Vesuvius first erupted, he took a boat into the bay to get a closer look. However, he received a letter from Rectina (the wife of a friend of his), who was trapped and fearful for her life. Pliny decided to sail closer to see if he could rescue her and any others. Ash, pumice and blackened stones fell as he neared the shore, but Pliny continued on until he landed at Stabiae. However, the next day, on 25 August, Pliny the Elder died, perhaps due to a cloud of sulphur gas or from a heart attack.

The second day

The first eruption lasted all day and that night, or early the next morning, pyroclastic flows started from Vesuvius. They reached terrifying speeds and burnt everything in their path. The volcanic ash darkened the skies as the day went on, turning day into night, adding to the terror. A toxic cloud of hot ash and gas then descended on Pompeii, killing anyone in its wake and preserving much of the city.

Pliny the Younger

Pliny the Younger, the nephew of Pliny the Elder, lived with his uncle in Misenum, the other side of the Bay of Naples and around 19 miles (30 km) from Vesuvius. He was an eyewitness to the eruption of Mount Vesuvius, and wrote letters to his friend Tacitus, describing what he saw. Pliny the Elder had asked his nephew to accompany him on the boat but Pliny the Younger declined, as he had studies to finish. It would be a decision that probably saved his life. Pliny the Younger went on to describe the huge cloud that descended, the ash and the screams of people who perished in Pompeii.

The fate of Pompeii and its discovery

On the first day, the eruption sent volcanic ash and burning rock down on Pompeii; experts believe that about 1.5 million tonnes of ash and rock shot out of the volcano every second. A huge toxic cloud also descended on Pompeii and the surrounding area. The next day, another explosion resulted in huge pyroclastic flows that covered Pompeii and surrounding cities and towns, killing everyone left. Pompeii remained buried under volcanic ash and pumice until 1595, when workers digging an aqueduct stumbled upon it. However, no further work was done until 1748, when archaeologists rediscovered it. The volcanic ash had preserved much of the city. Casts were made of the bodies, with over 1,000 in total to view, with the victims in the exact pose they died in as they were overcome by fumes or engulfed in the molten flow. Much of what we know about Roman life comes from the remains of Pompeii.

Key words

Stratovolcano: A type of classic cone-shaped volcano.
Pumice: Volcanic rock.
Pyroclastic flow: Fast-moving current of hot gas and rock that flows from a volcano.

Important dates

24 August, AD 79: Mount Vesuvius erupts.
25 August, AD 79: Pliny the Elder dies.

Important people

Pliny the Elder: Official in the Roman court, killed during the eruption.
Pliny the Younger: Nephew of Pliny the Elder; eyewitness to the eruption.
Tacitus: Roman historian and recipient of Pliny the Younger's letters.

Useful links

www.history.com/this-day-in-history/eruption-of-mount-vesuvius-begins
www.youtube.com/watch?v=dY_3ggKg0Bc Animation of the eruption.

Lesson 1 What are natural disasters?

Getting started

In groups, pupils come up with as many natural disasters as they can. Which do they think is the most powerful and dangerous?

Class activities

- Show a short presentation (e.g. PowerPoint) of different natural disasters. Look on a world map and fill in what natural disasters have occurred and where.
- Explain that natural disasters still strike suddenly and cause devastating damage and loss of life; investigate recent examples around the world.

Plenary material

Pupils write down three natural disasters and one key fact about each of them.

Lesson 2 Why live near a volcano?

Getting started

Many people in the world live under threat from natural disasters. Which natural disaster would pupils least like to experience and why?

Class activities

- Pose the class a question: why would people live near a volcano? Let each group feed back their answers.
- Explain that the land around a volcano is very fertile. Why would this be useful? Lead a group discussion.

Plenary material

Pupils consider the question: does the benefit of living near a volcano outweigh the danger? After all, there are millions of people living near Vesuvius today, and it could erupt again.

Lesson 3 Witness to the eruption

Getting started
Show pupils the painting *The Destruction of Pompeii and Herculaneum* by John Martin, 1822. What words and phrases can they find to describe what they see?

Class activities
- Read the class an account from Pliny the Younger. How similar is it to the painting?
- Using the painting and some phrases from Pliny the Younger's letters, pupils write their own eyewitness account of the eruption. Put some key words on the board if necessary to help them.

Plenary material
Pose the following question: why are eyewitness accounts useful?

Further activities for pupils

- What is Pompeii like to visit now?
- Write a series of diary entries from Pliny the Elder and Younger, outlining what they experienced.
- How do artefacts help us? What do they tell us about Roman life? Research, draw and explain.

Further research for pupils

Pompeii…Buried Alive! by Edith Kunhardt and Michael Eagle.
www.eyewitnesstohistory.com/pompeii.htm Contains eyewitness accounts of the eruption by Pliny the Younger.

Cross-curricular links

Art and design: Pupils draw their own interpretation of the eruption.
English: Pupils imagine they were in Pompeii when Vesuvius erupted. Write a creative account.
Computing: Design a fact sheet all about Pompeii then and now.
Geography: Draw on a map of the world the locations of major natural disasters past and present.
Science: Investigate how casts were made of the bodies and how we know what Pompeii looked like.
Drama: Act out the moment when Mount Vesuvius erupts. Include the eyewitnesses.

Progression

1. Pupils can say what happened in Pompeii in AD 79.
2. Pupils can name a number of natural disasters.
3. Pupils understand why people would live near a volcano.
4. Pupils can explain how the people of Pompeii died.
5. Pupils understand how eyewitness accounts help us understand the past.
6. Pupils understand how artefacts help our understanding of past civilisations.

The Battle of Hastings

In 30 seconds. . .

It is 1066. Edward the Confessor dies and four people want his position as king of England – Harold Godwinson; Edgar Atheling; William, Duke of Normandy and Harald Hardrada. Edgar is too young and Harold Godwinson takes the throne. After beating Hardrada, he faces William at Hastings. William has more troops and they are all professional, whereas Harold has his fearsome housecarls but also many fyrds. The Saxons are able to repel early attacks due to a good position on Senlac Hill, but then the Normans pretend to run away, causing the Saxons to chase them, thus leaving their good position. They are slaughtered on the flat ground and Harold dies. William has won and is king of England.

What do I need to know?

The four contenders

With no son to follow as heir, the death of Edward the Confessor saw four people contend the throne. Edgar Atheling, the king's nephew, was too young at 14 to be an effective king, with the Danish, French and Norse threats on the horizon. Instead, the Witenagemot (or Witan for short) proclaimed Edward's brother-in-law Harold Godwinson, the powerful Earl of Wessex, as the new king. However, William, Duke of Normandy believed that he should be the king; indeed, William said that Harold had made a sacred oath on some relics that he would support William. (This was due to William helping Harold in France a few years before.) Meanwhile, Harald Hardrada, the king of Norway, believed that he should be king of England, due to an earlier agreement between the previous king of Norway (Magnus the Good) and the previous king of England before Edward the Confessor (Harthacnut). The agreement was said to be that if Harthacnut died childless, he agreed that Magnus and his descendants would be king. As the uncle of Magnus, Harald believed that Edward the Confessor was an imposter and that the throne was rightfully his. Harold Godwinson, the Saxon king of England, now faced the threat of invasion from both Harald Hardrada and the Vikings, and William and the Normans.

A tricky decision

Unsure of who would invade first, Harold Godwinson found it impossible to be in two places at once; William would be landing on the south coast, whereas Hardrada would arrive further north. Hardrada landed in Yorkshire and teamed up with Tostig, who was Harold Godwinson's exiled brother. Harold Godwinson was faced with a tricky situation: should he stay where he was, waiting for William to invade, but let Harald Hardrada consolidate his position in Yorkshire? Or should he march north to face the Viking king, thus leaving the south coast unprotected against the inevitable invasion by William? Caught in an impossible dilemma, Harold chose to head north to face the immediate threat from Harald Hardrada – perhaps he hoped to beat him and get back before William invaded.

The Battle of Stamford Bridge

Harold Godwinson marched north and caught Hardrada and Tostig completely by surprise. Legend has it that a lone Viking warrior desperately held the bridge against the English before being cut down, as Hardrada rushed to arrange his troops. With many of the Viking troops not wearing their chain mail or helmets, the Saxon army won convincingly, and both Hardrada and Tostig were killed. However, having marched his men 180 miles (290 km) in just four days to face Hardrada, Harold Godwinson now had to turn his weary troops around and march them back south to face William.

Preparing for the Battle of Hastings

William landed on the south coast near Pevensey and prepared for battle. He built the first motte and bailey castle and set fire to houses to make way for his army and also to upset Harold – the area that he was burning was part of Harold's Wessex territory. Confident after beating the Vikings and angry at William setting fire to the villages, Harold marched south, covering almost 200 miles (320 km) in just four days. Arriving at Hastings, Harold's men would have been tired, outnumbered and facing a well-trained and rested army.

King of the hill

Harold took up a good position at the top of Senlac Hill, protected by marshes on the sides. His housecarls and fyrds formed a tight shield wall that repelled William's footsoldiers, archers and cavalry. At this stage, it looked like Harold would prevail if his men held their discipline and stood their ground in this position.

Trick or fluke?

With William's troops failing to break the shield wall, a rumour went around that William had been killed. Looking to spur his men on and quash the rumour, William removed his helmet to show he was still alive. When some of his troops started to run away, part of the Saxon shield wall broke and gave chase. However, when they reached the flat ground, the Normans turned around and slaughtered them. This happened twice more. It was a trick that the Normans had used before in France and it proved to be crucial. With the shield wall weakened, the Norman archers fired again and Harold was hit in the eye, as legend has it. He was also hacked to pieces by knights, losing a leg in the process. With Harold dead, the rest of the Saxon army fled and William was victorious. He had won the Battle of Hastings and the Norman reign had begun.

Why did William win?

There are a number of reasons that are attributed to William winning.

1. Harold and his men were tired after marching up to fight the Vikings then heading back again without resting.
2. William's troops were rested and professional soldiers, whereas Harold had many untrained fyrds who lacked discipline and could not fill the gaps effectively once the shield wall had broken.
3. Harold's men fell for the Norman tactic of retreating, forcing them to leave their strong position on Senlac Hill.

Key words

Witenagemot: An assembly that advised the king; also known as the Witan.
Housecarls: Household troops in service to the king.
Fyrds: Peasants who could be called up to fight; unprofessional soldiers.
Shield wall: Soldiers form a wall of shields, standing together shoulder to shoulder.

Important dates

5 January 1066: Edward the Confessor dies.
6 January 1066: Harold Godwinson is named king.
25 September 1066: Battle of Stamford Bridge. Harald Hardrada is killed.
14 October 1066: Battle of Hastings. Harold Godwinson is killed.

Important people

Edward the Confessor: King of England who died in January 1066, leaving no heir.
Harold Godwinson: Earl of Wessex and a powerful nobleman; later the last Anglo-Saxon king of England. Brother-in-law to Edward.
Edgar Atheling: Nephew of Edward but only a teenager when Edward died.
William, Duke of Normandy: Powerful and experienced French nobleman.
Harald Hardrada: King of Norway, a fearsome and formidable Viking warrior.

Interesting fact

Historians are not certain why the Saxons left their shield wall; the popular theory is that the Normans deliberately ran away, thus luring them from the safety of their position on Senlac Hill. However, they may have just been running away! Another theory is that the fyrds saw an opportunity to win, and in victory they would have been free to help themselves to any booty they could grab: horses, weapons, armour.

Useful links

www.battle1066.com Extensive and excellent site on everything to do with the era.

Lesson 1 Who should be king?

Getting started

Put the class into groups of four or so. Explain that one pupil from each group is going to be given an incredible prize. How do they decide who it shall be? Are they happy to let one of their group claim it or do they all want the winning prize? Explain that this was the case in 1066, when Edward the Confessor died and four men each thought they should be king of England.

Class activities

- Ask the class what qualities were needed to be a good king in medieval times.
- Look at a fact file about each contender: how many of the qualities do they possess?
  (Bloomsbury Online Resource 2B)
- List the good and bad qualities of each contender. Who is the most suitable?
- Take a class vote on who should be king in 1066.

Plenary material

The teacher plays the role of a mystery contender for the throne; the pupils have to deduce which contender the teacher is (by asking closed questions). Then they can split into smaller groups and take turns being a contender, with the rest of their group guessing which they are.

Lesson 2 Waiting for the invasion

Getting started

Split the class into three groups: one group represents Harold Godwinson and his army; the second group represents William, Duke of Normandy and his troops; the third represents Harald Hardrada and his troops. Set Hardrada in the north and William in the south. What problem does Godwinson have? Ask pupils what they would do if they were in charge of Godwinson's force.

Class activities

- Explain that Hardrada landed first and Harold Godwinson marched up to meet him and fight at the Battle of Stamford Bridge. Make a short presentation (e.g. PowerPoint).
- When should William invade? Pupils fill in a sheet about the Battle of Stamford Bridge and William arriving. **(Bloomsbury Online Resource 2C)**

Plenary material

What should Harold Godwinson do? Spilt the class into small groups to decide.

Lesson 3 Should Harold have waited?

Getting started
Show pupils a picture from the Bayeux Tapestry, without telling them what it shows (where William is building a motte and bailey castle and burning houses to make way for his army). In groups, they describe what they can see and what it might mean.

Class activities
- Explain that Harold's men are tired after marching up to fight the Vikings and then winning the battle. Why might it be a good idea to rest before heading south to face William? The pupils fill in speech bubbles of Harold explaining why he should wait.
- Look at what William did when he landed: show the Bayeux Tapestry and annotate it.
- Ask the class why Harold rushed down to face William. Can they think of any reasons? (William burning houses, Harold confident after winning at Stamford Bridge, Harold wanted to catch William before he could prepare properly.)

Plenary material
Pupils imagine they get to ask Harold three questions. What questions would they ask him?

Further activities for pupils

- Discuss: What did Harold need to do to win the Battle of Hastings? What did William need to do?
- How did William trick Harold's men from their strong position, and what happened?
- Look at the three main reasons for William winning, and state which was the most important.
- Colour in your own version of the Bayeux Tapestry and explain what is happening in each picture. **(Bloomsbury Online Resource 2D)**
- Watch the excellent animated version of the Bayeux Tapestry that shows William's preparation and the Battle of Hastings. (Teacher's note: warning – it contains a little bit of blood, so watch it first to ensure it is suitable for younger pupils.) Find it at: **www.youtube.com/watch?v=LtGoBZ4D4_E**

Further research for pupils

Great Events: The Battle of Hastings by Gillian Clements.
Visit: **www.english-heritage.org.uk/visit/places/1066-battle-of-hastings-abbey-and-battlefield/** Battle of Hastings, Abbey and Battlefield. Find it at TN33 0AD.

Cross-curricular links

Art and design: Create a storyboard of the Battle of Hastings. **(Bloomsbury Online Resource 2E)**
English: Imagine you are a soldier in either William's or Harold's army. Write a series of diary entries leading up to the Battle of Hastings.
Religious studies: Investigate the sacred oath that Harold made to William. Should Harold have kept his promise to William?
Computing: Design a poster encouraging people to fight for Harold. Think about slogans or reasons that they should sign up to join you.
Geography: On a map, plot the journey Harold and his men took to fight first Harald Hardrada and then William. Also, look at the layout of the battlefield at Hastings and explain why Harold had such a good position on Senlac Hill.
Drama: Write a short script or improvise the Battle of Hastings.
PE: Split the class into three groups: one each for Hardrada, Godwinson and William. Godwinson's group has to run a distance to fight Hardrada, before running back without a rest to face William. Pupils should appreciate how tired Harold Hardrada's men would have been when fighting at Hastings.

Progression

1. Pupils know who the four contenders for the throne were in 1066.
2. Pupils recognise the good and bad qualities of each contender.
3. Pupils can explain why one of the four contenders is best suited for the job of king.
4. Pupils can put main events into a chronological order.
5. Pupils can explain why Harold faced a dilemma after winning at Stamford Bridge.
6. Pupils understand the strengths and weaknesses of both sides before the Battle of Hastings.
7. Pupils can explain reasons why William won the Battle of Hastings and rank them in order of importance.

The Gunpowder Plot and Bonfire Night

In 30 seconds. . .

James I was king and had upset both the Puritans and Catholics, but it was the Catholics who acted first. They planned to blow up the Houses of Parliament and the King as he opened the new session on 5 November. They rented a cellar underneath Parliament and loaded it with gunpowder, but it was searched the night before and Guy Fawkes, one of the conspirators, was found. After being tortured, he gave the names of his co-conspirators and they were killed instantly or captured. Those that were captured, including Fawkes, were later hanged, drawn and quartered. To commemorate this occasion, effigies of Fawkes are made and bonfires lit on 5 November.

What do I need to know?

Why some people were unhappy

King James I, the son of the Catholic Mary, Queen of Scots, was very different to the previous monarch, Elizabeth I. For a start, he believed in Divine Right, which managed to upset both Catholics and Puritans. Although he had been lenient on Catholics to start with, he soon adopted a more strict approach. Some of them decided that the only way to change things would be to get rid of the king – *permanently*.

The plan of action

Some wealthy Catholics, led by Robert Catesby and Thomas Percy, planned to blow up Parliament when the king opened the new session on 5 November 1605. Their initial plan had been to tunnel under Parliament but this proved too difficult and dangerous. They managed to rent a room under the Houses of Parliament and started loading it up with barrels of gunpowder. Guy Fawkes, a weapons specialist, was in charge of this, having fought as a mercenary in Europe.

What went wrong

One of the conspirators, Francis Tresham, was worried that his brother-in-law, Lord Monteagle, would be killed in the blast. Therefore, he wrote a letter warning him not to attend Parliament on that day. However, Lord Monteagle was suspicious and handed the letter to Robert Cecil. Cecil organised a search of the rooms under Parliament and Guy Fawkes was discovered. At first, Fawkes said his name was John Johnson but after being tortured for three days, including a session on the rack, he confessed all. The co-conspirators were tracked down to a house in Leicestershire and many were killed in a gunfight. Those that were captured alive were taken back to London to be executed.

Was it a conspiracy?

There are some people who think that the government may have known about the plot. Consider:

- All gunpowder was kept under lock and key in the Tower of London.
- How would they get over 60 barrels of gunpowder into the cellar without being seen?
- When the conspirators were found in a country house, the order was shoot to kill, not capture. When one of the main men was killed, the man who shot him was paid handsomely.
- The man who rented the cellar mysteriously died just before the conspirators needed it.
- Francis Tresham, who sent the letter of warning, died under strange circumstances, probably poisoned.

How we remember it today

Each year on 5 November we still commemorate the Gunpowder Plot with bonfires and fireworks. This is to remember how close the Catholic plotters came to killing the king and changing the course of British history.

Key words

Divine Right: A belief that a king is answerable only to God and thus men have to obey their monarch.
Treason: Crime against the monarch, punishable by execution.
Catholic: Christians who follow the Pope in Rome.
Protestant: Christians who split from the Catholic Church, in *protest* at how it was being run.
Protestantism: Movement started by Martin Luther in 1517.
Puritan: Strict type of Protestant (the word can refer to the Church or behaviour).
Hanged, drawn and quartered: Penalty for treason for a non-noble/royal. First the person was hanged until half-dead, then their insides were drawn out while still alive, before being chopped into four pieces.

Important dates

4 November 1605: Guy Fawkes is discovered by troops in a cellar under the Houses of Parliament.
8 November 1605: After being tortured, Guy Fawkes confesses and gives the names of his co-conspirators.

Important people

James I: King at the time; son of Mary, Queen of Scots and the father to the future King Charles I.
Robert Catesby: One of the main conspirators who thought up the plot.
Thomas Percy: Another of the main conspirators who thought up the plot.
Guy Fawkes: The conspirator who was caught in the cellar below Parliament.
Robert Cecil: Chief minister to King James I.
Francis Tresham: The conspirator who sent a letter to Lord Monteagle.
Lord Monteagle: Brother-in-law to Francis Tresham, who passed the letter to Robert Cecil.

Useful links

www.bbc.co.uk/history/the_gunpowder_plot BBC documentary on the Gunpowder Plot.
www.theschoolrun.com/homework-help/guy-fawkes-and-bonfire-night

Lesson 1 We all love 5 November!

Getting started
Get the class to list the sorts of activities that are done on Bonfire Night.

Class activities
- Show the class a picture of a typical Bonfire Night.
- The pupils label a picture of what happens on Bonfire Night.

Plenary material
In groups, pupils discuss dangers of bonfires, sparklers and fireworks; then feed back.

Lesson 2 Kill the king!

Getting started
Ask the class why we have Bonfire Night. Record answers on the board.

Class activities
- Explain how important religion was in the seventeenth century by briefly describing the religious rollercoaster that took place after Henry VIII split from the Pope and made himself Head of the Church in England. His son Edward VI subsequently made the country Protestant; Edward was succeeded by Mary I, who restored Catholicism and the Pope, burning almost 300 Protestants during her reign; followed by Elizabeth I, who changed it back to Protestant again.
- Introduce James I and why he was so unpopular. Ask the class what options the Puritans and Catholics had if they were so unhappy with James I; explain that some Puritans sailed to America on the *Mayflower* to start a new life. Did they have to kill the king?
- Pupils fill in speech bubbles of what a Puritan and Catholic might say about James I.

Plenary material
The class imagine they were Catholics back in 1605 and vote on what they would do.

Lesson 3 Keeping it secret

Getting started
Ask the class what the plotters would need in order to be successful – not just a successful explosion, but keeping the plot secret.

Class activities
- Ask the class what the best way is to keep a secret: the fewer people that know, the better.
- Show a picture of the plotters. How easy would it be to keep a secret between eight people? Split the class into groups: in Group A, two of the group are told a secret that they have to keep from the other half who don't know it. In Group B, all but two of the pupils are told a secret that they have to keep hidden from the other two. Which group lasts longest?
- Explain what happened and how the plotters got caught. Look at what was in the letter to Lord Monteagle; what does it mean? Pupils rewrite the letter in modern-day language.

Plenary material
Was the letter written by Francis Tresham or somebody else? Discuss.

Further activities for pupils

- Imagine what would have happened if the plotters had been successful.
- Why do we still celebrate Bonfire Night? Does it have any importance or relevance today?

Further research for pupils

www.youtube.com/watch?v=fMNOnYxhpOY Horrible Histories take on the Gunpowder Plot.
Beginning History: The Gunpowder Plot by Liz Gogerly: A wonderful book for children aged 5–7.

Cross-curricular links

Art and design: Create a storyboard of the Gunpowder Plot and what happened.
(Bloomsbury Online Resource 2F)
English: Write a series of diary entries as Guy Fawkes or another one of the plotters.
Religious studies: Investigate the main differences between Catholics and Protestants.
Computing: Design a poster to get Catholics to join the plot against King James.
Geography: Print out a map of the Houses of Parliament and label key features and landmarks. Compare it with a map from the present day.
Science: Investigate how gunpowder is made and what it was first used for.
Drama: Write a short script or improvise Guy Fawkes and the Gunpowder Plot. Dramatise the trial.
Music: Invent a new song or rhyme along the lines of 'Remember, remember the Fifth of November, gunpowder, treason and plot. . .'

Progression

1. Pupils can state what happens on Bonfire Night.
2. Pupils can state what event is remembered when we celebrate Bonfire Night.
3. Pupils understand there was a plot against the king.
4. Pupils understand why the Catholics were upset with James.
5. Pupils understand that both Catholics and Puritans were upset with James.
6. Pupils can state what the Catholics hoped to achieve with the plot.
7. Pupils can suggest reasons why Fawkes was guilty but also why it may have been a conspiracy.

The Great Fire of London

In 30 seconds...

London in 1666 had been ravaged by the plague the year before, when another disaster struck: the wooden houses and narrow streets were a natural fire hazard and a fire in a baker's on Pudding Lane started the Fire of London. The initial lack of action from the mayor, combined with a strong wind and poor fire-fighting techniques, resulted in a huge blaze that raged for four days. A change in wind direction and the king's authorisation of firebreaks saw it eventually die out, but at a huge cost. Much of London was destroyed and many thousands were made homeless. Sir Christopher Wren planned a new London but people built where their homes had been before, thwarting his plans, although he managed to construct St Paul's Cathedral.

What do I need to know?

An accident waiting to happen

London had barely recovered from the Great Plague in 1665, which had decimated the population, killing thousands. Fire had been a constant threat to a city that was constructed mostly in wood; a law had been passed years before, stating that new buildings should be made out of brick or stone but not many paid attention as it was too expensive. Houses were also built very close together; in some cases, it was possible to reach over and shake hands with the person in the house opposite due to their proximity. So any fire would quickly spread from one building to another.

The fire starts

The fire started in Pudding Lane on 2 September 1666 in the house of Thomas Farriner, who was the king's baker. Although the exact cause is not known, it was probably due to an oven not being extinguished fully. The blaze started to spread downstairs and when the baker woke up to discover a fire in his house, he managed to get out. However, one of his maids was not so fortunate and became the first casualty. The Lord Mayor of London, Thomas Bloodworth, was stirred from his sleep and informed about the fire. However, he had enjoyed a pleasurable meal and consumed a large quantity of wine the night before and so was unimpressed at having been awoken for such a seemingly trivial matter; there were lots of fires in London and this one didn't seem remarkable in any way. Grumbling at his servant, he went back to bed. By the morning, the fire had got worse and could no longer be ignored.

The fire spreads

The fire continued to burn and move east in the strong wind, destroying everything in its path. Along Thames Street, there were warehouses full of tar, brandy, sugar and other flammable material that burnt fiercely. People waited until the last moment before fleeing their houses, hoping that their home would miraculously be spared. Some had boats and charged a fortune for people to put their belongings from their homes on the boats and escape down the Thames. The Lord Mayor, Thomas Bloodworth, knew by now that he had a major fire to deal with. One possible way to help stop it spreading would have been to pull down houses in its path to create a firebreak, but he was unwilling to do so; insurance did not cover loss by fire in those days – if he had commissioned houses to be pulled down, then he would have been responsible for the cost of rebuilding them, and Bloodworth did not want to have to pay for that. His error would end up costing the city far, far more. Bloodworth was replaced in charge by none other than King Charles II, and also his brother James, the Duke of York, who oversaw much of the work in person.

How the fire stopped

After five days, on 7 September, the wind changed direction. Up until that point, there was a fear that the fire would spread across the Thames and then set fire to the south of London but the change in wind direction took it away. Running out of material to burn as it was now going back on the path it had come, the fire died down and went out, aided by a wind that had finally died down.

Why was the fire so bad?

There are a number of reasons why the fire spread so fast and destroyed so much:

- It had been a hot summer so buildings were very dry.
- The wind was very strong, helping to spread the fire.
- The reaction of the Lord Mayor when he first heard about the fire was poor.
- The fire-fighting methods of the day were rather ineffective; there was no organised fire brigade.
- The Thames was low after a long, hot summer; this made collecting water difficult.
- The water pumps around London Bridge burnt and couldn't be used.
- People didn't authorise firebreaks early on as they were not covered by insurance. It took an order from the King to make it happen, promising to rebuild any houses destroyed by gunpowder to help stop the spread of the fire.

Rebuilding London

The fire caused a huge amount of damage; over 13,000 houses and around 87 churches were destroyed and between 70,000 and 100,000 people were left homeless. Sir Christopher Wren drew up plans for a new London, based on the wide piazza-style streets of Paris, but many Londoners rebuilt their homes before this could happen. However, Wren did manage to rebuild St Paul's Cathedral and a monument was built on the site where the fire first started. Despite the ferocity of the fire, not many people perished; estimates vary between five and eight in total. The fire did manage to destroy some of the disgusting rat-infested slums around London and new buildings had to be made out of stone or brick. Also, each parish had to provide their own fire-fighting equipment.

Important dates

2 September 1666: The fire starts in Pudding Lane.
5 September 1666: The fire finally goes out.

Important people

Charles II: The King of England in 1666.
James, Duke of York: The king's brother and future king.
Thomas Farriner: The king's baker, whose house the fire started in.
Thomas Bloodworth: Lord Mayor of London.
Samuel Pepys: Royal official who kept a diary during the Great Plague and Fire of London, providing eyewitness accounts of the disasters.
Sir Christopher Wren: Famous architect who designed St Paul's Cathedral.
John Evelyn: Famous architect who drew up plans for a new London.

Useful links

www.theschoolrun.com/homework-help/great-fire-london Useful information, facts and some pictures to look at.
www.everyschool.co.uk/history-key-stage-1-fire-of-london.html Quite a few different sites on the Fire of London, including interactive material.

Lesson 1 Where did it start?

Getting started
How did fires start back in the Stuart era? Talk about open fires for heat and light and the dangers associated with them.

Class activities
- Describe the types of houses in London in 1666. Ask the class why London might be at risk from a fire.
- Show a map of London circa 1666. Ask pupils to find Pudding Lane, Fish Street and Thames Street and label them.

Plenary material
Ask pupils why the Lord Mayor wasn't overly bothered when he first heard about the fire. Pupils fill in a speech bubble of what he might say.

Lesson 2 How do we know what happened?

Getting started
Ask pupils to explain an incident they saw with their own eyes yesterday. Explain this is called an eyewitness account. Why are these useful?

Class activities
- Explain that Samuel Pepys was an eyewitness to the fire and wrote a diary of what he saw and experienced. Read through some of his diary extracts.
- What do the diary extracts tell us about the fire and how people reacted? Pupils work in groups to find interesting phrases and words and then feed back.

Plenary material
Pupils work in pairs: one tells the other a fact or description they can remember from Pepys' diary. They then switch roles and repeat the exercise.

Lesson 3 The fire spreads

Getting started
Get pupils to line up, within arm's length of each other. Tell the pupil at one end they represent the fire starting in the baker's house. The other pupils represent other Stuart houses. The first pupil raises their arm and touches the pupil next to them, who makes a sound like a fire and then does the same. Watch how quickly the fire spreads to all the houses!

Class activities
- Give pupils a list of factors that contributed to the fire spreading so quickly, and read through them. **(Bloomsbury Online Resource 2G)**
- Ask pupils to put the list in order of importance and to explain their most important reason.

Plenary material
Take a class vote on the most and least important reason for the fire spreading so quickly.

Further activities for pupils

- Look at houses from the seventeenth century and the material used. Why did the fire spread so fast?
- Investigate fire-fighting techniques in 1666. How effective were they?
- Explore reasons why the fire eventually stopped. Was it just down to luck?
- How did they rebuild London?

Further research for pupils

iPad: *Charlie and the Great Fire of London*, ABC Melody Editions, an interactive book.
www.themonument.info Visit the Monument, London.

Cross-curricular links

Art and design: Draw or paint a picture of the raging fire.
English: Imagine you are an eyewitness to the fire. Write a series of diary entries like Samuel Pepys.
Computing: Design a poster showing how they fought fires in the seventeenth century.
Geography: Plot the course of the fire on a map of seventeenth-century London.
Drama: Write a short script showing the main events of the Fire of London.

Progression

1. Pupils know what city the fire started in.
2. Pupils know where the fire started.
3. Pupils understand why the fire spread so quickly.
4. Pupils understand what an eyewitness account is and why they are useful.
5. Pupils can explain why the fire was difficult to put out.
6. Pupils understand the changes to London that happened after the fire.

The first aeroplane flight

In 30 seconds. . .

People had long looked at the sky and wished to fly and there were many futile attempts to build the first aeroplane. Brothers Orville and Wilbur Wright owned a bicycle shop and were scientific enthusiasts. They began experimenting with their own designs for flight and moved to Kitty Hawk in North Carolina, USA, to test out their research. On 17 December 1903, Orville flew for 120 feet (36.6 metres) at a height of 20 feet (6 metres), with the flight lasting 12 seconds. This was the first powered flight in a heavier-than-air plane.

What do I need to know?

'If you are looking for perfect safety, you will do well to sit on a fence and watch the birds; but if you really wish to learn, you must mount a machine and become acquainted with its tricks by actual trial.'

Wilbur Wright

'After a while they shook hands, and we couldn't help notice how they held on to each other's hand, sort o'like they hated to let go; like two folks parting who weren't sure they'd ever see each other again.'

John T. Daniels, Kitty Hawk lifesaving crewman, recalling the moments before the first flight.

Fascination with flight

Humankind had long gazed at the birds and wished to emulate them. As far back as the fifteenth century, inventor and artist Leonardo da Vinci had made sketches and instructions for an aerial screw that worked like a helicopter, although he never tested his invention. He also designed a flying machine, the 'ornithopter', with a 33-foot (10-metre) wingspan! Although humans had flown before the Wright brothers made their historic flight, it had been in airships filled with gas that was lighter than air: Frenchman Henri Gifford was the first to fly in an airship in 1852. This design was taken a step further by the German Count Ferdinand von Zeppelin, who completed his first airship in 1900. These airships would go on to be used in the First World War as the infamous Zeppelins, huge crafts that could drop bombs. However, the race was still on to invent and successfully test a powered flight in a heavier-than-air plane. This would happen in America.

Early life

Orville and Wilbur Wright had always been fascinated by mechanics and Orville in particular spent hours fiddling with mechanical objects and investigating how they worked. With the bicycle craze sweeping the nation from England, the Wright brothers opened their own bike shop. At first they repaired them, their knowledge of mechanics standing them in good stead. Later, they designed their own bicycles and started selling them. This knowledge of how bicycles worked certainly helped them as they started to investigate the possibility of flying: both planes and bikes needed to share the same lightweight design and balance, as well as other attributes.

Designing a plane

By the late 1890s, there were many people racing to be the first to make a powered flight. Some engineers focused on the problem of the engine; others used models to perfect their ideas; the rest experimented with gliders. The Wright brothers used this last approach, trying out their ideas with a series of gliders, having been inspired by the glider pioneer Otto Lilienthal. They built their glider and travelled to Kitty Hawk in North Carolina to test it. Kitty Hawk was perfect for flying a glider, as it had wide, open spaces and strong winds. They spent a long time designing the wings, working on 'wing warping', where the wings were at slightly different angles; this made one of them rise and the plane bank, so they needed to steer it to compensate. After their first glider performed reasonably successfully in 1900, they returned to Kitty Hawk in 1901 but encountered problems with their new glider. After conducting more aeronautical research, the brothers returned in 1902 with a much improved glider; this was due to it having a movable rudder as opposed to a fixed one. The Wright brothers now had an aircraft that they could control.

Making history

Their 1902 glider was very successful and the brothers made hundreds of flights, often gliding over 600 feet (183 metres). Spurred on by this, they set about building a plane with an engine and two propellers. Due to its size and weight, the plane had to be launched down a 60-foot (18-metre) track. On 14 December, they were ready to go. The brothers tossed a coin to see who would be the pilot, with Wilbur winning. However, 40 feet (12 metres) down the track, the plane lurched and stalled, and the damage was enough to postpone what would be the maiden flight. Three days later on 17 December, Orville took the controls and they tried again. This time, the plane flew 120 feet (36.6 metres) and was airborne for 12 seconds – the first time a human being had flown. They took turns making a number of flights that day, with Wilbur managing to stay in the air for 59 seconds, travelling 852 feet (260 metres).

Key words

Kitty Hawk: The town in North Carolina, USA, where the Wright brothers made their first flight.
The Wright *Flyer*: The first heavier-than-air powered aircraft.

Important dates

1867: Wilbur Wright is born.
1871: Orville Wright is born.
1892: The brothers open a bike shop.
1900: They test their first glider successfully at Kitty Hawk.
1901: They encounter problems with their new glider.
1902: They use a glider with a movable rudder, making it a controllable plane.
1903: They make the first powered flight in a heavier-than-air plane (17 December).

Important people

Wilbur Wright (1867–1912): Older of the Wright brothers. Wilbur won the coin toss to make the first flight, but the plane was damaged before it could take off. After his brother had made the first flight, Wilbur had another turn, staying in the air for almost a minute, travelling 852 feet. Wilbur later travelled to Europe in 1908 to sell his aeroplanes, where he and his brother became minor celebrities. After returning to the USA, he became a successful businessman before dying of typhoid fever in 1912.

Orville Wright (1871–1948): Younger brother of Wilbur. Orville made the first flight in a heavier-than-air powered aircraft. He followed his brother to Europe and also became a successful businessman. However, he lacked the business brain of Wilbur and sold the Wright company in 1915 a few years after Wilbur had died. Orville died in 1948 after having a second heart attack.

Leonardo da Vinci (1452–1519): Famous Italian painter, sculptor, draftsman (someone who makes detailed technical drawings) and inventor. Although da Vinci is most famous for painting the *Mona Lisa* and *The Last Supper*, he also made around 13,000 pages of notes and drawings; these included designs for flying machines, war machines, architectural, plant and anatomical drawings. A true Renaissance genius, da Vinci's ideas for a flying machine were designed around 400 years before the Wright brothers made their first flight.

Otto Lilienthal (1848–1896): German aviator who made a number of successful flights in gliders. A civil engineer, the success of Lilienthal's flights inspired the Wright brothers and got many others interested in flight.

Interesting fact

Although they were pioneering inventors, neither Wilbur nor Orville attended college – but their sister Katharine did.

Useful links

www.da-vinci-inventions.com/flying-machine.aspx
www.britannica.com/EBchecked/topic/210191/history-of-flight
https://airandspace.si.edu/exhibitions/wright-brothers/online/who/1895/biketoflight.cfm
http://airandspace.si.edu/explore-and-learn/topics/wright-brothers.cfm

---

Lesson 1 The importance of flying

Getting started
Ask pupils what places they have been to on holiday or where they would like to go. Get them to list how they would travel to that destination. Do most of them fly?

Class activities
- Give pupils a series of pictures of aeroplanes from different time periods, and a separate series of dates of the years these planes were produced. Jumble up the dates and ask them to label each plane with the date they think it was made.
- Go through the answers on the board, explaining how planes gradually developed from the Wright brothers' plane to the jets of today.
- On a timeline on the board, plot the development of planes to see the chronological order.

Plenary material
Which of the planes would pupils most like to fly? Take feedback.

Lesson 2 Learning to fly

Getting started
Show pupils the design of da Vinci's ornithopter. Can they guess when it was made?

Class activities
- Pupils imagine they live in the fifteenth century in the time of Leonardo da Vinci. They have to design their own way of enabling humans to fly without using modern mechanics or motors. Ask them to label their designs.
- Explain that people had tried for many years to find a method to fly but had been unsuccessful. Why had this not succeeded? Look at early designs, with wings strapped to arms, and explain that the human body is too heavy to fly with wings – unless of course they are giant wings, in which case they would be too heavy for the person to use!

Plenary material
What materials do the pupils need to add to their designs to enable them to fly? Take feedback.

Lesson 3 The first aeroplane flight

Getting started
Ask pupils how a bicycle is similar to the Wright *Flyer*; give them hints until they understand the concept of balance and a lightweight material.

Class activities
- Hand out templates for making a paper plane or demonstrate slowly. Pupils each make a plane and test its flight.
- Experiment with reusable adhesive tack and paperclips to alter the balance of the plane and record any differences.
- Pupils sketch their design and comment on how weight affected the flight.

Plenary material
Show pupils a picture of the Wright *Flyer*; ask them to point out characteristics, and similarities and differences to a modern plane.

Further activities for pupils

- Investigate early pioneers of flight before the Wright brothers.
- Watch footage of the first aeroplane flight (see Further research for pupils).
- Investigate famous flyers who followed on after the Wright brothers.
- Investigate how technology allowed planes to evolve. Compare the Wright *Flyer* with a *Sopwith Camel*, a 15-year difference.

Further research for pupils

www.youtube.com/watch?v=T5o-fhBKf8Y Clip from British Pathé.
The Wright Brothers and the Science of Flight: The Explosion Zone by Ian Graham and David Antram.
TV series: *Animated Hero Classics: The Wright Brothers*

Cross-curricular links

Art and design: Design and colour your own plane.
English: Imagine you are one of the Wright brothers. Write a series of diary entries, finishing with how you feel making the first flight.
Computing: Investigate the early pioneers of flight, including von Zeppelin.
Geography: Find Kitty Hawk on a map and label some other historical moments in aviation and flights made (Amy Johnson etc.).
Science: Compare the wing of the Kitty Hawk to that of a bird. Are there any similarities?
Drama: Create a radio/TV show reporting live from Kitty Hawk as the Wright Brothers make their first flight. Include reporters in the studio and in Kitty Hawk, the brothers, sceptics, witnesses etc. Record it and play it back to the class.

Progression

1. Pupils know who made the first aeroplane flight.
2. Pupils understand that planes have developed over the years.
3. Pupils can identify planes from different eras.
4. Pupils can identify planes from different eras and recognise what makes them different.
5. Pupils understand the importance of balance in a plane.
6. Pupils can explain the problems with early flight and how the Wright brothers managed to overcome them and be successful.

First World War remembrance

In 30 seconds. . .

The First World War, also known as World War One or the Great War, lasted from 1914 –1918. Although tension had been building in Europe for some time, the assassination of Archduke Franz Ferdinand triggered hostilities. During the conflict, much of it fought in France, around 10 million men died. The horrendous loss of life and the sheer size, scale and nature of the conflict caused it to be remembered on the anniversary of the day that the guns finally fell silent. Each year on the eleventh hour of the eleventh day of the eleventh month (Armistice day), a service of remembrance is held; not just for the First World War, but for all conflicts since then that have claimed the lives of both combatants and civilians.

What do I need to know?

Why the First World War started

Tension had been building in Europe for many years: countries raced to build up their territories around the world and were jealous of those which had a larger empire than them. They were also allied to other countries, meaning they would defend one another in a conflict. All it needed was a spark to set it off, and this happened in Sarajavo on 28 June 1914. Archduke Franz Ferdinand and his wife Sophie were visiting Sarajevo and were the target for a group of assassins; the Serbs were unhappy at the way Austria–Hungary was ruling them, and Ferdinand was next in line to the throne. The group of assassins was called the Black Hand gang and, after a number of failed attempts, Gavrilo Princip shot Ferdinand and his wife at point-blank range. Austria–Hungary declared war on Serbia. Serbia was an ally of Russia, which therefore declared war on Austria–Hungary. Germany was an ally of Austria–Hungary and therefore declared war on Russia. France was an ally of Russia, so declared war on Germany. Germany invaded Belgium, which was neutral. This act, combined with a treaty with France, caused Britain to declare war on Germany. The first global war had started.

The two sides

Although there were many more countries involved in the First World War, the two main alliances in 1914 were known as the Triple Alliance (Germany, Austria–Hungary and Italy) and the Triple Entente (Britain, France and Russia). These alliances had stood since the 1800s. Italy entered the war *against* Austria–Hungary in 1915.

Why it was so bad

Initially intended to be a fast-moving war, the failure of the Schlieffen Plan for a quick German victory meant that the two sides dug in and it became a static war; the onus was on removing the other side and it became a war of attrition. Technology had progressed to create new weapons that resulted in huge losses for both sides. Artillery shells, machine guns, snipers, gas, planes and the nature of trench warfare meant that men lost their lives on a scale never seen before. Pals battalions had been set up to encourage friends and colleagues to join up and fight together but these were disbanded after villages lost all their young men. In Britain, conscription was brought in to bolster flagging volunteer numbers. The war finally ended on 11 November 1918. By the time the last shot was fired, over 10 million soldiers had died, and 7 million civilians.

How do we know what it was like?

The technological advancements that made terrible weapons possible also gave us cameras, so we are able to see photographs and footage of the war. The footage looks grainy and of poor quality compared to the high definition we are used to today, but it gives us an understanding of what conditions were like for the soldiers. There are primary accounts of those who fought in the war, as well as countless books written by historians. There were many wonderful poets who fought during the war, with many of them dying, and their words provide a haunting picture of life on the Western Front.

Why we remember

Every year on 11 November, Remembrance Day, we remember those who died during the First World War with a remembrance service. We remember those who made the ultimate sacrifice, those who had loves, hopes and dreams dashed and ruined. It is also a time for remembering all those who have died in wars since then, combatants and civilians. During the service, passages are read that remind us of the sacrifices made in the war. The poppy is worn as a symbol of remembrance and poems are often read that were written by soldiers who fought in the trenches. The 'last post' is sounded, followed by a two-minute silence at 11am.

Key words

The Great War: Another name for the First World War, often used before the Second World War.
Armstice: An agreement between opposing forces to stop fighting.
Ally: A country that is united with another country with an agreement.

Important dates

1914:
28 June: Archduke Franz Ferdinand is assassinated.
4 August: Britain declares war on Germany.
19 October: First Battle of Ypres

1915:
22 April: Second Battle of Ypres. Germany uses poison gas for the first time.

1916:
21 February: Battle of Verdun; Germany inflicts terrible losses on France.
25 May: Conscription is passed as law in Britain.
1 July: The Battle of the Somme starts. On the first day, there are about 60,000 casualties, dead or wounded, making it the worst day in British military history.

1917:
6 April: USA declares war on Germany.
29 October: German sailors' mutiny.
11 November: Armistice Day. The Peace Treaty is signed and comes into effect at 11am.

Important people

Archduke Franz Ferdinand: Heir to the Austro-Hungarian throne. His assassination was the trigger that started the First World War.

Gavrilo Princip: Member of Serbian terrorist group 'The Black Hand' who shot and killed Franz Ferdinand and his wife Sophie.

Franz Josef: Emperor of Austria and king of Hungary.

George V: King of the United Kingdom.

Kaiser Wilhelm II: Kaiser of Germany.

Tsar Nicholas II: Tsar of Russia.

Wilfred Owen (1893–1918): Owen wrote many famous poems during the war, including 'Dulce et Decorum Est' and 'Anthem for Doomed Youth.' Undergoing treatment for shell shock, he met Siegfried Sassoon, one of his literary heroes, who encouraged Owen to convey his experiences of the war through poetry. Now regarded as one of the greatest poets from the First World War, he was virtually unknown when he was killed – just a week before the war ended.

Siegfried Sassoon (1886–1967): Sassoon earned the nickname 'Mad Jack' for his daring and almost suicidal bravery during the war, resulting in being awarded a number of medals, among them the Military Cross. Sassoon was already a famous writer and poet during the war, and met other poets including Wilfred Owen and Robert Graves when convalescing in England after suffering from shell shock. Famous works include 'The General' and 'Suicide in the Trenches.'

John McCrae (1872–1918): Canadian doctor whose most famous work is 'In Flanders Fields,' inspired by the death of his close friend Alexis Helmer. He died of pneumonia and meningitis in 1918.

Rupert Brooke (1887–1915): Brooke was a published poet before the war broke out. His poems often displayed the optimism felt at the start of the war, in stark contrast to those of Sassoon. Brooke's most famous poem was probably 'The Soldier.' He died in 1915 from an infection caused by a mosquito bite.

Interesting fact

Poppies often grow on ground that has been disturbed, and the terrain in France and Belgium during the First World War was ravaged by shellfire. A Canadian soldier, John McCrae, visited a friend's grave in Ypres in Belgium in 1915 (an area known as Flanders) and noticed all the poppies that had grown in the fields. He wrote his famous poem 'In Flanders Fields', which is often read out at remembrance services.

Useful links

http://firstworldwar.com/index.htm

Lesson 1 Why do we wear poppies?

Getting started
Show the class a picture of a poppy. Ask pupils to discuss in groups why we wear a poppy.

Class activities
- Explain that the money raised by the selling of poppies goes to servicemen and women across the Commonwealth. Tell pupils why we use poppies, and read the first verse of 'In Flanders Fields', asking them to comment on the language: which words and phrases stand out and why.
- Pupils make their own poppies and stick them under the first two lines of the poem.

Plenary material
In groups, pupils come up with an acrostic using the word 'poppy'.

Lesson 2 Allies argy-bargy!

Getting started
Ask pupils to discuss in groups if they have ever stood up for one of their friends. When they feed back, ask if by doing so this has led to any other problem.

Class activities
- Explain the term 'allies' and how they work (they agree to support and help each other, to back one another up).
- Hand out the list of allies from 1914. **(Bloomsbury Online Resource 2H)**
- Pupils cut them out and sort them into the two sides.
- Pupils colour in a map of Europe to see who opposed whom at the start of the First World War.

Plenary material
Do pupils think that allies should stand up for each other if it means having to go to war? They discuss in groups and feed back to the class.

Lesson 3 Life in the trenches

Getting started
Ask pupils to imagine digging a big hole and living in it all year. Discuss and feed back to the class.

Class activities
- Show the class a picture of a trench. How would it feel to be in the trench?
- Identify main features of a trench and explain that rats and lice lived with the soldiers. Explain that there was the constant danger of shellfire or even a gas attack.
- Pupils imagine they are a soldier in a trench and write about how it would feel.

Plenary material
Split pupils into small groups. Give each group a set of folded pieces of paper: each scrap of paper has one feature of a trench written on it. Pupils pick one piece of paper and describe what the trench feature is without saying the name. The group have to guess the feature.

Further activities for pupils

- Analyse at some famous First World War poems.
- Create and illustrate a timeline of the First World War.

Further research for pupils

Horrible Histories videos.
The Story of the First World War for Children 1914–1918 by John Malam, suitable for ages 7 and above.
iPad: *WW1 For Kids*, suitable for ages 9–11.

Cross-curricular links

Art and design: Design a poster encouraging men to sign up to fight in 1914.
English: Write a series of diary entries, imagining you are a soldier in the trenches.
Computing: Create a fact file on the different weapons used in the First World War.
Geography: Make a list of all the countries that fought in the First World War.
Science: Investigate new machines that were invented between 1914 and 1918.
Drama: Write a short playscript set in a trench, and perform and record it.
Music: Listen to *The Last Post* and describe emotions as you hear the music.
PE: Have a game of Trenchball. **(Bloomsbury Online Resource 21)**

Progression

1. Pupils know when the First World War started and ended.
2. Pupils can explain why we have a remembrance service.
3. Pupils can list some of the features of a remembrance service.
4. Pupils can explain what happens in a remembrance service.

3 The lives of significant individuals in the past

What does the curriculum say?

- *Pupils should study the lives of individuals who have contributed to national and international achievements. Some should be used to compare aspects of life in different periods (for example, Elizabeth I and Queen Victoria, Christopher Columbus and Neil Armstrong, William Caxton and Tim Berners-Lee, Pieter Bruegel the Elder and LS Lowry, Rosa Parks and Emily Davison, Mary Seacole and/or Florence Nightingale and Edith Cavell).*

Florence Nightingale, Mary Seacole and Edith Cavell

In 30 seconds...

All three of these women dedicated their lives to nursing, training other nurses and helping the sick and wounded. Florence Nightingale travelled to Crimea in the 1850s to work in a hospital near the front line, where she was shocked at the insanitary conditions that accounted for many soldiers dying. Mary Seacole's frequent travels had given her a wealth of knowledge that she used to treat people on the front line in Crimea, tending soldiers from both sides. Edith Cavell was a nurse during the First World War who also tended soldiers from both sides in her hospital in Belgium before being shot by the Germans for helping Allied soldiers (soldiers who fought on the same side as Britain, France and Russia against Germany and their allies) to escape into Holland.

What do I need to know?

Florence Nightingale

Florence was born in Florence, Italy, and was named after her birthplace. She was born into a wealthy family, and had what she termed 'calls from God' to reduce human suffering. Deciding that nursing would be a good way to serve both humankind and God, Florence was dismayed to find that her parents disapproved of the idea of their daughter nursing, as they felt it was below a woman of her stature in society. However, Florence would not give in, and eventually her parents relented. Florence then travelled to Kaiserswerth in Germany to train as a nurse in 1851. In 1853, now back in London, she took up the post of Superintendent of the Institution for Sick Gentlewomen (governesses) in Distressed Circumstances, but she felt that her skills would be better used to train nurses as opposed to efficiently running and improving the hospital. She would soon get her opportunity.

War broke out between Russia and Turkey in 1853 and the next year Britain and France, allies of Turkey, joined in. Reports in the London *Times* newspaper by William Howard Russell of conditions in the hospitals shocked people back in England. Florence travelled to the Barrack Hospital in Scutari (a few miles from the front line in the Crimean Peninsula), where she received a frosty welcome. Florence was shocked at the dirty and crowded conditions, poor medical supplies and lack of effective care or treatment. She organised the wards to be cleaned, equipment to be bought and the patients cared for more efficiently. She also stressed the importance of cleanliness, bathing and changing the dressings, which became standard practice. Wandering the wards during the night gave her the nickname 'Lady with the Lamp'. When the war ended, Florence returned to England in 1856. The Nightingale Fund was established and enough money was raised to open the Nightingale School of Nursing at St Thomas' Hospital in London in 1860. Florence also wrote the influential *Notes on Nursing*, which outlined ways of caring for people at home and is still in print today. When she died in 1910, her parents refused a state funeral and burial in Westminster Abbey and, after a service at St Paul's Cathedral, she was buried in East Wellow, Hampshire.

Why we remember Florence Nightingale

Florence Nightingale showed that with clean conditions and trained staff, patients got better more quickly. She invented modern nursing and her work still influences medical professionals today.

Mary Seacole

Mary was born in Kingston, Jamaica, to a Jamaican mother and a Scottish father. Her mother ran a boarding house in Kingston and Mary used to help her nurse sick people. Mary's mother believed in the use of herbal medicine and Mary helped treat people with cholera and yellow fever. Mary travelled extensively, to Cuba, the Bahamas, Panama and Haiti, picking up local medical knowledge. She used this knowledge in conjunction with European medical ideas. When Britain joined the Crimean War against Russia in 1854, Mary decided that she wanted to help, but it would not be that straightforward. It has been argued by some historians that Mary was more of a businesswoman than a nurse, as she had no formal training and spent most of her time selling goods to officers and soldiers, rather than tending sick or injured soldiers. Opinion is still divided.

In 1854, Mary went to London and asked the British army to help; they refused, as there was a general disapproval of women being involved in medicine. However, after conditions in the Crimea were publicised in the London *Times*, this hard line softened and Florence Nightingale headed over to Scutari. Mary applied to join Florence Nightingale's team, but was refused; perhaps because of her age (50), ethnicity or lack of formal medical training. This did not deter Mary, so she made her own way to the Crimea, at her own expense. After visiting Florence Nightingale in Scutari, Mary set up the British Hotel (called 'Mrs Seacole's hut' by others), where she sold food and drink to soldiers, also running a canteen. She would also patrol close to the battlefield with two mules: one would be carrying food and drink and the other medical supplies. Mary tended the wounded and would help any soldier she found injured, from either side. After the war, Mary returned to England and wrote a book chronicling her adventures; it became a bestseller and she lived in some comfort until she died in 1881.

Why we remember Mary Seacole

Mary Seacole tended those who were sick or injured regardless of which side they were on; she saw them all as human beings that needed help. As a woman of mixed race, she had to combat two prejudices of the time and was also a successful businesswoman.

Edith Cavell

Born in Norfolk in 1865, Edith joined the nursing profession when she was 20, before moving to Belgium where she was appointed the matron of the Berkendael Medical Institute in Brussels in 1907. When war broke out in 1914 and Germany invaded Belgium, the Berkendael Institute was converted into a hospital to look after soldiers of all nationalities. When the First World War started, the clinic was changed to a Red Cross Hospital and soldiers from both sides received treatment. When Germany took Brussels, Edith would treat Germans and captured Allied soldiers, who would then be prisoners of war. However, Edith helped injured Allied soldiers escape from Belgium into neutral Holland, a process that was extremely risky – the penalty for helping prisoners escape was death. Yet Edith was undaunted and continued to be involved in moving Allied soldiers across the border. Two of the team who helped organise the escapes were captured and questioned, and eventually the Germans came to interrogate Edith. Edith told her interrogators the truth and was put into solitary confinement to await the death sentence. Edith was calm on the day of her execution, even forgiving those who were about to kill her. She was buried at Norwich Cathedral and there is a statue commemorating her near Trafalgar Square in London.

Why we remember Edith Cavell

Edith Cavell cared for all soldiers, whether they were from Britain, France, Germany or Austria; to her, they were injured men that needed helping. Some people did not think that she should be helping soldiers from the other side, but to her, where they came from did not matter; they were injured and needed aid. Her death was used by the government for propaganda purposes against the Germans and there are many statues remembering her. The Cavell Nurses' Trust was set up in 1917, a charity that helps nurses and midwives who have been injured or are sick.

Important dates

Florence Nightingale:
1820: Florence Nightingale is born (12 May).
1837: Florence feels God is calling her to work and starts to take an interest in nursing.
1851: Florence starts her nursing training in Germany.
1853: She becomes superintendent for a hospital in Harley Street.
1854: Britain enters the Crimean War. Florence observes the horrific conditions in the field hospital at Scutari.
1860: She establishes the Nightingale Training School for nurses at St Thomas' Hospital.
1860: Her ideas on nursing, *Notes on Nursing*, is published. It is still influential today.
1910: Florence Nightingale dies (13 August).

Mary Seacole:
1805: Mary Seacole is born (23 November).
1857: Mary publishes her memoirs, *The Wonderful Adventures of Mrs Seacole in Many Lands*.

Edith Cavell:
1865: Edith Cavell is born (4 December).
1915: Edith Cavell is shot by firing squad (12 October).

Important people

Florence Nightingale (1820–1910): Pioneering nurse who travelled to Scutari to treat injured British soldiers during the Crimean War. Appalled by the filthy conditions in the hospitals, Nightingale showed that improved medical care, cleanliness and sanitation could save the lives of many soldiers.

Mary Seacole (1805–1881): Seacole practised in herbal medicine before making her own way to the Crimea after being refused permission to join Florence Nightingale's team. She sold goods at the British Hotel and tended to injured soldiers from both sides.

Edith Cavell (1865–1915): Worked at a Red Cross hospital in Brussels during the First World War, treating injured soldiers of all nationalities. After helping Allied soldiers escape into neutral Holland, Cavell was arrested and shot by the Germans.

William Howard Russell (1821–1907): Journalist who covered the Crimean War for the *Times*. His vivid descriptions of the fighting, the plight of the soldiers and the terrible medical conditions shocked people back in Britain. His account of the Battle of Balaclava in 1854 inspired Alfred Lord Tennyson to write his famous poem, 'Charge of the Light Brigade'.

Useful links

www.maryseacole.info/?Introduction:Florence_Nightingale_and_Mary_Seacole_Timeline
http://historysheroes.e2bn.org/hero/timeline/86 Detailed site about Edith Cavell.
www.theschoolrun.com/homework-help/mary-seacole Lots of easy-to-digest facts about Mary Seacole.
http://spartacus-educational.com/REseacole.htm Primary sources on Mary Seacole.
http://www.nationalarchives.gov.uk/education/resources/florence-nightingale/ Contains teaching ideas on Florence Nightingale.

Lesson 1 What makes us famous?

Getting started
Ask pupils to imagine they are famous when they are older and known throughout the world. Tell them to write down what it is they would like to be famous for. For now, they are to keep their answers a secret.

Class activities
- Show the class a picture of a celebrity actor or sportsperson. Discuss why they are famous – is it for something that benefits others, or just their own personal life?
- Explain that the pupils are going to be looking at people who were famous for helping others. How might we do this today?
- Explain that the three people they are going to study were famous for helping others during a time of war. Pupils write down the sorts of things that they could do to help in wartime.

Plenary material
Put some categories of fame on the board and ask pupils to feed back the answer they wrote for the starter activity. How many are selfless acts and how many for more personal gain?

Lesson 2 What did Florence Nightingale improve?

Getting started

Show a picture of a hospital in Scutari. Pupils discuss in groups how it is different to a hospital today.

Class activities

- Look at the picture of the hospital in Scutari. Explain that Florence Nightingale was unhappy at the conditions. Why were so many soldiers dying?
- What sorts of things would Florence Nightingale have liked to have changed or improved? If pupils need help, offer them some key words like *beds, clean dressings, clean floors, proper treatment* etc. to stimulate discussion.
- Look at a picture of Florence Nightingale with a lamp. What key features and changes can the pupils see?

Plenary material

Pupils order the following factors in order of importance for saving lives: proper treatment; clean dressings; clean areas and beds.

Lesson 3 A welcome sight on the battlefield

Getting started

Explain that you are going to be looking at the life of somebody who helped soldiers in a war. What sort of help or things would soldiers need? (Not just treatment for wounds, but food, drink, luxuries, clothes, etc.) Feed back in small groups.

Class activities

- Explain that Mary Seacole was born in Jamaica. How would she have travelled to England in Victorian times, and what would the journey have been like?
- Look at Mary's early life and how she learnt to use herbal medicines. Do we still use herbal medicines today?
- Explain that Mary wanted to go to the Crimea. What reasons would she have for doing this? Pupils fill in speech bubbles.
- Pupils fill in what could be in the British Hotel and who it would be for.
  (Bloomsbury Online Resource 3A)

Plenary material

Pupils imagine they are in another country. What item of food or drink would they miss the most if it was no longer available?

Further activities for pupils

- Construct a timeline for both Florence Nightingale and Mary Seacole. What are their similarities and differences?
- Was Edith Cavell a hero or a traitor for helping soldiers of both sides?
- Look at how Florence Nightingale improved medical care and conditions.
- Write a letter as Florence Nightingale to the London *Times*, saying what life is like in Scutari and the sorts of supplies you need to make the hospital better.

Further research for pupils

Florence Nightingale by Lucy Lethbridge and Karen Donnelly.
Comparing People from the Past: Mary Seacole, Florence Nightingale and Edith Cavell, by Nick Hunter.

Cross-curricular links

Art and design: Design a 'thank you' card from a soldier written to Florence Nightingale, Mary Seacole or Edith Cavell, expressing gratitude for helping them.
English: Write a story about when Mary Seacole met Florence Nightingale and what they may have said to each other.
Computing: Create a fact file about Florence Nightingale, Mary Seacole or Edith Cavell.
Art and design: Design a poster showing the poor conditions in Scutari before Florence Nightingale.
Geography: Trace the travels of Mary Seacole. See where the Crimea is and find out more about the area where the war was fought.
Science: Investigate the cause of cholera, why it was so dangerous and how it was treated.
Drama: Write and record a TV/radio-style news programme about one of the women; include reporters describing where the women work and the conditions/dangers.

Progression

1. Pupils understand who Florence Nightingale, Mary Seacole and Edith Cavell were.
2. Pupils understand that conditions were not very good at the start of the Crimean War.
3. Pupils can explain how Florence Nightingale improved conditions for injured soldiers.
4. Pupils recognise why Mary Seacole went to the Crimea.
5. Pupils can explain why Edith Cavell helped all wounded soldiers.
6. Pupils can list the three women in order of importance, and explain their decision.

Queen Elizabeth I and Queen Victoria

In 30 seconds. . .

Elizabeth I and Queen Victoria have often been hailed as Britian's greatest monarchs, and had a lot in common; both were women occupying a role that usually saw a male monarch and both their reigns saw the country grow in strength and military might. Elizabeth oversaw the birth of the British Empire as the country started to flex its muscles in Europe, and the empire reached its impressive peak under Victoria, when it was said that the sun never set on the British Empire. Both queens had a long and successful reign and opinion is divided as to which of the two has been Britian's best monarch.

Queen Elizabeth I

> 'I have already joined myself in marriage to a husband, namely the kingdom of England.'
>
> *Elizabeth to Parliament*

What do I need to know?

Tough Tudor times

Elizabeth was born in 1533, the daughter of Henry VIII and his second wife, Anne Boleyn. When Henry died in 1547, Elizabeth's half-brother Edward, Henry's only son, became king. A Protestant like Elizabeth, Edward was a sickly child and, after turning the country Protestant, died of tuberculosis in 1553. Mary, Henry's eldest child and the daughter of his first wife, Catherine of Aragon, was next in line and turned the country back to Catholicism, burning almost 300 Protestants in the process. There were a number of plots against Mary, and Elizabeth was even put in the Tower of London, suspected of involvement in Wyatt's Rebellion. Wyatt's plan had been to replace Mary on the throne with Elizabeth, but Elizabeth protested her innocence and Wyatt refused to implicate her even under torture. When Mary died in 1558, Elizabeth became queen at the age of 25, but she had many problems to deal with and it looked unlikely that she would survive for long.

Factors Elizabeth had to deal with

Religion

England had been unsettled, with Henry splitting from the Pope, Edward turning England Protestant and then Mary turning it back to Catholic. In a time when to openly flaunt religious views against the monarch could result in being burnt at the stake, people in England probably didn't know what to think. Elizabeth, a Protestant, opted for a middle road; she tolerated Puritans and Catholics as long as they attended church each week and didn't cause trouble. She famously said, 'I have no desire to make windows into men's souls', and had the title Supreme Governor of the Church in England, a more ambiguous and therefore less problematic title than Henry VIII had, as Head of the Church in England.

The poor

There was the constant problem of poor people and beggars. This was not a new problem and was due to a number of factors: poor harvests, high food prices, enclosure and sheep farming. Elizabeth got Parliament to pass a law that meant beggars had to go back to the parish where they were born. They were also split into different categories of poor – deserving or undeserving. The deserving poor, who included orphans, wounded soldiers and the old, would be helped. The undeserving poor would be whipped and punished. The Poor Laws passed under Elizabeth formed the basis of how the government addressed the issue of poverty for over 200 years.

Her image

In the days when the strength of a monarch was judged by how they looked in portraits, it was important that Elizabeth always looked strong and in command in the pictures she had painted. She also went on many progresses, travelling around the country, often on horseback, so her subjects could see their queen.

Mary, Queen of Scots

Elizabeth's cousin, Mary, Queen of Scots, led a colourful life; she had fled from Scotland to England, looking to her cousin for sanctuary after a tempestuous series of events that involved three husbands, two murders and having a child. Elizabeth was worried that Mary had her eye on the throne of England, and put her under house arrest for 19 years. Mary became the focal point for Catholic plots and after Elizabeth's spymaster, Walsingham, found evidence that Mary was involved in the Babington Plot in 1586, Elizabeth reluctantly signed Mary's death warrant. In doing so, she was sentencing to death her own cousin, an anointed queen and a Catholic with powerful friends; but as long as Mary was alive, plots against Elizabeth would continue. Elizabeth's ministers were very relieved and hurried to Fotheringhay, where Mary was held, with the warrant before Elizabeth could change her mind again.

The Spanish Armada

The execution of Mary, Queen of Scots was the trigger for the Spanish Armada, but trouble had been brewing for a long time. Elizabeth had refused Philip II's hand in marriage and was a Protestant as well; he wanted to bring England back to the Catholic fold. Elizabeth had sent troops to help the Protestant Dutch fight against the Spanish invaders, partly in support of a fellow Protestant nation and partly to stop Spain gaining a colony so close to England that would then provide an ideal launch pad for an invasion. Elizabeth's privateer Francis Drake had raided Spanish ships laden with treasure on their way back from the New World, relieving them of their precious cargo. This infuriated Philip even more, who thought Drake was like a ghost as he could never be found! After Drake had sailed into Cadiz harbour in Spain and set some ships on fire, delaying the Armada for a year, it finally set off in 1588 under the guidance of the Duke of Medina Sidonia after the original admiral, Santa Cruz, had died. Philip II's plan was simple: avoid any battle at sea unless absolutely necessary, and sail to pick up the Duke of Parma and 30,000 experienced Spanish troops stationed in the Netherlands and ferry them across the channel to England. After being sighted, with beacons being lit around the coast to warn of the Armada's arrival, the English navy set off in pursuit. The fast and agile English ships fought at a distance using cannons, while the Spanish ships, full of soldiers, tried to get

close in order to use grappling hooks to board the English ships. Despite firing lots of cannon balls, little damage was done to the Spanish. Unable to stop the Spanish fleet, the English followed them as the Spanish sailed on in a giant crescent shape. When the Spanish moored at Calais, word had only just got through to the Duke of Parma and it would take weeks to assemble his fighting force and get them to where the Armada was moored. The English did not know this, but they knew they had to scatter or destroy the Spanish ships before the Duke of Parma and his army arrived.

Spain's defeat

Drake came up with a plan and set eight ships on fire and let them drift towards the moored Armada; the Spanish thought the fireships were hellburners, a fearsome weapon that they had experienced firsthand at the Siege of Antwerp in 1585. In their panic to avoid the fireships, the Spanish cut their anchors and headed back out to sea. Now at the mercy of the wind, they drifted before meeting the English ships in the Battle of Gravelines. This major battle of the Spanish Armada saw little damage done to either side, with the Spanish ships heading steadily north with the wind; this took them away from where Parma was, so eventually Medina Sidonia decided to head back to Spain, his invasion plans in tatters. With the wind against them and the English ships preventing them going back the way they had come, the Spanish had to go the long way back around Scotland and Ireland. Storms and gales sank many of their ships, and those who were shipwrecked in Ireland were either killed or held for ransom if they were nobles. Although more armadas were planned, none came as close to invading England as the one in 1588. As Spain's power and dominance as a European power started to fade, England's started to grow into the empire that would eventually peak under Queen Victoria's rule.

Marriage

Although there were rumours that Elizabeth may marry, she never did. She certainly had favourites, including Robert Dudley and the Earl of Essex, Robert Devereux, but she stayed single until her death in 1603. Elizabeth had named James Stuart, the son of Mary, Queen of Scots, as her heir.

Achievements

Elizabeth reigned for 45 years and provided some stability after the short reigns of Edward and Mary. She defeated a number of Catholic plots and provided a religion that satisfied many, as well as creating the Anglican Church. She defeated the Spanish Armada, brought some control over Ireland, and her Poor Laws lasted over 200 years. However, she failed to tackle the economic and social problems which dogged the 1590s. Puritans and Catholics continued to be a threat; as she did not marry, the Tudor line finished with her; her relationship with Parliament would lead to bigger problems with the Stuart kings that followed.

Famous Tudor travellers

Sir Francis Drake and Sir Walter Raleigh were two famous sailors and explorers who made a name for themselves during Elizabeth's reign. Drake was the first Englishman to circumnavigate the globe, and also sailed to Africa to join the slave trade with his cousin John Hawkins. After being ambushed by the Spanish and seeing many of his men killed, Drake developed an enduring hatred of the Spanish. As a privateer, he raided their treasure ships and was second in command of the English navy in 1588 when the Spanish Armada was launched. Raleigh was credited with introducing the potato and tobacco to England, although this is debated. He was looked upon fondly by Elizabeth, although she did fall out with him when he married Elizabeth Throckmorton, one of her maids of honour, without telling Elizabeth. However, she forgave him and he continued to explore the seas, searching for the famous city of El Dorado. He fell from grace during the reign of Elizabeth's successor, James I, and was eventually executed.

Key words

Protestant: Those who split from the Catholic Church in *protest* at how it was being run.
Catholic: Those who follow the Pope as head of their Church.
Puritan: Strict Protestants who wanted to purify the Church.
Enclosure: Land fenced in to graze sheep.
Hellburners: Boats filled with gunpowder and metal, used by Dutch rebels against the Spanish to great effect.
Privateer: Privately owned ship, sanctioned by Elizabeth to hassle and prey on Spanish ships, stealing their cargo. Or, as the Spanish understandably called these privateers, pirates!

Important dates

1533: Elizabeth is born at Greenwich (7 September).
1558: Elizabeth becomes Queen.
1587: Mary, Queen of Scots is executed at Fotheringhay.
1588: The Spanish Armada is sent.
1603: Elizabeth I dies.

Important people

Henry VIII: Powerful Tudor King and father of Elizabeth I.
Catherine of Aragon: Henry's first wife, mother of Mary Tudor.
Mary Tudor: Catholic half-sister of Elizabeth, also known as 'Bloody Mary'.
Anne Boleyn: Elizabeth's mother, Henry's second wife; executed.
Jane Seymour: Henry's third and favourite wife.
Mary, Queen of Scots: Mary Stuart, Catholic queen and Elizabeth's cousin.
Sir Francis Walsingham: Elizabeth's spymaster.
Sir William Cecil: Lord Burghley, Elizabeth's trusted chief minister.
Philip II: Powerful Catholic king of Spain; was married to Mary Tudor and sent the Armada to conquer England.
James Stuart: Son of Mary, Queen of Scots, whom Elizabeth named as heir.

Useful links

www.elizabethi.org Site dedicated to Elizabeth I.
www.bbc.co.uk/schools/primaryhistory/famouspeople/elizabeth_i/

Queen Victoria

What do I need to know?

Victoria became queen at just 18 years old, when her uncle, King William IV, died; she reigned for 64 years. She married her cousin, Prince Albert of Saxe-Coburg, when she was 21, and they had nine children. The Victorian Age is named after her, and anything dating from the 1800s is referred to as Victorian. She was queen during a time when Britain was expanding its empire to become the most powerful global force, and her country was at the centre of the Industrial Revolution.

Early life

Victoria's father, the fourth son of King George III, died when she was just a baby. The king died a few days afterwards and her uncle became George IV. When he died without a legitimate heir, Victoria was next in line and she was informed of his death when she was just 18 years old. Victoria did not go to school when she was younger, instead being educated at home by a governess. She met her German cousin Albert when she was 17 and married him a few years later in 1840.

Family life

Victorians often had large families and Queen Victoria was no different; she had nine children with Albert, five boys and four girls. Many of her children married into royalty and by the time of her Diamond Jubilee in 1897, Victoria had 29 grandchildren.

Time for a change

The 1800s saw a continuing exodus from rural areas to the cities; the Industrial Revolution was in full swing and things would never be the same again. Machines took the place of manual labour and old rural ways of making a living could not compete with the new machines. Before the Industrial Revolution, many people lived and worked under the domestic system (also known as the cottage industry). This involved working on the land and fields and making textiles at home.

Machines and factories

The Industrial Revolution saw the invention of new machines that could do the work of many people. The demand for goods was high, both at home and abroad, as the British Empire grew and grew. This vast empire provided not only a market for goods but also a source of raw materials unavailable in Britain. Huge cotton and wool mills sprang up and people flocked to the cities to get jobs. Work was long and hard in the factories, and accidents were commonplace. Without any safety regulations or insurance, those injured would lose their job and resort to begging in the street. Children were also sent to work in the factories and life was hard and dangerous for them; they earned less than adults, worked long hours under strict conditions and would be fined and beaten for the slightest infraction.

Travel

There was a transport revolution as well, as bumpy and hazardous roads were transformed by turnpike trusts which repaired and maintained them. In the 1700s, most people got from one place to another by walking but, later on, horse-drawn carriages were common. Canals sprang up all over the place, with many people racing to get involved in canal mania, looking to make their fortune. A lot of them lost all their money, but canals ruled for a time, making it possible to transport fragile goods along manmade waterways, and they were dug all over the country. The arrival of the train signalled the end of the canals, as trains could transport more goods at a much faster pace, as well as ensuring that perishable goods arrived in good condition. They also transported people, although third-class carriages were not for the faint-hearted! The trains also saw seaside towns and resorts grow as people started to take holidays and travel to the coastal areas for a break. Railways were made by navvies, tough men who led a hard and dangerous life digging out countless tonnes of rock and dirt to make way for the tracks. Not everyone welcomed the arrival of the train, afraid that it would ruin the countryside and scare wildlife, but there was no going back and nothing could stop the expansion.

Victorian health

All the factories springing up in the cities led factory owners to build housing for their workers, called back-to-back houses. Conditions were terrible in the overcrowded houses, with a whole street often sharing a single water pump and toilet. This led to sewage leaking into the water supply, leading in turn to outbreaks of cholera that killed thousands. It was not until 1854, when John Snow removed a water pump in London's Soho, that the connection between dirty water and the disease was found. Not even the rich were safe from the dirty conditions; Prince Albert died of typhoid in 1861, aged 42, and Victoria was devastated. She dressed in black for the rest of her life and was rarely seen in public after that. Some factory owners took better care of their workers, building villages for their employees to live in more comfort. Around his mill near Bradford, Titus Salt built decent housing that had piped water and indoor toilets. In Victorian times, operations were very dangerous affairs, with no anaesthetic until 1847, when James Simpson, a Scottish doctor, discovered the liquid anaesthetic chloroform, which he tested on himself and two friends. In 1865, Joseph Lister invented an antiseptic spray which combated infection, and operating theatres started to become more hygienic.

School

Few children went to school in 1837; poor children were expected to join their parents in working to support their family. Richer children might be taught by a governess, or boys could be sent to a boarding school like Eton or Harrow. There were charity schools, Sunday schools and dame schools for poorer children, and soon ragged schools started appearing in the poorer areas. The 1870 Education Act saw school boards set up to start schools in areas where there were not enough of them, and the 1880 Education Act stated that all children between the ages of five and ten had to attend school. Victorian schools were very strict, with the cane and dunce hat regularly used. Pupils wrote on a slate, which they could wipe clean, and eventually used paper and inkwells.

Growth of the empire

During Victoria's reign, the British Empire doubled in size and Britain became the most powerful trading nation in the world. It was said that 'the sun never set on the British Empire', and with colonies as far afield as Australia, Canada, parts of Africa and the Far East and India (among others), it is easy to see why. Understandably, not all nations took well to being ruled by the British. The native peoples of Australia and New Zealand were ravaged through a combination of force and disease, and there were uprisings in India, including a violent rebellion in 1857. Raw materials, such as cotton, tea and wool, were imported from Britain's colonies and then made into goods in the factories before being exported to other countries. India was called the 'jewel in the crown' of the British Empire, and Victoria was officially named Empress of India in 1877.

Important dates

1819: Victoria is born at Kensington Palace, named Alexandrina Victoria (24 May).
1837: Victoria becomes Queen (20 June).
1840: Victoria marries Prince Albert.
1851: The Great Exhibition takes place.
1852: Albert buys Balmoral castle for Victoria.
1861: Prince Albert dies of typhoid.
1877: Victoria is made Empress of India.
1887: Victoria celebrates her Golden Jubilee.
1897: Victoria celebrates her Diamond Jubilee.
1901: Victoria dies at Osborne House on the Isle of Wight (22 January).

Important people

Edward, Duke of Kent: Victoria's father.
Princess Victoria of Saxe-Coburg: Victoria's mother.
Robert Peel: Founder of the Metropolitan Police Force, and a prime minister.
Isambard Kingdom Brunel: Famous engineer.
Benjamin Disraeli: Prime minister twice during Victoria's reign.
John Snow: Discovered the cause of cholera.
James Simpson: Doctor who first used chloroform as an anaesthetic.
Joseph Lister: Pioneer of antiseptic.

Useful links

www.britroyals.com/kings.asp?id=victoria Includes a detailed timeline.
www.funtrivia.com/en/subtopics/The-First-Empress-of-India-99661.html Good set of questions and answers on Victoria.

Lesson 1 Meet the queens

Getting started
Ask the class what they know about Queen Elizabeth I and Queen Victoria. They can collate ideas in small groups and then feed back to the rest of the class.

Class activities
- Explain that the two famous queens lived in different times. Show them a well-known picture of each (the Armada picture for Elizabeth, and the 1846 portrait of Victoria with her family) and see if they can identify which queen came first.
- Pupils plot on a timeline the reigns of both queens.
- Looking at the portraits, pupils identify features of the monarch's clothing and anything else the portraits tell us about them.

Plenary material
Pupils each write one interesting fact they have found out about each of the queens.

Lesson 2 Tudor blind date

Getting started
Ask the class if they know who any of the current royals are married to. Why is it important that the monarch has children?

Class activities
- Look at a family tree from Victoria. Can pupils trace the various monarchs until the present?
- Explain that they are to act as a Royal Advisor to Elizabeth I. What sort of man would they advise her to marry and why? (English, foreign, powerful, rich, royal, etc.)
- Design a short Tudor blind date presentation and hand out voting slips for pupils to fill in. They have to pick which contender they would advise Elizabeth to marry. (The contenders could be Philip II of Spain; Francois, Duke of Alençon; and Robert Dudley.)
- Explain that Elizabeth didn't marry; she was 'married to her kingdom'.

Plenary material
In groups, pupils come up with ideas why Elizabeth did not marry.

Lesson 3 Victorian inventions

Getting started
In groups, pupils list any inventions they can think of that came from Victorian times.

Class activities
- Explain that there were many inventions during Victorian times in various fields.
- Hand out a sheet on Victorian inventions and ask pupils to fill in what they think they are.
  (Bloomsbury Online Resource 3B)
- Show a presentation on inventions and ask the class to fill in any other details.

Plenary material
If pupils were alive during Victorian times, which invention would they like to have invented?

Further activities for pupils

Elizabeth

- Look at portraits of Elizabeth and how they changed over the years. Why was her image so important, and what can you find out about the pictures?
- Investigate the life of Sir Francis Drake and imagine you are on one of his ships.
- Look at the problems Elizabeth faced and how she dealt with them. (Create a presentation showing her problems, giving pupils three options to choose from to advise the queen.)
- Imagine you are on an English or Spanish ship during the Spanish Armada, and write diary entries.
- Look at the plays that William Shakespeare wrote and performed at the Globe Theatre.
- Investigate Tudor houses and the difference between rich and poor homes.

Victoria

- Look at the changes from early to late Victorian times under the headings transport, work, housing, health, law & order. Which heading had the biggest change over the time period?
- Investigate the life and engineering designs of Isambard Kingdom Brunel.
- Look at Victorian schools and imagine the class has been transported back to Victorian times for the day. Use slates, an inkwell and recite work Victorian-style. Ask the children to stand up in silence when an adult walks into the room, and to put their hand up before standing to ask or answer a question.
- Have a Victorian Day at school: all dress up as various Victorian people; lessons follow Victorian themes; serve a Victorian lunch.
- Look at how the British Empire spread; investigate the sorts of raw materials imported from colonies and then what they were made into in the factories and where the exported goods were sent.

Further research for pupils

The Virgin Queen (1955): A wonderful film, with Bette Davis playing Elizabeth.
Cue for Treason by Geoffrey Trease, a fictional story about a plot to kill Elizabeth.
Hetty Feather by Jacqueline Wilson, set in Victorian times.

Cross-curricular links

Art and design: Create a poster about either Elizabeth or Victoria, showing some of the famous incidents that took place during their reign.

English: Write a series of diary entries as Elizabeth or Victoria. Include some of the famous people/ events that happened in each reign. Write a short story set in the reign of Elizabeth or Victoria, focusing on one event.

Religious studies: Investigate Elizabeth's 'middle way'; look at the beliefs of Puritans and Catholics and how they opposed the Queen.

Computing: Create a booklet on a famous Tudor or Victorian.

Geography: Look at the routes that Drake or Raleigh took. On a world map, shade in countries that made up the British Empire during Victoria's reign.

Science: Investigate some Victorian inventions that stretched scientific boundaries.

Drama: Imagine you are Philip II. Write and perform a short play about why you are so upset with Elizabeth I.

PE: Investigate drill exercises done by Victorian schoolchildren and try them out in class.

Progression

1. Pupils recognise that Elizabeth and Victoria reigned for a long time.
2. Pupils can name some events during the reigns of Elizabeth and Victoria.
3. Pupils can identify problems faced during Elizabeth's reign.
4. Pupils recognise the importance of the Industrial Revolution and how it changed lives.
5. Pupils can identify objects and famous people during the two reigns.

Christopher Columbus and Neil Armstrong

In 30 seconds...

Both Christopher Columbus and Neil Armstrong were pioneers of their time; Columbus landed in the Americas in 1492, and Armstrong landed on the Moon in 1969. Columbus was looking for the Far East when he landed in the Bahamas and explored the area, looking for untold riches, and taking slaves back to Spain. Although people from Europe had been to the Americas before Columbus, it was he who opened it up as a trade route to Europe, and it would never be the same again. Russia became the first country to send a person into space in 1961, but America was determined to put the first man on the Moon and it achieved this when Neil Armstrong stepped onto the surface of the Moon in 1969. Humankind had conquered a new frontier.

What do I need to know?

A bold plan

Italian explorer Christopher Columbus was determined to find a new route to the Far East from Europe; it was a long, arduous and dangerous journey across land and Columbus believed that he would be able to reach his destination by sailing west from Europe. At that time, ships had to sail from Europe around Africa to get to the Far East and Columbus was sure that by merely setting off in a westerly direction, he would reach his destination. Columbus needed patronage and a lot of money to support such a voyage; European rulers were keen to sponsor explorers, who would discover new lands and hopefully vast riches in their name. Columbus approached several monarchs who turned him down, before Ferdinand and Isabella of Spain agreed to fund the expedition. If all went to plan, the three of them would get fame and fortune and be able to further the spread of Catholicism.

The New World

In trying to find the Far East across the Atlantic, Columbus ended up in the New World, landing in the Bahamas in 1492. Believing he was near India, he mistakenly referred to the people there as 'Red Indians', an incorrect and misleading name that has stuck to this day (cowboy films may be partly to blame). The islands he landed in were therefore named the West Indies, but Columbus was disappointed not to find the spices, riches and gold that he was after. Disillusioned, he sailed back to Spain but returned later in 1493, sending back hundreds of slaves. He returned again in 1498 to find the original settlement where he had left his brothers, Hispaniola (present-day Dominican Republic and Haiti), in revolt; Columbus barely escaped with his life.

Consequences of his discovery

The arrival of Columbus and Europeans to the Americas would have disastrous consequences for the indigenous people; not only were many taken as slaves and their population drastically reduced by diseases brought by the new arrivals, such as smallpox, that they had no resistance to, but it paved the way for future exploration and exploitation of the land, natural resources and people. Columbus did not get the recognition in his lifetime for opening up this gateway, and died a few years after a third trip across the Atlantic, landing in what is now Panama.

Race for space

Throughout the late 1950s, the Cold War between Russia and the USA had included the race to space and both nations claimed significant scalps. Russia was the first to strike, with *Sputnik* becoming the first artificial satellite in space in 1957. After Russian cosmonaut Yuri Gagarin became the first human to orbit the Earth, the USA stepped up its effort. American president John F. Kennedy boldly predicted in 1961 that the USA would put a man on the Moon by the end of the decade. He was right.

First steps

Neil Armstrong had served as a navy pilot in the Korean War, flying 78 combat missions, before serving as a test pilot and engineer for NACA, which later became NASA. After the first manned spacecraft, *Apollo 8*, orbited the Moon in 1968, the stage was set to take it one step further and put a man on the Moon. Michael Collins and Buzz Aldrin joined Neil Armstrong on the Apollo 11 mission and, after landing on the Moon on 20 July 1969, Neil Armstrong became the first human to step on the Moon. 'That's one small step for man, one giant leap for mankind,' Armstrong famously remarked as he stepped onto the Moon's surface. Armstrong and Aldrin collected samples and took photographs for a couple of hours before heading back to the ship. Collins had stayed aboard the command module. After landing in the Pacific Ocean and being picked up by the navy, Armstrong and the rest of the crew were put in quarantine for three weeks. All three astronauts were greeted as returning heroes and the USA had won the biggest prize in the Space Race.

How Columbus and Armstrong are similar

Both Columbus and Armstrong were explorers who took a gamble; both expeditions could have ended in disaster and death. Both men were daring and brave and their missions were funded by governments. However, Columbus and many explorers of his day were driven by personal gain and greed, which resulted in many deaths, including their own crew and the native people they came across. Also, Armstrong landed somewhere that humankind had never visited before, whereas there were indigenous people in the New World as well as Viking explorers who had found their way there hundreds of years before.

Key words

Santa Maria: Flagship of Columbus.
NASA: National Aeronautics and Space Administration.

Important dates

1957: Russia launches the artificial satellite *Sputnik* into space (4 October).
1961: Russian cosmonaut Yuri Gagarin becomes the first human to orbit Earth (April).
1969: Apollo 11 is launched (16 July).

1969: Neil Armstrong takes the first steps on the Moon (20 July).
1969: The Apollo 11 mission returns to Earth (24 July).
2012: Neil Armstrong dies (25 August).

Important people

Christopher Columbus (1451–1506): Italian explorer and navigator, famous for landing in the New World in 1492.

Ferdinand and Isabella: King and Queen of Spain, who sponsored of Columbus on the expedition that saw him land in the Bahamas in 1492.

John Cabot (c.1450–c.1499): Italian navigator and explorer, funded by Henry VII of England to discover new lands for England. Cabot landed in North America in 1497 while seeking a route to Asia, and thought he'd successfully landed in Asia.

Leif Eriksson (c.960–c.1020): Viking explorer who lived in Greenland. After sailing from Norway back to Greenland in AD1000, his ship sailed off course and Eriksson landed in what is believed to be North America, which he described as Vinland, due to the grapes growing there and the fertile land.

Yuri Gagarin (1934–1968): Russian pilot and cosmonaut who became the first man in space when he orbited the Earth in 1961.

Neil Armstrong (1930–2012): American astronaut and pilot who, in 1969, became the first man to walk on the Moon.

Buzz Aldrin (born 1935): American astronaut and the second man to walk on the Moon. Aldrin was on the same mission as Neil Armstrong.

Michael Collins (born 1930): American astronaut and the third man on the Apollo 11 mission, along with Neil Armstrong and Buzz Aldrin. Collins did not set foot on the Moon but stayed on the command module.

Interesting fact

Columbus was not the first European to 'discover' the New World, as Viking explorers had landed in what is now Greenland and Newfoundland in the eleventh century.

Useful links

www.bbc.co.uk/schools/primaryhistory/famouspeople/christopher_columbus/
www.history.com/topics/neil-armstrong
www.ducksters.com/biography/explorers/neil_armstrong.php
www.eyewitnesstohistory.com/columbus.htm Extracts from Columbus's journal.

Lesson 1 Sea and Space Race

Getting started
Ask pupils in groups to list all the different ways they can think of to travel to destinations. Get them to list them in order of speed, from slowest to fastest.

Class activities
- Explain that humankind has been into exploration for a long time. Ask the class to feed back what explorers they have heard of over the ages.
- Ask pupils where there is left to explore. Is there anywhere left on Earth, or is it just into space?
- Briefly tell the class about Columbus and Armstrong: two pioneering explorers separated by almost 500 years.
- In groups, pupils find similarities and differences between exploration in 1492 and in 1969. What is the most significant similarity and the most significant difference?

Plenary material
Pupils imagine they are an explorer. Which would they rather be – one from 1492 or one from 1969?

Lesson 2 All aboard the *Santa Maria*

Getting started
Ask pupils what is the longest journey they have ever been on. Where were they going?

Class activities
- Show the class a picture of the *Santa Maria* or a similar vessel. What features can they identify? Pupils work in groups and then feed back.
- Explain that Columbus and his crew would be at sea for a long time. What would they need for such a long trip?
- In groups, pupils make a list of things they would need, split into three categories: urgent, useful, luxury.
- Pupils feed back their ideas and make a list on the board. Can the class agree on what their ship should be loaded up with for the journey?

Plenary material
If the class were going on a long journey by plane/car/on foot, what single most important item would they take with them for each?

Lesson 3 Space Race

Getting started

Ask the class what is the most incredible thing they can imagine doing when they are older – something that is impossible to do at their current age.

Class activities

• Explain the importance of the Space Race, and what was at stake.
• Explain that although the Americans had lost the race to get the first human to orbit the Earth, they were determined to get the first man on the Moon.
• Hand pupils a template of a spaceship (or they can draw their own). Ask them to list the things they would need for a trip to the Moon.
• Once they have finished, ask them to feed back their examples and discuss whether they are realistic or not. Which are the five best things they suggested?

Plenary material

If pupils could visit a distant planet, what would they like to bring back with them?

Further activities for pupils

• Plot on a timeline important events in the lives of Columbus and Armstrong.
• Look at the excitement of exploration; where would they like to explore if they could go anywhere?
• Look at the problems faced by both explorers; which of them faced the more testing circumstances?
• Look at and list the accomplishments of both explorers; which of them was the greatest explorer?
• As a class, write and record a news programme reporting on either/both explorers: include interviews with the explorer(s), other members of the crew and (in the case of Columbus) the indigenous people.

Further research for pupils

Columbus (1949), directed by David MacDonald.
In the Shadow of the Moon (2007), directed by David Sington.
Christopher Columbus by Minna Lacey and David Cuzik.
Comparing People from the Past: Christopher Columbus and Neil Armstrong by Nick Hunter.
iPad: *Apollo 11 Science Story for Kids* (for ages 3–10).
The Journey of Christopher Columbus HD – Children's Story Book: Contains some mini-games.

Cross-curricular links

Art and design: Create a poster advertising for crew for either the *Santa Maria* or Apollo 11.
English: Write a story or series of diary entries from the point of view of either Columbus or Armstrong.
Computing: In groups, create a presentation (e.g. PowerPoint) about one of the explorers.
Geography: On a map, plot the route that Columbus took in 1497 to land in the Bahamas, and annotate or illustrate it.
Science: Look at how much science had improved from 1492 to 1969; with this in mind, design a spaceship for the future.
Drama: In groups, imagine you are part of the crew of Columbus or Armstrong as you set off and eventually reach your destination.

Progression

1. Pupils can identify the two famous explorers and place them in chronological order.
2. Pupils can explain why explorers choose to do what they do.
3. Pupils recognise the differences between Columbus and Armstrong.
4. Pupils can describe similarities between the two explorers.
5. Pupils can identify the dangers that each explorer faced.

William Caxton and Tim Berners-Lee

In 30 seconds. . .

William Caxton and Tim Berners-Lee were separated by over 500 years, but their impact on their generation was huge. William Caxton was the first English printer, who translated and published many works. Tim Berners-Lee is the inventor of the World Wide Web. Both men used the technology of the day to create a means to get information across on a level not seen before.

What do I need to know?

William Caxton

Caxton was born in the early 1420s in Kent and became apprentice to Robert Large, a merchant in London. He later moved to Bruges, where he became involved in the burgeoning wool trade. After serving as the Governor of the English Nation of Merchant Adventurers, Caxton moved to Cologne to learn the art of printing. Although printing had been invented by the Chinese in the eleventh century, it didn't spread to Europe until the fifteenth century, with Johann Gutenberg. Returning to Bruges in 1472, Caxton teamed up with a calligrapher called Colard Mansion and they set up their own printing press. Caxton was a publisher and translator (he was able to translate French, Latin and Dutch), and the first book he printed in 1475 was an English translation of *The Recuyell of the Histories of Troye*. This was the first book ever published in English! Moving back to England in 1476, Caxton set up his own printing press in Westminster and published over 100 books. Information was thus made more readily available and accessible, due to the relative speed of production compared to laboriously copying text out by hand as had been done previously.

Tim Berners-Lee

Born on 8 June 1955 in London, Tim Berners-Lee graduated from Oxford University and was working as a software consultant at the European Organization for Nuclear Research when he came up with his idea: he wanted researchers to be able to share their ideas. This was then developed to enable people to share their ideas globally, and the World Wide Web was born. Berners-Lee also created the first Web browser and editor; then, in 1991, the first website was launched that explained all about the World Wide Web. Berners-Lee's idea was that people the world over would use the World Wide Web to share resources, information and ideas, pooling their knowledge to help one another. The Internet and the Web have now become fixtures in our lives.

The march of technology

Caxton and Berners-Lee each introduced a new technology that had a huge impact on lives and society; both the printing press and the World Wide Web enabled information to be accessed and digested on a scale unheard of before they came along. These days, pupils cannot imagine a life without the array of gadgets that keep them entertained all hours of the day: games consoles; on-demand TV, iPads and smartphones. Looking at the changes that have happened in just the last 20 years, it should not be a surprise if those in another 20 years' time look back at today's technology and wonder how we ever coped.

Key words

HTTP: Hypertext transfer protocol; enables you to click on a link and be taken to a location.
URL: Universal resource locator an address for a webpage.
HTML: Hypertext markup language; this enables links to be put into documents.

Important dates

1475: Caxton sets up his first printing press.
1475: Caxton publishes his first book in English.
1476: Caxton sets up his own printing press.
1990: Berners-Lee sets up key concepts: HTTP, URLs and HTML.
1990: Berners-Lee creates the first Web browser.
1991: Berners-Lee launches the first website and the World Wide Web.

Important people

Johann Gutenberg (c.1398–1468): German printer who invented the moveable type printing press. Up until that point, books had to be written by hand or block printed.
William Caxton (c.1420–1491): English writer and printer who, after learning the new ways of printing on the continent, returned to England and set up his own printing press.
Colard Mansion (c.1440–1484): Flemish scribe and printer who worked with Caxton in Bruges.
Tim Berners-Lee (born 1955): English scientist and inventor of the World Wide Web. Berners-Lee created it so people could share ideas globally.

Useful links

www.biographyonline.net/writers/william-caxton.html
www.spacemaninyourschool.co.uk/free-lesson-3/4586785585 Information, ideas and a workshop.

Lesson 1 Communication through the ages

Getting started
Pupils work in groups and list communication methods. Which do they value most?

Class activities
- Show a PPT of various means of communication through the ages. Ask the pupils to identify each and explain how they are used.
- Ask the pupils to chronologically plot the means of communication on a timeline.
- In groups, pupils discuss and list the good and bad points of each.

Plenary material
In groups, pupils are given one piece of communication technology to discuss and then do a short oral presentation on it.

Lesson 2 How to spread the word

Getting started
Pupils discuss in groups how they would spread a message to the whole school as quickly as possible. They then feed back to the class.

Class activities
- Pupils imagine they live before the invention of the printing press. How are books written?
- Show pupils pictures of medieval handwritten books. Ask them to comment on what they see and pose the question: what problems are there with this process?
- If they lived in 1475, how would the pupils spread a message to the rest of their town/village?
- Explain how the printing press worked and ask the class to discuss in groups the advantages over handwritten books.
- Feed back and record the best answers.

Plenary material
Can pupils think of anything bad about the printing press? (Answers should include the publishing of forbidden works at the time.)

Lesson 3 March of technology

Getting started
Ask pupils what piece of technology they could not live without: television, phone, iPad or games console. Record answers as a class in a table.

Class activities
- Show the class pictures of an early radio; an iPad; a ZX Spectrum; a CD player; a television; a Playstation 4.
- Ask them to ask three questions about each and then see if they can answer their own questions in groups.
- Pupils plot the invention of each gadget chronologically on a timeline.
- Ask the class how people would have felt when each of the gadgets first appeared. Can they think why some people may have disapproved of the gadgets?

Plenary material
The class has to vote for one of the gadgets to never have existed. Which would they choose and why?

Further activities for pupils

- Explore which method of communication made the greatest impact at the time, and why.
- Pupils invent their own piece of communication technology for the future.
- Investigate how Berners-Lee intended the World Wide Web to be used, and how it is used now. How might it be used in the future?
- Does the Internet hold too much power? Is information too readily available? How would pupils limit its accessibility and power? Present ideas visually on a sheet of A3 or a PowerPoint presentation.
- If we had to live without either the printing press or the Internet, which should it be?

Further research for pupils

History Heroes: Tim Berners-Lee by Damian Harvey.

Cross-curricular links

Art and design: Create your own printing press with the help of the art teacher.
English: Imagine a world without the Internet and write a short story about how you would get information. Then write another short story about a world with no printing press.
Computing: Create your own webpage with information about your hobbies.
Religious studies: Investigate the sort of material that was circulated from the new printing press that got its authors into trouble, like Tyndale, Luther, etc.
Geography: Trace the journey of the printing press as it spread across Europe and the world.
Science: Investigate how long it took to produce a book by hand compared to the early printing press.
Drama: Write and perform a short play about how useful either the printing press or the Internet is.

Progression

1. Pupils understand and can explain what the printing press is.
2. Pupils have an understanding of how we use the Internet today.
3. Pupils can explain how books were produced before the printing press, and the lengthy process involved.
4. Pupils understand how the Internet was initially intended to be used.
5. Pupils can explain how important the printing press was and how it helped spread ideas, both popular and unpopular.
6. Pupils can present a case for and against too much information being available via the Internet.

Alexander the Great and Genghis Khan

In 30 seconds. . .

Both Alexander the Great and Genghis Khan were fearsome warriors who each established control in their own country before they conquered many nations, ruling a huge empire by the time they died. Alexander, born into royalty, rose to conquer Persia and Egypt, creating a kingdom stretching from the Mediterranean to the border of India before he died at the age of 32. Genghis Khan rose from humble beginnings before uniting the warring Mongol tribes and ruling an empire that included large parts of Asia and China. His descendants would expand the empire into the largest empire the world has seen.

Alexander the Great

What do I need to know?

The young warrior

The young Alexander, born to King Philip II and Queen Olympia, had Aristotle as a tutor and commanded cavalry at 18 years old. Alexander succeeded his father as king after gaining the support of the Macedonian army, and led by example on the battlefield. His ability to adapt and improvise was outstanding and he proved an irresistible force in both siege and open warfare. After his father died, there were revolts by the Illyrians, Thracians and Greeks, who saw a chance to gain their freedom. Alexander was ruthless in putting these rebellions down. Upon reaching Thebes in Greece, Alexander offered the Greeks the chance to surrender but they refused, believing that more Greeks would join the revolt. Alexander killed 6,000 Theban citizens and sold 30,000 more into slavery. After he had dealt with internal threats and problems, Alexander turned his attention to the massive Persian Empire.

Conquering the Persians

The first conflict was the Battle of Granicus, with the Persian army containing around 24,000 men compared to around 47,000 men under the command of Alexander. It proved to be a rout, although the Greeks in the Persian army refused to yield, resulting in thousands of them dying. Alexander then moved south across Asia Minor and conquered the coastal areas. At the Battle of Issus, Alexander faced the Persian King Darius III, whose army greatly outnumbered his. However, the Persians were powerless against the Macedonian phalanx, and tens of thousands were killed. Darius fled, leaving his family behind, but Alexander treated them as royalty. Sieges at Tyre and Gaza followed, momentary delays to an unstoppable Macedonian force, before Darius offered Alexander a truce, offering areas of the Persian Empire. Alexander refused, wanting it all. The two leaders faced each other at the Battle of Gaugamela, in what is now northern Iraq, where the Persians again heavily outnumbered Alexander's men. Encouraged to attack the Persians at night, Alexander refused, wanting to beat Darius in a fair fight that would leave the Persian king under no doubt who the superior man was. Alexander took charge of one wing of his army, and his general Parmenio led the other. Although Parmenio came under severe pressure, Alexander broke through on his side, causing Darius to flee again. Alexander then occupied Babylon and the Persian capital of Persepolis, where he was named King of Persia. Alexander continued to chase Darius but found him dead, having been assassinated by Bessus. Alexander gave Darius a royal funeral before chasing after Bessus, eventually catching and killing him.

A changing man

Some Macedonians were concerned at Alexander increasingly adapting oriental ways and customs, and this led to a plot to kill him. Led by Philotas, the conspiracy was discovered and Philotas was tortured and killed, followed by his father, Parmenio, which proved an unpopular act as the old general was greatly respected. Alexander was prone to wild mood swings and outbursts of temper, due to his heavy drinking, and he killed his close friend Cleitus in a drunken brawl, which he later regretted. He also executed Callisthenes, a famous Greek historian and nephew to his old tutor Aristotle, for conspiring against him: Callisthenes and others had earlier defeated a motion by Alexander to make Europeans prostrate themselves in front of him, following the oriental tradition. The army marched on, into India, where they faced an army with elephants at the battle of Hydaspes, led by King Porus. Once again, Alexander was victorious but his army heard stories of larger armies heading their way, with more elephants and chariots. They voiced their concern to Alexander and he reluctantly decided to head back to Persia. Alexander was seriously injured on the way back to the sea fighting the Malli tribe, an arrow piercing his breastplate and heavily wounding him in the chest. He recovered and the Macedonians reached the Indus river and built a thousand ships to sail back. Crossing the Gerdosian desert, thousands of his soldiers died from heat and exhaustion before reaching Susa. At Opis, Alexander ordered 10,000 of his troops to head back to Macedonia, which was unpopular with his troops and they let him know. Alexander then gave a famous speech, reminding that his troops that if it had not been for him and his father, they would still be in Macedonia, fearful of those around them instead of having conquered so much of the world. This appeased them and the 10,000 headed back to Macedonia. Before Alexander could embark on his planned Arabian campaign, he contracted a fever and died at the age of just 33.

His legacy

Alexander achieved the incredible feat of never losing a battle. As generals tended to do in those days, he would lead from the front, setting the example and putting his own life in danger time after time, resulting in many wounds over the years. His empire spanned three continents and covered about 2 million square miles (over 5 million square kilometres).

Key words

Sarissa: 18–20-foot (5.5-metre) long pike.
Phalanx: Closely-packed rank of soldiers.

Important dates

356 BC: Alexander is born in Pella, in what is now Macedonia (July).
336 BC: His father Philip is assassinated and Alexander becomes king.
333 BC: Battle of Issus.
331 BC: Alexander reaches Egypt.
331 BC: Battle of Gaugamela (1 October).
327 BC: Alexander reaches India.
326 BC: Alexander defeats King Porus.
323 BC: Alexander dies (7 June).

Important people

Parmenio: Second in command to Alexander.
Darius III: Persian king.
Bessus: Persian nobleman.
Philotas: Conspirator and son of Parmenio.
Cleitus: Macedonian noble.
Roxane: Wife of Alexander.
Aristotle: Tutor to a young Alexander.

Genghis Khan

From humble beginnings

Genghis Khan was originally called Temujin and had a very hard early life. His father was poisoned by the Tatars, another tribe, and Temujin, his three brothers, baby sister and mother were thrown out of the tribe to fend for themselves. Temujin was later captured by another tribe and only managed to escape after being helped by a guard, who would later become one of his generals. At this time, Mongolia was split into many tribes and they often fought one another. Raiding parties, revenge attacks and plundering happened often. Temujin saw the chance to unite them and gradually built up one tribe: a defeated tribe would have the choice to be loyal to him or die. (Not much of an option.) But he cared for orphans and often gave defeated opponents the chance to be part of his new tribe. He also rewarded and promoted his men for their ability and loyalty, rather than how important their family name was.

Ruling the empire

Genghis Khan had the largest land empire in history, ruling over nearly 12 million square miles (more than 31 million square kilometres) of territory. His first campaign outside Mongolia was in north-west China against the Xi Xia kingdom. The Xi Xia ruler surrendered in 1209 and the Mongols then headed north, attacking the Jin dynasty. The Mongols swept all before them in the countryside, with thousands of peasants heading to the cities for sanctuary. This then caused food shortages, and the Jin army resorted to killing thousands of their own peasants to preserve the food stocks. Eventually, in 1215, Genghis seized the capital Zhongdu (what is now Beijing), although after the Jin ruler upset Genghis, he destroyed the city completely, levelling it to the ground. In 1219, Genghis turned his attention to the Khwarezm Empire, in what is now Iran, Afghanistan, Uzbekistan and Turkmenistan. They had incurred the wrath of the khan (chief of tribes) after the governor of Otrar had gone back on a trade agreement, killing the merchants before murdering the ambassadors Genghis had sent. Although they were outnumbered, the Mongols swept all before them, keeping those who were beneficial to them, like carpenters and soldiers, and killing the rest who could not be trusted or who had no use. When Genghis caught up with the governor, he killed him by pouring molten silver over his ears, eyes and mouth.

Brutal or revolutionary?

Genghis Khan's Mongolian army mostly fought on horseback, being tremendous riders, having learnt to handle horses when they were children. They used a bow as their main weapon, the body of it reinforced with horn and sinew to increase the power. The Mongols could shoot with remarkable accuracy from a galloping horse, steering the charging animal with just their knees and often firing at the split second that the hooves were all in mid-air. Genghis granted diplomatic immunity to foreign ambassadors and allowed people to worship freely, with Christians, Muslims and Buddhists among the ranks of his followers. Genghis learnt new technology from captured enemies and used it to besiege cities. Everyone had to follow the Yassa, a code for civilians and soldiers with strict penalties if broken. He set up yam routes and his generals were trusted to command whole tumans, often being sent on a mission that could last years. But he was without doubt a brutal and vicious man, killing whole cities that refused to surrender. He used captured prisoners at the front of his armies to soak up enemy fire and did not stop until all were beaten or dead.

End of an era, but the start of another

Genghis Khan died under mysterious circumstances, with nobody entirely sure how he met his end, although most sources point to a fall from his horse in 1227. His empire at his death included much of Asia and China, but his descendants, Ogedei and Kublai, extended it even further. He merged the civilisations of East and West and established the first international postal system. He was a man to be feared (he was responsible for the death of millions), but one capable of sparing a brave enemy his life and even making him a general in his army.

Key words

Yassa: A legal code that all the mongols had to follow, with strict penalties for those who broke it.
Yam: A set of relay routes for messengers, providing a communication network. There were stations every few miles with fresh horses and riders, so messages could be delivered as quickly as possible.
Tuman: A military unit consisting of 10,000 men.

Important dates

1162: Temujin is born.
1171: After the death of his father, Temujin and his family are banished from their tribe.
1206: Temujin is renamed Genghis Khan.
1209: The Mongols defeat the Xi Xia in China.
1215: The Mongols defeat Zhongda after starving the city as a way of forcing them to give in.
1219: After the Shah Muhammad of the Khwarizm Empire shuns a trade agreement and murders the mongol emissaries, Genghis responds by launching a massive assault on the Persian Empire. Many cities are destroyed, including Samakand and Bukhura.
1227: Genghis Khan dies (18 August).

Important people

Yesugei: Genghis Khan's father. (Also known as Yesukhai.)
Ogedei: Third son and successor to Genghis.
Kublai: Grandson of Genghis.

Interesting fact 1

Mongol attacks may have reduced the world's population by as much as 11 per cent!

Interesting fact 2

Genghis Khan would promote men with skill and talent, including beaten opponents, to generals.

Useful links

www.ducksters.com/biography/alexander_the_great.php Facts about Alexander the Great.
www.history.com/topics/genghis-khan
www.history.com/news/history-lists/10-things-you-may-not-know-about-genghis-khan

Lesson 1 Being a great ruler

Getting started
Ask pupils what qualities you need to be a great ruler. Take feedback and record answers on the board.

Class activities
- Explain that the class will be studying two great rulers from many years ago, both of whom had huge empires.
- Ask pupils to create a 'Wanted' poster for a great ruler that would lead by example and take his troops into battle.
- Tell them to draw the type of leader needed and list some of the qualities he (or she) would need.

Plenary material
Discuss as a class how a leader is different today than years ago. Can each group/table come up with one difference?

Lesson 2 Two different upbringings

Getting started

Ask the class why they go to school and why they learn the things and skills they do. What is it all in preparation for?

Class activities

- Explain that the young Alexander, born into a royal family, would have been prepared from an early age to be king. (Best training; best tutors; wealthy lifestyle etc.) What sorts of things may he have done?
- Tell the class about life on the harsh plains of Mongolia and the hardships Temujin (Genghis) faced as a young man.
- Ask pupils to discuss in groups how Temujin's upbringing would have differed from theirs.
- Ask them to produce a speech by either of the young warriors, stating how their upbringing will help them become a great ruler.

Plenary material

Ask the class to vote on whether the upbringing of Alexander or Temujin is better for a strong leader.

Lesson 3 Two different starting places

Getting started

Each table/pair is given three facts/statements: one about Alexander the Great, one about Genghis Khan and one that is to do with neither of them. Pupils have to sort them correctly.

Class activities

- Explain that Alexander the Great and Genghis Khan lived in two very different places with different climates. After explaining where Macedonia and Mongolia are, ask the pupils what they know about each area.
- Show the class a picture of Macedonia. What can they deduce from the picture? Ask if any of them have visited Greece.
- Show the class a picture of Mongolia. What can they deduce from the picture?
- Show the pictures of Macedonia and Mongolia side by side, or hand out copies to each table. Pupils compare them and find similarities/differences.

Plenary material

Pupils discuss in small groups which place would be harder to live in, and why. Which do they vote for? What criteria do they use?

Further activities for pupils

- Look at the different fighting styles of the Macedonians and Mongols: weapons; armour; way of fighting; tactics, etc.
- Look at key battles for both Alexander and Genghis and how they were able to win against a force of superior numbers.
- Investigate some of the famous generals under each great ruler.
- Look at the spread of each empire: how easy would it be to keep control over a big empire?

Further research for pupils

http://greece.mrdonn.org/alexander.html Includes games about Ancient Greece.
http://mongols.mrdonn.org/index.html Lots of great information on the Mongols.
www.eyewitnesstohistory.com/alexander.htm Account of Alexander defeating the Persians.
www.eyewitnesstohistory.com/alexanderdeath.htm Death of Alexander the Great.
www.eyewitnesstohistory.com/khan.htm Kublai Khan in battle.
Alexander the Great (1956), directed by Robert Rossen.
Alexander the Great: The Life of a King and Conqueror by Anita Ganeri and Rob Shone.
Genghis Khan: 13th-Century Mongolian Tyrant by Enid Goldberg and Norman Itzkowitz.
iPad: *Defend From Mongol* (Tang Hao).

Cross-curricular links

Art and design: Design a poster about either Alexander or Genghis Khan, showing them in full battle.
English: Write a story about Alexander or Genghis Khan, either as one of their warriors in a winning battle, or as a defeated soldier of their enemy. Describe what happens.
Religious studies: Investigate the religious beliefs of both men, including the countries they took over.
Computing: Design a fact file on one of the leaders with a list of their accomplishments.
Geography: On a map, colour in the empires of each and list the countries they took.
Science: Investigate some of the weapons and siege engines used.
Drama: Act out some of the key moments in both men's lives.
PE: In the playground, try to recreate some of the battles, using the movement of troops that the great leaders used to ensure victory.

Progression

1. Pupils know where Alexander the Great came from and that he never lost a battle.
2. Pupils know where Genghis Khan came from and that he had a huge empire.
3. Pupils can describe some features of how the two different armies fought.
4. Pupils can recount some key events from the lives of Alexander and Genghis Khan.
5. Pupils can explain how the upbringing of each leader helped to shape him.

4 Significant events, people and places

What does the curriculum say?

- *Pupils should be taught about significant historical events, people and places in their own locality.*

First World War remembrance: a local study and war memorials

In 30 seconds. . .

The First World War saw almost no village left untouched; the number of war memorials in towns and villages attests to the ultimate price that so many residents paid. There is hardly a town or village in the UK that does not have some record of those who lost their lives.

What do I need to know?

Remembering the fallen

Although mention of a war memorial conjures up an image of the familiar stone monument engraved with the names of the fallen, there are other venues that record the names. Schools list the names of past pupils who went on to fight, for some as soon as they had finished their final year at the school. Churches, train stations, factories and public buildings also have rolls of honour to remember those who died. Studying local war memorials reveals that there are often men from the same family who died, listed one after the other.

Famous memorials

There are many famous memorials: the Cenotaph in Whitehall; the Thiepval Memorial in the Somme region; the Menin Gate in Ypres; the grave of the Unknown Warrior in Westminster Abbey. There are over 70,000 names of British and South African soldiers inscribed at Thiepval, who have no known grave; when one of them is identified, they are given a proper burial and their name is deleted from the monument. At the Menin Gate in Ypres, there are over 54,000 names of men with no known grave, and the Last Post is played every night at 8pm. This has happened on a daily basis since 1927.

Local war memorials

There should be many war memorials near your school; some are more obvious than others, so look around at public buildings that may display the names of those who fell in the Great War. Train stations, post offices, other schools that are old enough to have provided ex-pupils who fought in the war. Look at the different styles, size and shape they have; were they built locally? War memorials can also be plaques, wreaths, books or a decorative garden or tree planted in remembrance.

Key words

The Great War: The First World War, also known as World War One. It was called the Great War until the Second World War started.
Cenotaph: From the Greek, meaning 'empty tomb' or monument.
Thiepval: Famous Thiepval Memorial in France.
Menin Gate: Famous war memorial in Ypres, where they play the Last Post every evening.

Important dates

3 August 1914: Britain declares war on Germany.
11 November 1918: The Armstice is signed, coming into effect at 11am.

Interesting fact 1

There are also many animal war memorials; eight million horses, mules and donkeys died in the First World War, as well as many dogs, pigeons and canaries. *War Horse*, written by famous children's author Michael Morpurgo, was made into a theatre show and blockbuster film.

Interesting fact 2

'Thankful Villages' were villages in the UK that sent men to fight in the war and all of them returned safely. One estimate lists 52 in England and Wales, with none in Scotland or Ireland. There are also 14 'Doubly Thankful Villages' – villages that sent men to fight in both the First and Second World Wars, and all of them returned safely.

Useful links

www.iwm.org.uk/memorials/search Site from the Imperial War Museum; find your local war memorials.
www.learnaboutwarmemorials.org/download/pub/300.3/ Some helpful information and ideas for lessons/activities from the War Memorial Trust.

Lesson 1 Famous memorials

Getting started

Pose the question to the class: what is a memorial? Working in groups, pupils see what answers they can come up with. What examples do they give? Give them a hint if needed.

Class activities

- Show the class a picture of the Thiepval Memorial. Ask pupils to describe it and list their ideas on the board.
- Explain that there are over 70,000 names inscribed on the memorial. Why is that? Show pupils a picture of engraved names from Thiepval.
- Explain that war memorials come in all different shapes and sizes; show examples.
- Show a picture of the Menin Gate. What are the similarities/differences with Thiepval?
- Play pupils a rendition of the Last Post, which is played every night at the Menin Gate. Pupils write down how it makes them feel as they hear it. Explain why it is played.

Plenary material

Pupils discuss and vote on which memorial is more impressive and why: Thiepval or Menin Gate? Collate their votes and see which one is more popular.

Lesson 2 Local memorials

Getting started

To recap from the last lesson, put pupils into pairs or groups. Ask them to write down what they can remember about the Thiepval and Menin Gate memorials – at least three facts/features for each.

Class activities

- Explain that while there are many famous iconic war memorials, there are thousands of much smaller ones, some of which they probably pass by each day without realising!
- Ask the class if they have seen any local war memorials. What types have they seen?
- Show the class local war memorials from the area.
- Ask pupils to write down what features they see: names, symbols, dates, size, material, etc.
- Explain that those who fought came from all walks of life and are thus remembered in many different memorials.

Plenary material

Split the class into small groups. Write down different types of war memorial on three pieces of paper (public memorial; famous memorial; school memorial). One pupil takes a piece of paper; the rest of the group can ask one question at a time that has to be answered with yes or no. At the end, they try to guess which type of memorial it is; then choose a new piece of paper and repeat.

Lesson 3 Animal memorials

Getting started
Write the following words on the board: *horse, dog, canary, pigeon.* Pupils work in groups to discuss what role these animals may have had in the First World War.

Class activities
- Explain that not all war memorials were for soldiers who died in battle; there are memorials to commemorate the lives of animals too.
- Show the class pictures of the jobs the animals listed above did in the First World War. Can pupils identify what the animals are doing?
- Do they think that animals should be remembered with a memorial? Encourage them to try to think of a reason both for and against.

Plenary material
You pick one of the jobs that an animal did in the First World War and think of five statements about that particular job; the first statement gives little away but each subsequent statement reveals more. After making each statement, ask pupils to guess which animal it is. Give points according to how quickly they guess.

Further activities for pupils

- Investigate 'Thankful Villages' and 'Doubly Thankful Villages'. Do they still have monuments?
- Visit a local memorial; sketch it; list its features. Are there any names from the same family?
- Research the different symbols on war memorials. What different religious symbols can you find?
- Research different types of war memorials.
- Pupils design their own war memorial to commemorate the fallen.

Cross-curricular links

Art and design: Design your own 3D war memorial.
English: Write an acrostic poem using either 'Thiepval' or 'Menin Gate'.
Religious studies: Research the different religious symbols on war memorials.
Computing: Design a new war memorial and write a fitting phrase that could go on it.
Geography: On a map of your locality, plot where the war memorials are situated.

Progression

1. Pupils can explain what a war memorial is and who is remembered.
2. Pupils can identify a famous war memorial.
3. Pupils can identify some of the features of a war memorial.
4. Pupils recognise that there are different types of war memorials.

The church: who is remembered there and why?

In 30 seconds. . .

In an increasingly secular society, a visit to the church can at times feel like a step back through time. In the building and grounds of a church, monuments, plaques and graves remember people from the past. A church service helps the congregation to remember the life and times of Jesus Christ.

What do I need to know?

Things to see

Churches have monuments and graves to remember the general public as well as anyone who made a more telling contribution to the local community. Looking at the gravestones from years ago reveals the life expectancy of people from that time. There might be particular first names that are rarely heard these days. Some of the graves may reveal more details about the person: where they lived, what they did or how they may have died if it was during a period of war. Inside the church, there are often plaques to see, with information about men and women who contributed to the life of the church.

Remembering Jesus

Churches are also used for services that remember the life and times of Jesus Christ. Daily services are held, and there are special services throughout the year at important times in the Christian calendar, such as Advent, Christmas, Lent, Easter and Harvest Festival.

Key words

Advent: The first season in the Christian year leading up to Christmas, including the four Sundays before this.
Christmas: Christian festival celebrating the birth of Jesus Christ on 25 December.
Lent: A period of 40 days before Easter to commemorate Jesus Christ's time spent in the wilderness. Some Christians give up certain foods, activities or luxuries for the 40 days of Lent in remembrance of what Christ went through.
Easter: A very important Christian festival that celebrates the resurrection of Jesus Christ.
Harvest Festival: A celebration of food grown on the land after the harvest, thanking God for all we have, and usually held in September.

Useful links

www.findachurch.co.uk Search for a church near you, with a database of over 45,000 churches.
www.ukcensusonline.com/index.php UK census online.

Lesson 1 What is a church?

Getting started
Ask pupils to write down a place that is special to them and say why. They feed back to the rest of their group. Poll the results to see if one particular place gets the most mentions.

Class activities
- Explain that a church is very important to many people, both now and in the past.
- Ask pupils if they can name any different Christian denominations. Explain that there is religious freedom in the UK for people to worship how they like. However, there used to be conflict and tension between Protestants and Catholics, and there still is in some parts of the world.
- Show a picture of the outside of a church: what features can the pupils identify?
- Show a picture of a gravestone: what information can pupils deduce about the person from the information on the gravestone?

Plenary material
Play a game of Hangman, using the following words: *Christian, Protestant, Catholic, Anglican, Baptist, Methodist.*

Lesson 2 Who is remembered in our church?

Getting started
Ask pupils why we remember some people from years ago and not others. What is it that makes them worth remembering? Many will probably mention famous people.

Class activities
- Explain that it is not always rich or famous people who are remembered; mention the earlier work done on war memorials – the names on the memorials were not of famous or rich people, but of people who had been a part of the local community and were remembered for what they did.
- Research who is buried or is commemorated at your local church. Present the class with a list of a number of people; pupils then use computers to research their lives. This can form a project.
- Pupils produce a fact file about some of the people who are remembered in the local church: where they lived, their job, their family, how they died etc.

Plenary material
Each pupil stands up and recites one fact that they have learnt about someone who is remembered in their local church.

Lesson 3 Visit to the church

Getting started
The pupils get into groups and come up with one thing that they want to find out when they visit their local church.

Class activities
- On arriving at the church, pupils ask questions to find out what sort of church it is; what features determine the type of church it is, and who worships there.
- Pupils find and write down the names and details of people outside the church who are buried in the graveyard. Ask them to see how many they can find with the same surname.
- Inside the church, pupils see who is commemorated there. They write down their details and why they are remembered.

Plenary material
Back at school, each group feeds back one interesting fact they found out about their visit to the local church.

Further activities for pupils

- Investigate buildings in the locality that were built during Victorian times or before. Who used to live there and what purpose did the buildings serve?
- Study a census from the area and find out more about who used to live around the school.

Cross-curricular links

Art and design: Paint a picture of the local church.
English: Write an account of a visit to the local church.
Religious studies: Research facts about the local church and who worships there.
Computing: Create a fact file on somebody who is commemorated or remembered in the local church.
Geography: On a map of the local area, plot famous buildings, old buildings, the church, etc.

Progression

1. Pupils understand that people are remembered and commemorated in a church.
2. Pupils can identify facts about people remembered in the local church.
3. Pupils understand there are different types of churches, depending on who worships there.
4. Pupils can identify and explain the significance of buildings in the locality.

Part 2:
Lower Key Stage 2

5 Changes in Britain from the Stone Age to the Iron Age

What does the curriculum say?

- *Non-statutory examples include: late Neolithic hunter-gatherers and early farmers, for example, Skara Brae; Bronze Age religion, technology and travel, for example, Stonehenge; Iron Age hill forts: tribal kingdoms, farming, art and culture.*

Hunter-gatherers and early farmers

In 30 seconds...

The three main periods of prehistory are generally divided into Stone Age, Bronze Age and Iron Age. The hunter-gatherers were from the Mesolithic Age (Middle Stone Age), and farming started to develop towards the end of this period. The Neolithic (New Stone Age) saw farming take the place of hunter-gathering. This period is known as the Neolithic Revolution.

What do I need to know?

Hunter-gatherers

The last Ice Age came to an end around 12,000 years ago. Up until that time, life for early humans was difficult due to the extreme conditions; the covering of ice meant that some plants would not grow and there was not much wood to build shelters from. Early humans made tools out of bone and antlers; caught fish; dug up roots; ate nuts, berries and fruit; and killed and skinned animals. As well as smaller animals like deer, they hunted larger prey like mammoths in groups, ambushing the huge beasts in pits before killing them with spears. When the last Ice Age ended, forests grew. These forests were home to many animals, which meant that early humans did not have to travel so far to hunt. They spent more time making tools, and in their homes, which became more permanent.

Star Carr

Dating back to around 9000 BC, the Mesolithic settlement Star Carr is situated in North Yorkshire, south of Scarborough. Originally, the site was on the bank of a lake, surrounded by woods. Excavation of the site began in 1948 and it unearthed a huge amount of artefacts preserved in the peat, resulting in the most important archaeological find from the Mesolithic era. Among the objects found were a number of barbed points made from antlers, and antler frontlets, which were worn as a headdress; they could have been used for some hunting disguise or religious ceremony.

Early farmers

Farming came to Britain in two ways: the indigenous people started herding animals and settling more, coupled with an influx of people from other countries who landed on Britain's shores. Most of it was down to the Mesolithic people adapting new methods and spreading these across the country. This was not an immediate phenomenon but took 2,000 years to spread across the whole of the country. During the New Stone Age (Neolithic), around 4000 BC, the first sheep, goats and cattle were brought to Britain from the continent, as well as corn which was then planted to grow crops. Early farmers would build villages close to a water supply and clear woodland to create grazing for their animals. They also kept the first dogs, domesticating an animal that had first been bred from wolves, and pigs were bred from wild boar. Animals were used to provide milk and meat, and crops such as wheat, barley and corn were grown.

Skara Brae

In 1850, a storm in Orkney off the north-east coast of Scotland revealed a Neolithic village called Skara Brae. Whereas most Neolithic people built their homes out of wood, the people at Skara Brae used stone, thus preserving it for archaeologists to discover so much about these Neolithic farmers. They lived there between 3200 and 2500 BC, farming cattle and sheep, fishing, and growing barley and wheat. Their houses had stone walls with a small doorway and stone dressers, where they kept more valuable possessions. The roofs would have been made of thick moss and the houses were partially underground to help protect them from the wind. Stone and bone tools were used, with a separate workshop crafting these tools. There are eight dwellings preserved at Skara Brae, with the houses having a square room, a fireplace, stone beds and a shelved dresser.

Why is it called the Neolithic Revolution?

We call it the Neolithic Revolution because it changed the way people lived; gone were the hunter-gatherers, who had to follow the animals they preyed on in order to survive. Instead, they stayed in one place, making the land work for them. This was not an easy life, with woodland needing to be cleared for animals to graze; land needing to be cleared for crops; the crops needing to be protected and some requiring further preparation before they could be eaten. Although it was harder work than hunting and gathering, it provided a more settled way of life and communities started to spring up.

Key words

New Stone Age: Also called the Neolithic Age.
Star Carr: Mesolithic settlement in North Yorkshire.
Skara Brae: Neolithic village in Orkney.

Important dates

9000 BC: Mesolithic people live at Star Carr.
c.10,000 BC: The last Ice Age ends.
6000 BC: Britain separates from the European mainland due to ice melting.
5000–4000 BC: Farming begins in Britain.
3200–2500 BC: Neolithic farmers live at Skara Brae.

Useful links

www.orkneyjar.com/history/skarabrae/ Investigate the Neolithic site.
http://teachinghistory100.org/objects/about_the_object/mesolithic_headdress Information, pictures and teaching ideas about the objects found at Star Carr.
www.timemaps.com/hunter-gatherer Good site with links to other aspects, such as the coming of farming.

Lesson 1 Hunter-gatherers

Getting started
Ask pupils what they have for their snack at break time. In groups, they discuss whether it is something that could be found in the wild (a piece of fruit) or something manufactured. See if they can guess which items could have been collected by a hunter-gatherer.

Class activities
- Write the phrase 'hunter-gatherer' on the board and invite children to feed back what they think of when they picture a hunter-gatherer.
- Under a new heading of 'tools', discuss what sort of tools hunter-gatherers would have had at the time. Ask pupils what these tools would have been used for. Alternatively, write a list of tools on one side and their purpose on the other side and ask pupils to match them up correctly.
- Show some pictures of early tools: ask pupils to identify them and what each was used for.
- Pupils design their own hunter-gatherer settlement, ensuring there is enough for their tribe to survive on: fresh water, animals, shelter, plants, etc.

Plenary material
Pupils show their settlement to the rest of their group and explain why it is the best place to live.

Lesson 2 Hunting a mammoth

Getting started
Explain to the class that they are going to be hunting today. With pupils working in groups, ask them to list what they will need for it to be a successful hunt. (Working as a team.)

Class activities
- Put a picture of a woolly mammoth on the board: ask pupils why these animals were hunted.
- Collect feedback from the class; explain all the ways the mammoth was used. Ask the pupils if they can now see how important the animal was to the hunter-gatherers.
- What dangers would there be in hunting a mammoth?
- In groups of four or five, pupils design their own board game called Hunt the Mammoth; it could be a Snakes and Ladders-type game, or one involving cards that are picked up when landing on a certain square.

Plenary material
Read out various statements about hunter-gatherers and mammoths – pupils write *true* or *false* in the back of their books.

Lesson 3 Star Carr

Getting started
Tell the class that they are going to be archaeologists today. To start with, what can they find out about the things that are in the bin and recycling bin in the classroom or at home?

Class activities
- Explain that you are going to be looking at Star Carr. Ask pupils to list the important features of a Mesolithic settlement – what would they need to survive?
- Describe the situation of Star Carr: on the banks of a lake surrounded by woodland. Why would these surroundings be useful to hunter-gatherers? Show a picture of Star Carr and how it would have looked at the time of the settlement.
- Explain that many items were found at Star Carr. On the board, show the picture of the antler headdress found at Star Carr: ask pupils what it is. After revealing more about it, ask: why would it have been worn? For what purpose? (Hunting, religion, etc.) The class can even act it out.
- Look at some of the other objects found at Star Carr: what do they tell us about the people who lived there? Pupils can draw and label some of them, before describing what the objects reveal about the lives of the hunter-gatherers.

Plenary material
Working in groups, one pupil thinks of an object they have studied and the rest of the group has to guess what it is by asking a question that can only be answered with *yes* or *no*. They get to ask three questions before the object is revealed.

Further activities for pupils

- www.bbc.co.uk/scotland/learning/primary/skarabrae/ Fun site on Skara Brae with lots of activities for pupils.
- What problems would there have been during each season for the settlement at Star Carr?
- Introduction to farming: look at how farming methods arrived and started to spread around the country. What were the advantages of farming? Were there any disadvantages?

Further research for pupils

www.butserancientfarm.co.uk A wonderful Iron Age settlement in Hampshire; great for school trips.
www.yorkshiremuseum.org.uk Yorkshire Museum has a display on Star Carr.
www.historic-scotland.gov.uk/index.htm Visit this site for information on Skara Brae.

Cross-curricular links

Art and design: Paint or draw a picture of a mammoth hunt – the gorier, the better!
English: Write a series of diary entries pretending you are a hunter-gatherer at Star Carr.
Computing: Design on computer a map of Star Carr, as seen from above.
Geography: Design a hunter-gatherer settlement. What geographical features make it the best place?
Science: Investigate how the artefacts at Star Carr were so well preserved.
Drama: Wearing headdresses, act out a hunting party or a ritual.

Progression

1. Pupils understand some of the ways hunter-gatherers lived in the Mesolithic era.
2. Pupils can identify some of the tools used by hunter-gatherers.
3. Pupils recognise the geographical features of a Mesolithic settlement.
4. Pupils can explain the advantages of farming over hunter-gathering.
5. Pupils can see the disadvantages of farming over hunter-gathering.

Iron Age hill forts

In 30 seconds. . .

The Celts built hill forts for protection from enemies, with deep ditches, steep banks and palisades to help keep attackers out. Being situated on the top of a hill made them easier to defend, as well as providing the people with an excellent view of the surrounding countryside. Hill forts varied in size, with some only used as a sanctuary when under attack. Others, like the massive Maiden Castle, were bustling settlements, with whole villages contained within their imposing walls.

What do I need to know?

The Iron Age

By this time, metal had started to be used to make weapons and tools: first copper, then bronze and finally iron. Bronze (a mixture of copper and tin) was better than copper, but bent easily and did not stay sharp for long. Iron ore was in more plentiful supply than copper or tin but required very hot temperatures and lots of hammering and heating to beat it into shape. However, once made, iron tools and weapons were far superior. This resulted in trees being cleared more quickly with iron axes, soil being cultivated more effectively with ploughs and shovels, and weapons doing more damage.

Who were the Celts?

The Celts originated from central and western Europe, before arriving in Britain in around 500 BC. They had been the dominant race in Europe and soon became the same in Britain. Although the popular image of the Celts is of a warlike and fierce people, they were in fact a well-organised society, experienced in working with both bronze and iron. They had their own laws, tribes and chiefs, with most Celtic people being farmers. As a race, they were tall and fair, with blue eyes. Long-haired, the men also had long moustaches, and the women wove their hair in braids.

How did they live?

The Celts lived in wattle and daub huts with thatched roofs, with the chief usually having the biggest house. They farmed the land, and their communities would have storage pits, granaries, workshops and animal pens.

Hill forts

Hill forts were built for two main reasons: as a place to seek refuge when under attack, and as more permanent settlements, containing villages within their walls. They were built on a hill to provide a commanding view of the surrounding countryside, thus enabling the Celts to spot threats more easily. Earth would be piled up to form high banks, with wooden palisades built to offer further protection, and ditches would be dug. In some areas, stone walls were built, with platforms and guard towers for warriors. The larger hill forts were permanently occupied, with stores for grain, enclosures for animals, workshops for blacksmiths, and a shrine for worship.

Maiden Castle

Situated in Dorset, Maiden Castle had been a settlement long before the Iron Age: it was originally built in around 3000 BC and, around 450–350 BC, Iron Age Celts extended it. It covers about 47 acres (19 hectares) and has ramparts rising to 20 foot (6 metres) in places. It had double and triple ramparts for extra defence, with the entrances not lined up, thus making forced entry more difficult. It would have been a thriving community, with a marketplace where home-grown goods as well as imported items like wine, glass and oil could be sold. At the time of the Roman invasion of AD 43, Maiden Castle was occupied by the Durotriges tribe.

Other types of Celtic homes

In Scotland and Ireland, Celts sometimes lived in a crannog; these roundhouses were built in a loch or marsh, situated on an artificial island and accessible only by boat, which made them very difficult to attack. A broch was made of stone and it had thick walls and a small door, making it hard to attack. Built only in Scotland, brochs were shaped like towers and were between 15 and 42 feet (5 and 13 metres) high, comprising two storeys and sometimes an underground chamber. They may have been built for defensive purposes or by the local chief to show his stature and importance. An earth house was built into the ground, with natural protection provided by the earth, and would have been difficult to see. Wheelhouses, also found only in Scotland, were stone dwellings with walls like spokes that split the space into rooms.

Key words

Hill fort: Built on high ground, with ditches and banks of earth for protection.
Roundhouse: Typical dwelling of people in the Iron Age.
Palisades: Wooden fence built around a hill fort for added protection.
Maiden Castle: Huge Iron Age hill fort, from the Celtic *mai dun*, meaning 'great hill'.
Crannog: An artificial island, with one or two roundhouses on top.
Broch: Found only in Scotland; a stone tower with thick walls.
Wheelhouse: Also only in Scotland; a stone house with smaller rooms around the edge of it divided by spoke-like walls.

Important dates

500 BC: The Celts spread from mainland Europe to other parts of Europe and Britain.
450–350 BC: Maiden Castle is extended as an Iron Age fort.

> ## Interesting fact
>
> Some hill forts started life in the Neolithic period and were originally built to protect and pen in agricultural animals. From there, they started to expand, and more buildings were built inside.

Useful links

www.heritagedaily.com/2014/07/top-ten-iron-age-hill-forts-in-britain/100759 Ten hill forts to visit.

Lesson 1 Introduction to hill forts

Getting started
Tell the class that they are the leader of their Celtic tribe and they have to choose where to put their fort: do they put it next to a river, near a wood or on a hill? Poll to see which the most popular location was. Ask some of the pupils to feed back why they chose their location.

Class activities
- Ask the class what a hill fort is and record ideas on board. What sort of features would they expect to see?
- Explain and describe the main features of a hill fort.
- Hand out sheets for class to fill in. (**Bloomsbury Online Resource 5A**)
- Ask the class how the Celts would make these hill forts. (Wood, tools, etc.)

Plenary material
In small groups, pupils label the main features of a hill fort.

Lesson 2 Maiden Castle

Getting started
Recap features of a hill fort with a game of Hangman on the board.

Class activities
- Ask the class how big they think hill forts were. Then explain that they came in different sizes, with some of them able to shelter and protect whole communities.
- Find Maiden Castle on a map and show photographs of how it looks now. How would it have looked years ago? Pupils feed back ideas.
- Explain that there would have been a bustling market there. What sorts of goods would people have traded? Show pictures of goods; pupils label the pictures.
- Pupils draw and label Maiden Castle as it would have looked in 400 BC.

Plenary material
Split the class into small teams and ask them a series of questions about Maiden Castle, in a *true* or *false* style.

Lesson 3 Designing a hill fort

Getting started
Split the class into small groups: they have 30 seconds to list advantages of a hill fort.

Class activities
- Explain to the class that they are Celtic builders and they are going to design a hill fort.
- On the board, write a few key words in a spider diagram that pupils can use and refer to: *location*; *materials*; *size of community*; etc.
- Pupils plan their hill fort, ensuring there are enough natural resources nearby to support their Celtic community.
- They can either work individually or in small groups to draw/make their hill forts.
- Compare hill forts as a class. How are the designs different?

Plenary material
Explain that just as their own designs were different, so were Celtic hill forts; they were not all the same. Pose the question: is a bigger hill fort better than a small one? What are the advantages and disadvantages?

Further activities for pupils

- www.bbc.co.uk/wales/celts/ Lots of activities, games and stories on the Celts.
- www.bbc.co.uk/wales/celts/activities/buildahillfort.shtml Pupils can build their own hill fort.
- www.theschoolrun.com/homework-help/the-iron-age Useful information and a good video.
- Design your own board game for attacking and defending a hill fort.

Cross-curricular links

Art and design: Make a model of a hill fort.
English: Write a story about defending a hill fort.
Religious studies: Investigate the religious beliefs of the Celts.
Computing: In small groups, design a presentation on hill forts to present to the rest of the class.
Geography: Place on a map the ten hill forts listed in the Useful links website.

Progression

1. Pupils understand who built hill forts.
2. Pupils can identify some features of a hill fort.
3. Pupils can explain what went on inside a hill fort.
4. Pupils can identify advantages and disadvantages of a hill fort.
5. Pupils can identify the importance of location in building a hill fort.

6 The Roman Empire and its impact on Britain

What does the curriculum say?

- *Non-statutory examples include: Julius Caesar's attempted invasion in 55–54 BC; the Roman Empire by AD 42 and the power of its army; successful invasion by Claudius and conquest, including Hadrian's Wall; British resistance, for example, Boudicca; 'Romanisation' of Britain: sites such as Caerwent and the impact of technology, culture and beliefs, including early Christianity.*

Julius Cesar's attempted invasion in 55–54 BC

In 30 seconds. . .

Angered by the support that the Britons had given the Gauls against the mighty Roman army, famous Roman general Julius Caesar decided to invade the meddlesome island of Britain to teach its inhabitants a lesson. He was also interested in the silver, gold and tin mines. His first invasion in 55 BC was not a success, due to the poor weather and the fierceness of the Celtic warriors. Caesar returned a year later in 54 BC with a much bigger army, beating the British chieftain Cassivellaunus and putting the south-east of Britain under Roman control. However, it was a short stay as he soon had to return to Gaul to deal with more uprisings, and he took his Roman army back with him.

What do I need to know?

The first invasion

In 55 BC, the Romans were fighting in Gaul, in what is now France. In a tough and bloody conflict, the Roman general, Julius Caesar, heard that the Gauls were getting assistance from the Britons. This angered him and he was determined to teach the people of Britain a lesson; he was also no doubt interested in getting his hands on the lucrative silver, gold and tin mines in the country. Adding to these reasons the fact that the plentiful cornfields in Britain would help feed his vast army, the idea of an invasion became a reality. However, he had not had the chance to carry out reconnaissance of the island to gather its strengths and weaknesses, as well as the best places to land his ships. Having said that, Caesar had received word from the Celts that they would submit to him and Caesar had no reason to doubt this; after all, who could stand up to the might of the magnificently trained and disciplined Roman army?

An unfriendly welcome

In 55 BC, on the night of 25 August, Caesar sailed across the Strait of Dover with 10,000 men and 500 cavalry in 80 ships, with the Britons watching from the cliffs and tailing them as they sailed closer. Caesar then realised that the Celts had no intention of surrendering, as the Britons waved their weapons in the air and issued war cries. Many of the Britons rode in chariots and the Romans were wary of leaving their ships until a standard bearer from the 10th Legion jumped into the water, triggering the rest of them to follow. A fierce battle commenced in the shallow water as the Romans fought their way ashore. Their advance through the waist-high water was made more difficult by their armour weighing them down, and many fell before they could reach the shore. However, once on dry land, the disciplined and experienced Roman soldiers formed up and gained the upper hand in the battle, and the Britons fled inland. The Celts sent some chieftains, who apologised for the aggressive welcome and promised loyalty to Caesar. At this point, it looked as though Caesar would have an easy conquest of the island. His ships with his cavalry appeared in the distance, but then fate intervened as storms blew them back towards Gaul, and Caesar was left without his cavalry. The fierce winds also destroyed many of Caesar's ships, which now lay in tatters. With the Romans thus marooned on a hostile land without the reinforcements of cavalry coming, the Celts sensed their chance to rise up again. A number of short skirmishes followed, with the Celts launching quick attacks on the Romans, who repelled them each time, sending the natives scurrying back to their forest hideouts. Meanwhile, the Romans repaired their battered ships, knowing that invasion that would have to wait. Less than four weeks after landing, they boarded their ships, loaded with some prisoners, and headed back to Gaul.

The second invasion

Caesar was determined to resume what he saw as unfinished business and the next year, in 54 BC, he assembled an even bigger invasion force. This time 25,000 infantry (five legions) and 2,000 cavalry boarded 800 ships, including an elephant; probably the first time such a creature had been seen in Britain. Arriving in July, Caesar landed unopposed and his troops marched ashore. He knew that the Celts would look to engage the Romans in guerrilla warfare, but Caesar wanted to meet them on an open battlefield, where the superior Roman tactics, weaponry and discipline would win out.

Foiled again by the weather

Heading towards Canterbury, Caesar learnt from captured prisoners that the British base was less than 10 miles (16 km) away. But luck was not on his side as again the inclement weather intervened to help the natives. A gale wrecked around 40 of Caesar's moored ships; he had to turn around and head back to the shore to inspect the damage, to salvage and repair what he could. The Celts continued to snap at the Romans, refusing to meet them in open battle. Caesar finally lost patience and left his fortified camp to flush the Britons out. Reaching the Thames, Caesar used the elephant, with archers on top, to cross the river, causing the terrified Celts to flee into the trees. Aware that autumn was approaching and winter would soon follow, Caesar knew he had to gain control soon or lose the chance. Using a captured chieftain's son, Caesar promised to return the man to his kingdom and some of the tribes started to desert their leader, Cassivellaunus. After one last failed attempt to beat the Romans, Cassivellaunus called for a truce. Caesar accepted and negotiated a very favourable treaty, which Cassivellaunus promised to keep. However, Caesar was keen to be gone from Britain; trouble had flared up in Gaul and he had to keep control there, even at the expense of leaving Britain. Plus, Caesar had no doubt had enough of the awful weather and the fierce and cunning Celtic warriors. Caesar gathered his force and, with a few more prisoners, they boarded their ships and sailed back to Gaul. Caesar would never return to Britain.

Was Caesar's invasion a success?

The invasion was a partial success, insofar as Caesar forced Cassivellaunus to negotiate a truce. However, the first invasion, while lauded as a success back in Rome, had been far from it. Nevertheless, in Rome this latest venture was greeted with 20 days of celebration and Caesar remarked that the purpose of the first invasion had been to pave the way for the next one, which would add Britain to the vast Roman Empire. Although the second invasion was more successful in terms of establishing temporary control over the fierce inhabitants, the Romans did not stay in Britain and so it must ultimately be termed unsuccessful. If anything, Caesar's invasions of Britain paved the way for the future conquest of the island, as the Romans eyed the lucrative minerals and strategic position of Britain, being so close to Gaul.

Key words

Gauls: French natives from Gaul.

Important dates

25 August, 55 BC: Caesar sails from Gaul, heading to Britain.
26 August, 55 BC: Caesar and the Romans land on British shores.
Summer, 54 BC: Second invasion of Britain by Caesar.
c. 26 September, 54 BC: Caesar leaves Britain.

Important people

Julius Caesar (100 BC–44 BC): Politician and general who, after winning huge amounts of territory for the Roman Empire, seized power in Rome and became a dictator. However, his ambition, power and success upset some of the Roman senate, and he was assassinated by a number of senators led by Cassius and Brutus.
Cassivellaunus: Powerful British chieftain who led a number of tribes in revolt against Julius Caesar. He was eventually betrayed but called for a truce, and it was agreed he would provide hostages and pay tribute to Rome.

Interesting fact 1

Julius Caesar is so famous as a great general and leader that some words meaning 'leader' have sprung from his name – *tsar* in Russian and *kaiser* in German.

Interesting fact 2

In 75 BC, Caesar was kidnapped by pirates. Eventually freed after a ransom was paid, he hunted them all down and executed them, as he had promised them he would do!

Useful links

www.bbc.co.uk/education/clips/zs2mhyc Short clip looking at why Caesar invaded.

Lesson 1 Time to invade

Getting started

On the board, list some facts about the life of Julius Caesar. Pupils can look at them for 30 seconds and then see how many they can remember, individually or in groups.

Class activities

- Explain to the class that they are going to be investigating why Julius Caesar first invaded Britain in 55 BC. Ask what the pupils know about Julius Caesar. Explain that he was a famous and powerful Roman general.
- Ask the class why the Romans might want to invade Britain. After hearing their ideas, explain that there were a few reasons why Caesar wanted to invade.
- Split the reasons into different headings and write them down: *resources*; *revenge*; *minerals*. Which do pupils think was the most important reason and why?
- Pupils write a letter from Julius Caesar to the Senate explaining why he wants to launch an invasion. Remind them to include as many reasons as they can.

Plenary material

The vote for the most important reason for invading Britain in 55 BC.

Lesson 2 Fighting the Celts

Getting started

On the board, show pupils a picture of a Celtic warrior for 30 seconds. Then take the picture down and ask them to write as many details as they can from memory.

Class activities

- Explain that the Celts were fierce warriors. Look at the picture of the Celt again and have the class label the main features of a Celtic warrior.
- Ask the class how the Celts would have fought. Ask them to write a short descriptive paragraph on a Celtic charge. List key words on the board if needed.
- Pose the question: should the Romans have been worried about the Celts? Have a class discussion, looking at both sides.

Plenary material

The teacher says a key word and the class describe its relevance to the Celts: for instance, *woad*; *chariot*; *tin*; *Gaul*; *braid*.

Lesson 3 The first invasion

Getting started
- Write three jumbled-up key words to do with a Celtic warrior on the board: make the first one easy and then get progressively harder. Pupils have to unscramble the first one correctly before moving on to the second one.

Class activities
- Recap why Caesar wanted to invade Britain. Ask the class to give reasons.
- Show a picture of a Roman soldier. In groups, pupils list as many features as they can.
- On a photocopied picture, pupils label the features of a Roman soldier.
- Compare the picture of a Celtic warrior with that of a Roman soldier. What are the similarities/differences?
- Looking at the two different types of soldier, which would win in a fight? Is there any circumstance that could make a fight between them more even or suggest a different outcome?
- Explain to the class what happened during the first invasion. This can also be used for a comprehension-style exercise.
- Pose the question: was Caesar's first invasion a success? Look for reasons both for and against. This can be used as a writing exercise, with Caesar arguing that it was a success, and a Celt arguing that it was not a success.

Plenary material
- Take a class vote: was the first invasion a success?

Further activities for pupils

- Investigate the second invasion.
- Look at the battle tactics of both the Romans and the Celts.
- Assess the importance of discipline when fighting, for both the Roman army and the Celts.
- Write a speech from Caesar to the Senate, arguing why your invasions were a success.
- Write a speech as Cassivellaunus, explaining why you have negotiated a truce. Make sure you don't anger your Celtic people!

Further research for pupils

Newspaper History: The Roman Record by Paul Dowswell, an imaginative and humorous take on how modern tabloid front pages would look if reporting on famous Roman events.
iPad: *Ancient Roman Timeline* (Richard Carlson): Free app – a timeline of a number of important events and people in Roman history.
Roman Forum (Codegrind AB): Free app – experience how the Roman Forum would have looked 2,000 years ago.

Cross-curricular links

Art and design: Paint a mask for a Celtic warrior. Design a cartoon strip about Caesar's invasions.
English: Write an account of the first invasion from the point of view of either a Roman soldier or a Celtic warrior.
Computing: Design a poster calling for Celts to join the battle against the invading Romans.
Geography: Plot on a map where the Romans landed, and the main Celtic strongholds.
Drama: Act out Caesar addressing the Senate on his return to Rome.
PE: Act out a battle between the organised Roman army and the more disorganised Celts.

Progression

1. Pupils know who was in charge of the first invasion in 55 BC.
2. Pupils can identify features of a Celtic warrior.
3. Pupils understand why the Romans invaded Britain.
4. Pupils can put reasons for the invasion into order of importance.
5. Pupils can reason whether the invasion was a success or not.

The Roman Empire by AD 42 and its army

In 30 seconds. . .

At the time of the invasion of Britain in AD 43, the Roman army was the most efficient, disciplined and effective army the ancient world had seen. There were two main types of soldiers: legionaries (Roman citizens) and auxiliaries (from conquered lands or border territories). All soldiers were well trained in fighting with different weapons, had the best equipment that was available and maintained their discipline in battle. Many of the soldiers were capable engineers and builders. All this resulted in an outstanding army.

What do I need to know?

Life in the army

Legionaries had to be born Roman citizens; they served in the army for 20 years, after which they would receive a pension or plot of land to farm. They wore iron-plate armour, with a helmet that had guards over the neck and cheeks. They were equipped with a short sword (*gladius*), dagger, shield and javelin or spear (*pilum*). The end of the spear was made of soft metal so it would bend upon impact, thus rendering it ineffective if thrown back in retaliation! Legionaries were also trained in building and engineering and were the most important soldiers in the Roman army. Auxiliaries were made up of men recruited from conquered lands. After serving for 25 years, they became Roman citizens. They were often put into the most dangerous situations in battle, as they were viewed as more expendable than the legionaries. However, they would often be useful in providing local knowledge about the area and they were very useful in the conquest of Britain. Auxiliaries were equipped with a longer sword and had oval shields, with units of cavalry, archers and slingers. Training for a legionary was hard and lasted four months. During this time, they would complete obstacle courses in full armour, fight mock battles with weighted weapons to help build up muscles and take part in long marches fully loaded with armour and equipment. They were trained in different types of fighting, building, engineering, riding and swimming. All of this meant that they were tremendously disciplined and thus more effective fighters when it mattered, able to follow orders in the heat of battle. Soldiers based in a fort would have training to keep them in shape, with weekly marches of up to 18 miles (30 kilometres) and drill practice twice a day. For a soldier on the move, life was harder; they would have to build a camp at the end of marching all day. They would be equipped with rations, a pot for cooking, spare clothes, a short spade and two wooden stakes to build a fence around the camp.

The size of the empire

After becoming the dominant power in the Mediterranean, the Romans realised that a bigger empire would bring ever greater treasures. With such a powerful army, the Roman Empire spread in all directions. Although it would reach its peak in around AD 117, by AD 42 it was already huge. Even before this, by the time Julius Caesar was murdered in 44 BC, the Roman Empire included Spain (Hispaniola), France (Gaul), Greece (Achaea) and coastal parts of North Africa. Under Octavian, the Romans added Egypt as a Roman province but failed to add Germany to the empire. However, under the new Emperor Tiberius, Rome managed to secure the Rhine frontier due to the work of the general Germanicus, who was rewarded by Tiberius. Caligula was the next emperor but he failed to add to the empire; he was succeeded by Claudius, who would expand the Roman Empire in AD 43 to include Mauretania, (what is today Morocco), Britain, Thrace (what are now the borders of Bulgaria, Greece and Turkey) and Lycia (southern coast of Turkey). The success of the Roman Empire depended on the might of the Roman army maintaining control over all the provinces, resisting uprisings and rebellions. This in turn created the conundrum: the further the empire spread, the more stretched the lines of communication became and the harder it was to keep control in so large an area, even with the expertise of the Roman army.

Key words

Legionary: A soldier who was born a Roman citizen.
Auxiliary: A soldier belonging to the tribes that the Romans had conquered.
Gladius: A short sword favoured by the Roman soldier.
Pilum: A javelin just over 6 feet (2 metres) long.
Legion: A legion contained between 5,000 and 6,000 soldiers.
Cohorts: A legion was divided into ten cohorts. Each cohort had six centuries, normally of around 80 men per century.
Centurion: Each centurion led about 80 men.
Aquilifer: The officer that carried the sacred eagle of their legion into battle.

Useful links

www.bbc.co.uk/schools/primaryhistory/romans/the_roman_army/ Lots of useful information.
www.romanarmy.net/pdf/Members%20Handbook%20%28Part%206%29-Drill%20Manual.pdf
A comprehensive list of drill commands.

Lesson 1 Building an empire

Getting started
Read out some Latin drill commands that would have been used to command the Roman army. Give pupils a list of them and ask them to practise saying them.

Class activities
- Show a picture of Italy on the board, labelling Rome. Tell pupils that Rome was the centre of the Roman Empire. Pose the question: if the pupils were the Roman Emperor, which direction would they go in to expand their empire, and why?
- Explain that the location of Rome meant that conquest was possible in many directions. Look at a map of the Roman Empire. What would be needed to conquer surrounding lands?
- Show the class a picture of the Roman army in formation, such as *testudo* (tortoise): in small groups, pupils feed back what the formation tells them about the Roman army.
- On one side of the board, list some of the key words, such as *legionaries*, *auxiliaries*, etc. and on the other side, list the definitions. In groups, pupils try to match them. Go through them.

Plenary material
Split the class into groups of however many key words are on the board. Tell each group they will be asked to explain a key word in one minute, but don't tell them which. Then assign a key word to each group, to explain to the rest of the class.

Lesson 2 Life in the army

Getting started
Write some of the key definitions from the last lesson on the board. In pairs, pupils write down the key words that match the definitions.

Class activities
- Explain that discipline was very important in the Roman army: even in the heat of battle, the soldiers followed orders without fail. Why was this so important?
- Write some of the Latin drill commands on the board: go through them with the class, so they understand how they sound and what they mean.
- Explain that they are going to be Roman soldiers today – they must be disciplined.
- Once they have learnt some basic drill commands, take the pupils to an area big enough to practise them, with the whole class acting as Roman soldiers. They can all hold a ruler as a *gladius*, or even make some weapons.
- Depending on how successful they are at the drill commands, try out a few battle formations.
- Once back in class, pupils write a short report on what it was like to be a Roman soldier.

Plenary material
Give the class a short test on Latin drill commands: tell them the definition, and they have to write down the command.

Lesson 3 Roman weapons

Getting started
Write some of the Latin names for Roman weapons on the board and ask pupils to practise saying them out loud in groups: *pilum, gladius, pugio, ballista, scorpio*, etc. Can they guess what any of them are?

Class activities
- Split pupils into small groups. Hand out photocopied pictures of the main weapons without the names. Ask pupils to describe the weapons and how they would be used.
- Hand out the English definitions; see if the pupils can pair them with the correct picture.
- Finally, hand out the Latin names of the weapons. Give pupils a few minutes to arrange them into groups, and then go through the correct Latin names.
- Hand out sheets for pupils to complete. **(Bloomsbury Online Resource 6A)**
- Can they think of any weaknesses of any of the weapons?

Plenary material
In groups, pupils discuss which Roman weapon is their favourite and why.

Further activities for pupils

- Using a timeline, chart the rise and eventual fall of the Roman Empire.
- Investigate some of the battles against the Gauls, Celts and barbarians: how were tactics important?

Further research for pupils

http://primaryfacts.com/1179/roman-army-facts/ Information, facts and a clip showing a Roman Legion at war!

http://primaryfacts.com/1177/roman-soldier-facts/ Includes a clip about discipline, weapons and clothing.

Spartacus (1960), directed by Stanley Kubrick, starring Kirk Douglas (not to be confused with the series of the same name, which is not suitable for children); *Ben Hur* (1959), directed by William Wyler.

The *Roman Mystery* books by Caroline Lawrence; a good starting point would be *The Thieves of Ostia*.

The Eagle of the Ninth by Rosemary Sutcliff: a novel about the missing 9th Legion, suitable for children aged 8 and above.

iPad: *Roads of Rome 2* (Realore): A game that combines strategy and time management.

There are many companies that will visit your school, such as **www.legion-fourteen.com/romans. htm** and **www.romantoursuk.com/schools.htm**.

Cross-curricular links

Art and design: Make a life-size Roman shield.

English: Write an account of being a Roman soldier in a battle. Write a series of diary entries on what it is like training to be a Roman soldier.

Computing: In groups, create a short presentation on life in the Roman army.

Geography: Colour in a map showing the expansion of the Roman Empire.

Science: Make a replica *ballista*, *trebuchet* or *scorpio*!

Drama: Learn some battle formations and fighting techniques.

Progression

1. Pupils understand that the Roman Empire was very large at its peak.
2. Pupils understand the importance of discipline and organisation in the Roman army.
3. Pupils can name the different types of soldiers in the Roman army.
4. Pupils can identify some of the weapons used by the Roman army.
5. Pupils can explain how the Roman army was such an effective fighting force.

Invasion by Claudius and conquest, Hadrian's Wall

In 30 seconds. . .

In AD 43, Claudius sent an army of 40,000 troops and several elephants to Britain. Many tribes, upon seeing the strength of the Roman army, made peace with the Romans, and the tribal capital of Colchester was taken. Britain was now under Roman control and would be so for the next 365 years. Years later, the emperor Hadrian visited Britain and, due to the constant skirmishes with tribes from the north (the Picts), ordered a wall to be built to keep them out. This was Hadrian's Wall.

What do I need to know?

Why did the Romans invade Britain again?

The Romans had been keeping an eye on Britain and saw it as unfinished business since Caesar had twice invaded with limited success. This time, there was no excuse for repeating what had happened before; the Romans wanted Britain as a province, to reap the benefits of the country as a trading post and to get their hands on the tin mines. Also, and perhaps more importantly, the new emperor Claudius was not seen as a particularly strong leader; he would have seen a successful conquest of Britain as a good way to silence his critics.

The Romans seize control

The Romans arrived in Britain, landing at Richborough with over 40,000 men, split equally between legionaries and auxiliaries. They were led by Aulus Plautius and fought a big battle against the Catuvellauni tribe along the banks of the River Medway. When the Britons fled across the Thames, the Romans followed, laying siege to the enemy stronghold of Camulodunum (Colchester) and eventually seizing it. After the capital was taken, a delighted Claudius led his troops in, riding on the back of an elephant. The Roman advance into Britain continued, though it took decades to get Wales under control. There were further major uprisings, the most famous spearheaded by Boudicca. The Romans never had total control of the whole of Britain; Scotland was never taken and the Romans did not send many troops to Ireland.

Why did the Romans build Hadrian's Wall?

The wall was built to keep out the Picts (Scots) from the north and took six years to build. Manned by the auxiliary troops, Hadrian's Wall was almost destroyed three times by the Picts and was guarded for around 250 years, making it a dangerous and lonely outpost for those who were stationed there. It stretched from the Tyne estuary to the Solway Firth, around 73 miles (79 Roman miles, or 117 km).

Features of Hadrian's Wall

A wall alone would not have been sufficient; the Romans added a series of forts that ran the length of Hadrian's Wall, occupied by auxiliary soldiers who patrolled the dangerous border wall. There was a big fort every 5 miles (8 kilometres), where up to 500 men could be stationed and called upon. There were also a number of smaller forts. Hadrian's Wall was built by legionaries, and it took around 15,000 of them to complete the job. It was truly a great engineering feat. The height of it varied, due to the rolling countryside that it cut across, but it was generally between 16 and 20 feet (5 and 6 metres) high and 10 feet (3 metres) wide, with a ditch running alongside the wall for added protection.

Key words

Colchester: Stronghold of Caratacus, a Catevellaunian prince.
Picts: A collection of tribes that lived in Scotland.
Hadrian's Wall: A defensive wall that stretched across the northern border, from the River Tyne to the Solway Firth.

Important dates

AD 43: The Romans successfully invade and conquer Britain.
AD 122: Hadrian arrives in Britain and starts to plan the building of Hadrian's Wall.

Important people

Caratacus: Chieftan of the Catuvellauni tribe who was captured and taken to Rome, but was then surprisingly pardoned and released after impressing Claudius with an impassioned speech.
Aulus Plautius: Roman politician and general who served as governor of Britain between AD 43 and 47.
Boudicca: Legendary leader of the Iceni tribe who led a revolt against the Romans. After a number of successes including Colchester and London, she was defeated and it is thought that she poisoned herself.
Claudius (10 BC–AD 54): Roman Emperor who oversaw the conquest of Britain.
Hadrian (76–138): Roman Emperor who oversaw the building of Hadrian's Wall.

Useful links

www.bbc.co.uk/history/ancient/british_prehistory/iron_01.shtml List of British tribes.

Lesson 1 Time to invade!

Getting started
Explain that the pupils are going to be in charge of a Roman invasion fleet: in groups, they list all they will need for a successful invasion of Britain.

Class activities
- On a timeline, show Julius Caesar's first invasion and then the invasion by Claudius in AD 43. Pose the question: why would Claudius want to invade Britain? (Give some hints if needed.)
- Ask the pupils why an invasion would make Claudius more popular. Is it still the case today?
- Explain the reasons behind the planned invasion in AD 43. In small groups, pupils prepare a speech by Claudius to be delivered to the rest of the class, acting as the Senate. Once each group has given their speech, the rest of the class can quiz them and ask questions.
- Individual writing exercise: write a speech by Claudius explaining why you are launching an invasion and what you hope to achieve.

Plenary material
Sum up the reasons for the invasion and take a vote on which was the most important.

Lesson 2 Who's in charge?

Getting started
Ask: who is in charge of the school? After pupils have written down their answers, ask which of them would take charge in your (the teacher's) absence. The class will probably write down lots of different names. Explain that they would not therefore be united; this was one of the problems when the Romans invaded Britain in 43 AD.

Class activities
- Show the class a map of Britain in AD 43 that also shows the different tribes.
- Hand out a photocopied map showing the tribes, and ask pupils to label and colour it in.
- Pose questions about the various tribes to do with their size and geographical location, with pupils writing statements about the map in their books.
- Ask pupils to think of other questions that they could ask other groups; they can do this orally.
- Pose the question: what advantages would the Romans have over the Celts in AD 43? Would there be any disadvantages?
- Writing activity: as a leader of one of the Celtic tribes, write about how you feel as the Romans start to invade. Are you feeling confident of repelling them?

Plenary material
Run a short quiz on some of the main tribes in Britain in AD 43.

Lesson 3 Hadrian's Wall

Getting started
Have a quick game of Hangman, using British tribes' names as the words.

Class activities
- Show the class a picture of Hadrian's Wall as it would have looked in Roman times. Pose the question: why would a wall be built?
- Explain the reason behind the building of the wall and a few facts about it. Pupils can research this in groups, using ICT if available.
- On the board, write the phrase *stationed at Hadrian's Wall* and ask pupils what it would have been like to be an auxiliary patrolling the wall. Record their answers on the board.
- Leaving their ideas on the board, tell the pupils to imagine they are an auxiliary on Hadrian's Wall and to write a letter home describing what it is like.

Plenary material
Pupils feed back to the rest of the class one phrase or sentence from their letters.

Further activities for pupils

- Investigate the path Claudius took when he landed in Britain.
- As a Celt, describe what it would have been like seeing an elephant for the first time.
- Investigate facts and figures about the building of Hadrian's Wall.

Further research for pupils

Roman Frontiers – Hadrian's Wall/Antonine Wall, documentary on Hadrian's Wall in England and the Antonine Wall in Scotland.
Across the Roman Wall by Theresa Breslin, a book suitable for Lower KS2.
iPad: *Roman army fortifications in Britain. Hadrian's Wall* (Jacek Chedor), a virtual 3D tour over some of the more impressive parts of Hadrian's Wall. (There is also a Lite version that is free.)
Visit: **www.visithadrianswall.co.uk** Hadrian's Wall.

Cross-curricular links

Art and design: Make a model of Hadrian's Wall or draw/paint a picture of it.
English: Write an account from the Picts about seeing and attacking Hadrian's Wall.
Computing: Create a poster advertising for jobs either building or patrolling Hadrian's Wall.
Geography: Trace the route Claudius took when he invaded. On a map, draw in Hadrian's Wall.
Drama: Do a series of news reports about either Claudius's invasion, or building and working on Hadrian's Wall. Perhaps record them using GarageBand, with groups doing it as a project.

Progression

1. Pupils can recall when Claudius invaded Britain.
2. Pupils can explain why Hadrian's Wall was built.
3. Pupils can give reasons why Claudius invaded Britain.
4. Pupils can explain reasons why Claudius was successful.

British resistance and Boudicca

In 30 seconds. . .

When the Romans invaded Britain first under Julius Caesar and then more successfully under Claudius, the British did not submit without a fight. Tribes that had up until that time been splintered united to fight the common foe. Caratacus, the son of the king of the Catuvellauni tribe, tried to stop the Roman invaders in skirmish raids but was eventually betrayed and defeated. More famously, Boudicca, queen of the Iceni tribe, led a huge revolt against the Romans. After seizing Colchester, she slaughtered many Romans and even Celts that were sympathetic to the Romans. Boudicca made the mistake of fighting the well-organised Romans in an open battle; 80,000 Celts were killed but her body was never found.

What do I need to know?

A fearsome welcome

The Celts had twice fought hard against Caesar when he had tried to invade, first in 55 BC and then a year later in 54 BC. By the time Claudius launched the next invasion in AD 43, the Celts were no closer to submitting without a fight. The Celts fought quite differently to the Romans; where the Romans were very organised and well drilled, relying on teamwork and discipline to win battle after battle, the Celts had a more primitive approach to fighting. Covered in blue woad, they would often ride to battle in a chariot and then fight on foot. Although they would be equipped with spears, shields and swords, they did not wear armour. They were extremely fierce and aggressive warriors but were not well organised or disciplined like the Romans. The Celts were better suited to adopting guerrilla tactics, using quick raids to snap at the more powerful Roman force rather than engaging them in open battle.

Caratacus

Caratacus was the son of the king of the Catuvellauni tribe (Cunobelinus), who resisted the Romans when they invaded in AD 43. Caratacus had his stronghold at Camulodunum (Colchester) and faced the advancing Roman army at the River Medway. Along with his brother Togodumnus, Caratacus fought and lost against the Romans in battle but managed to escape to South Wales. Here he led small groups of raiders against the Romans in fast hit-and-run raids, knowing that he would not stand a chance in an open battle. These guerrilla tactics proved a nuisance to the Romans but, buoyed by his success, Caratacus foolishly decided to face the Romans in battle and was defeated. He managed to escape and fled north to the Brigantes tribe, where he planned for future campaigns against the Romans. Cartimandua, the queen of the Brigantes tribe, was loyal to the Romans, though, and Caratacus was captured and taken to Rome. Paraded in front of the Roman Senate, Caratacus gave an impassioned speech and Claudius was so impressed, Caratacus was released and pardoned. He lived the rest of his life in Rome.

Boudicca

A more famous figure of British resistance was Boudicca, queen of the Iceni tribe in Norfolk. Her husband, Prasutagus, had made a treaty with the Romans but when he died, the Romans took all his land. Boudicca was supposedly beaten and her daughters attacked, resulting in her hatred for the Romans and lust for bloody revenge. In AD 60, she united the other tribes of East Anglia and marched towards Colchester. There was not a large Roman force there, as the majority of them were in Wales and their governor, Suetonius, was in Anglesey. When Boudicca and her army reached Colchester, they burnt it down and slaughtered thousands. Both Romans and those Celts who were friendly to them died in the carnage. The 9th Legion was defeated in battle, with only the cavalry escaping. The governor, General Suetonius Paulinus, marched with the 14th and 20th Legions to intercept Boudicca. However, he could not reach her in time: Boudicca reached London and Suetonius, hearing that his force in London was greatly outnumbered by Boudicca's army, ordered the small Roman army to leave the city. Boudicca therefore arrived in London to find it undefended, and her army looted the houses and massacred thousands of the townspeople. They went on to do the same to St Albans (Verulamium) before General Suetonius Paulinus met them in battle. The terrain suited the Romans: a narrow valley with a wood behind them, and open country in front. Although the Celts numbered around 80,000 to the Romans' 10,000, the Celts had brought their families in lines of wagons to watch what they assumed would be a famous victory. Once the battle started, the supremely trained Roman soldiers, with auxiliaries and legionaries, and cavalry on their flanks, destroyed the larger number of ill-disciplined Celts. Those who tried to flee were barred from doing so by the wagons full of their families, and the Roman troops showed no mercy to anyone there. Rather than be captured alive, Boudicca managed to escape to the woods, before taking poison and her own life. Her brave and bloody revolt was over.

Key words

Guerrilla tactics: Hit-and-run warfare by irregular (non-standard military) troops against a larger force.
Blue woad: A blue natural dye taken from the woad plant. Used by Celts and Picts, among- others.

Important dates

AD 43: Caratacus is defeated.
AD 50: Caratacus is captured.
AD 60: Boudicca revolts.

Important people

Caratacus: Fought the Romans using guerrilla tactics.
Boudicca: Queen of the Iceni tribe.
Suetonius: Roman governor.
Tacitus: Roman senator and historian.

Useful links

www.theschoolrun.com/homework-help/boudica Includes a video clip.

Lesson 1 What makes a good leader?

Getting started
Ask pupils to write down three words that would describe a good Celtic leader. Then go around the class, writing one answer from each pupil on the board. As they all have to write three down, there should not be too many repetitions.

Class activities
- Discuss with the class what was needed to be a strong leader of the Celts.
- Using the words that they have contributed on the board, pupils create a job advert/poster advertising the position of leader of the Celts.
- In small groups, pupils hold a mock job interview for the post. Issue each pupil with a Celtic name (using a Celtic name generator, or they make up their own) as well as various qualities: can they pass a difficult job interview to be king or queen of the Celts?

Plenary material
Pupils each have ten seconds to explain why their Celtic character would be the best fit for leader.

Lesson 2 Celtic warriors

Getting started
Recap the qualities needed to be a good leader. Each pupil stands up and says one quality before nominating the next person to stand up and contribute.

Class activities
- Show the class a picture of a Celtic warrior. Put pupils into small groups and ask them to describe what they see.
- Ask them to list any good points/advantages of fighting like a Celt.
- Ask them to list any bad points/disadvantages of fighting like a Celt.
- Pupils colour in and label a Celtic warrior.
- Pupils write a short report on how the Celts fought.

Plenary material
In groups or pairs, pupils write three short statements to sum up a Celtic warrior.

Lesson 3 Who was Boudicca?

Getting started

Recap the qualities needed to be the leader of the Celts. Could a woman be leader in those days?

Class activities

* Without mentioning the name *Boudicca*, read out the story of this fearsome Celtic leader and pose the question to pupils: was this leader a man or a woman? Take a vote.
* Show a picture of Boudicca and ask the class to describe what they see.
* Hand out photocopies of the life of Boudicca and ask pupils to complete a comic strip on her life. **(Bloomsbury Online Resource 6B)**

Plenary material

Show a jumbled-up version of Boudicca's life and ask pupils to put it into the right order.

Further activities for pupils

* Write an obituary for Boudicca.
* Create a newspaper front page reporting on Boudicca's revolt or defeat.
* Write a speech from Boudicca to rally all Celts behind her.
* Create a comic strip on the life of Caratacus.
* Imagine you are a Senator; explain why Caratacus impressed you with his speech.

Further research for pupils

Battlefield Britain: Boudicca's Revolt: An excellent TV series presented by Peter and Dan Snow.
Horrible Histories: Boudicca: As usual, *Horrible Histories* cover the material in their own inimitable way!
Arthur Archer and the Warrior Queen: 2 by Ben Molyneux.

Cross-curricular links

Art and design: Create a 'Wanted' poster for Boudicca, drawn by the Romans.
English: Write a letter from Boudicca to the Romans, saying why you are fighting back.
Computing: In pairs or small groups, create a presentation on Boudicca's or Caratacus' life.
Geography: Trace Boudicca's path of terror.
Drama: Write and perform a series of news programmes reporting on Boudicca's revolt and eventual defeat. Write them from either the Celts' or the Romans' point of view.

Progression

1. Pupils recognise that there was resistance to Roman rule.
2. Pupils can name one of the two Celtic leaders who resisted the Romans.
3. Pupils can recall facts about Boudicca and/or Caratacus.
4. Pupils recognise what made Boudicca a strong leader.
5. Pupils can explain why the Romans beat Caratacus and Boudicca.

7 Britain's settlement by Anglo-Saxons and Scots

What does the curriculum say?

- *Non-statutory examples include: Roman withdrawal from Britain c. AD 410 and the fall of the western Roman Empire; Scots invasions from Ireland to north Britain (now Scotland); Anglo-Saxon invasions, settlements and kingdoms: place names and village life; Anglo-Saxon art and culture; Christian conversion – Canterbury, Iona and Lindisfarne.*

Anglo-Saxon invasions, settlements and kingdoms: place names and village life

In 30 seconds. . .

When the Romans left Britain, the door was open for more invaders, who soon took advantage of the newly undefended country. Scots and Picts from the north and Angles, Saxons and Jutes from Germany and Denmark sailed across the North Sea. They were farmers, and soon settlements grew that gradually became larger until there were seven kingdoms in England.

What do I need to know?

The first arrivals

The Angles and Saxons (as well as other people) had often raided Britain in small parties but had been repelled by the Romans. However, in around AD 410, when the Romans left Britain, there was nothing to stop these new invaders from settling. The Angles came from north Germany, Norway, Denmark and Sweden. The Saxons came from Germany and Denmark. The Jutes came from Denmark too, from the same sort of area as the Angles. From north of the border came the Picts and Scots. This period is known as the Dark Ages, so called because there are so few accounts from the time: the invaders could not read or write so nothing was recorded. Most of what we know from this time is from archaeological finds or from the writing of Bede, who lived around 300 years later.

Hengist and Horsa

The British commander Vortigern hired Saxon mercenaries to help fight against the invading Picts from the north. Two of these Saxon leaders were Hengist and Horsa, who were paid in money and land to help repel the Picts. However, Hengist and Horsa liked what they saw and decided to stay; they rebelled against Vortigern, taking the land for themselves. After they defeated the Picts, more Saxons arrived, who were also given money and land in return for protecting the country. The invaders crossed the North Sea in narrow longboats that could carry about 40 men. As they navigated the rivers bringing them further inland, they ignored the towns left by the Romans and, being farmers, took the fertile lands for their homes. It was far easier to take by force the farmland that the Britons lived on rather than clearing the impenetrable forest that covered much of the island. Those who didn't flee were either killed or made slaves.

The Saxons settle

The Angles settled in East Anglia, the Midlands and Northumbria. England means 'land of the Angles' and East Anglia means 'the place of the east Angles'. The Saxons settled in Sussex, ('south Saxons'), Wessex ('west Saxons'), too large to be a county today, Essex ('east Saxons') and Middlesex ('middle Saxons'). The Jutes settled in Hampshire, Kent and the Isle of Wight. Settlements soon grew as they farmed the land and cut down trees to build their wooden houses, some with wattle and daub walls. The houses had thatched roofs and the settlements had fences around them to protect their inhabitants from wild animals and enemies.

Village life

Saxons ploughed the fields using heavy ploughs and grew barley, wheat, rye and oats. Some fields were left fallow to maintain soil nutrients for the next year, and their animals grazed on the grass. The core diet of the Saxons was bread, cheese, milk and eggs but they enjoyed pork and fish when they could. The poorer Saxons drank ale (a weak beer), while the richer families drank wine and mead (made with honey and water). The houses varied in size, with the lord (or *thane*) having the largest. The lord would give or rent land to the freemen, who would farm it and provide food as well as military service if required. Most of the villages had a meeting place and the hall would be the largest building in the village; it was here that the thane would host feasts for his guests. The poorer families would share their simple houses with their animals, with no windows or chimney for smoke from the fire to escape. One of the most important people in the village was the smith (blacksmith), who fashioned farming tools like spades, scythes and ploughshares as well as crafting weapons like swords and spears.

Kings and kingdoms

The many settlements established by the Anglo-Saxons gradually became small kingdoms and, by around AD 600, there were seven of them: Northumbria, Mercia, Wessex, East Anglia, Sussex, Essex and Kent. The first Anglo-Saxon kings were successful leaders who had led their warriors into England: Hengist and Horsa in Kent; Aelle in Sussex; Cerdic and Cynric in Wessex. These kings would pass written laws that their subjects had to obey, with harsh punishments for those who broke them. They also collected taxes from their people, had coins minted and led their men into battle. A king would be assisted in some of his decisions by the Witan, a council made up of his most important thanes (nobles) and bishops.

Key words

The Dark Ages: Early medieval period around the time AD 500–1000, so called because of the perceived barbarism and lack of knowledge and learning. However, this was not always the case.
Angles: Germanic tribe that invaded Britain (from what is now southwest Denmark), settling in Mercia and Northumbria.
Saxons: Another Germanic tribe that invaded Britain (from what is now northwest Germany), settling predominantly in East Anglia.
Jutes: Germanic tribe (from what is now Denmark) that settled on the south coast of Britain and in Wessex.
Picts: A collection of tribes that lived in Scotland.
Wattle and daub: A method of constructing walls using wood that is then patched with a mixture of water, mud, straw and dung.
Thane: A Saxon lord who owned a lot of land.
Witan: Also known as Witenagemot, a council that advised the king.

Important dates

c. AD 410: The Romans leave Britain.
AD 449: Hengist and Horsa arrive in Kent.

Important people

Vortigern: A leading ruler in Britain who hired Saxon mercenaries to help fight against the Picts.
Hengist: Saxon mercenary and one of the leaders of the first Anglo-Saxon settlers.
Horsa: Saxon mercenary and brother of Hengist.
Bede (c. 672–735): Famous English monk, theologian and historian whose *Ecclesiastical History of the English People* tells us much of what we know about the 'Dark Ages' and Anglo-Saxon life.

Interesting fact

Many towns and villages today are named after Saxon villages. Places ending in words including 'worth', 'ford', 'den', 'wick', 'bury', 'ham' and 'minster' all originate from Saxon times.

Useful links

www.localhistories.org/saxonlife.html
http://anglosaxondiscovery.ashmolean.org/index.html

Lesson 1 Invasion!

Getting started
Split pupils into pairs or groups and write *Picts*, *Scots*, *Jutes* and *Saxons* on the board. On the other side of the board, write where they came from in a random order: give pupils one minute to sort them and guess where they came from. Reveal the answers as the lesson continues.

Class activities
- Recap that the Romans had been a very efficient and organised fighting force that had prevented any other invaders from establishing themselves in Britain – like a fierce guard dog! What might happen if there was no guard dog?
- Pose the question: why did the Romans leave Britain? Explain that Rome itself was under threat: why would this result in the Romans leaving Britain?
- Look at a map that shows Britain and Europe: explain where the invaders came from.
- Hand out photocopied maps for pupils to colour in and label where each of the invaders originally came from.
- Pupils design a newspaper front page that describes the Anglo-Saxon invasion.
  (Bloomsbury Online Resource 7A)

Plenary material
Split the class into pairs. Assign these questions to each pair and pupils take turns explaining the answer to their partner: Why did the Romans leave Britain? Where did the invaders come from?

Lesson 2 Why did the Anglo-Saxons settle in Britain?

Getting started
Recap where the Anglo-Saxons came from and why they invaded.

Class activities
- Explain that the Anglo-Saxons came over for a few reasons: their land would flood and was therefore not suitable for farming; there was not enough land for everybody; the land in Britain was good for farming; the Romans had left. Pupils discuss and rate reasons in order of importance.
- Explain how the Anglo-Saxons arrived in their longboats and sailed up the rivers. How would the local people have felt when they saw these invaders arrive?
- Pupils imagine they are Britons watching the Anglo-Saxons arrive. They write a first-hand account of what happened when these invaders arrived.

Plenary material
In pairs, one pupil explains to the other the type of landscape the invaders came from and then their partner explains the benefit of the land in Britain. Then they swap. At the end, they can rate one another's explanations.

Lesson 3 Village life

Getting started
Pupils work in groups. Ask them to list the different Anglo-Saxon invaders; where they came from originally; and why they invaded.

Class activities
- Explain that Anglo-Saxons lived in villages and were farmers.
- Show the class a picture of an Anglo-Saxon village. What features can they identify?
- In groups or pairs, pupils research Anglo-Saxon village life.

Plenary material
Each pair/group feeds back to the rest of the class what they have found out.

Further activities for pupils

- Investigate Anglo-Saxon words and place names.
- Examine archaeological evidence from the Anglo-Saxons and what it tells us about daily life.
- Have an Anglo-Saxon school day!

Further research for pupils

http://pastexplorers.org.uk/village/ Explore an Anglo-Saxon village; great for pupils.
Wolf Girl by Theresa Tomlinson, adventure set in Anglo-Saxon times.
Visit: **https://www.weststow.org** West Stow Anglo-Saxon village in Suffolk.

Cross-curricular links

Art and design: Paint a picture showing Anglo-Saxon village life.
English: Write a series of diary entries about life in an Anglo-Saxon village.
Religious studies: Research the religious beliefs of the Anglo-Saxons.
Geography: Research modern names of places with Anglo-Saxon roots.
Science: Research Anglo-Saxon blacksmiths.
Drama: Act out the story of Hengist and Horsa.
Music: Make up a short song about Anglo-Saxon invaders.

Progression

1. Pupils can identify some of the invaders who arrived after the Romans.
2. Pupils can explain why the Anglo-Saxons settled in Britain.
3. Pupils can identify some features of Anglo-Saxon village life.
4. Pupils can explain different sections of Anglo-Saxon life.

Christian conversion: Canterbury, Iona and Lindisfarne

In 30 seconds. . .

Ignoring the Christianity that the Romans had introduced to Britain, the Anglo-Saxons were pagans who worshipped many gods. The monks Patrick and Columba converted parts of Ireland, Scotland and England to Christianity, establishing monasteries along the way. Pope Gregory sent Augustine to England to spread the word, and he later became the first Archbishop of Canterbury. The Synod of Whitby saw the traditions established by Celtic missionaries from Ireland abandoned, with Christians across the country now united in following the Roman Church.

What do I need to know?

A pagan way of life

Although the Romans had brought Christianity to Britain, the Anglo-Saxons were not Christians. Those natives who held on to Christian beliefs fled from the invading Anglo-Saxons and settled in Wales, Scotland and Cornwall. The Anglo-Saxons were pagans, who worshipped many gods. Woden was their chief god and the Saxons believed in all sorts of creatures like dragons, giants and other strange beasts.

Patrick and Columba

In AD 432, the British monk Patrick set off to Ireland to spread the word of God, converting the Irish to Christianity and later becoming St Patrick. Later, in AD 563, the Irish monk Columba sailed from Ireland to a small island off the west coast of Scotland called Iona. When he got there, he and other monks built a monastery, where they lived a simple life, worshipping and praying to God. They also travelled south into northern England to spread the word of God.

Pope Gregory, Canterbury and Lindisfarne

Legend has it that Pope Gregory was in the marketplace in Rome when he saw two young children who were slaves, with blonde hair and bright blue eyes. When informed that they were Angles, he remarked that they were indeed *angels* and perhaps the rest of the people on their island should be converted to Christianity. He entrusted the mission to Augustine, who travelled to Britain in AD 597 with 40 monks. Augustine met up with the local king, Ethelbert (also known as Aethelberht), in Kent; his wife Bertha was a Christian. The king was friendly to them but wary too, suspecting them of being able to do magic. Ethelbert allowed them to use an old Roman church in Canterbury and Pope Gregory made Augustine Archbishop of Canterbury in AD 601, in charge of all Christians in England. In AD 635, Oswald, the Anglo-Saxon king of Northumbria, who was a Christian, asked the monks of Iona to teach his people about Christianity. The monks, led by an Irish monk called Aidan, travelled to Northumbria and built a monastery on the island of Lindisfarne. They travelled around the north of England, spreading the word of God and converting the people to Christianity.

The Synod of Whitby

At this time, the Church of Ireland and Scotland (the Celtic Church) was different from the Roman Catholic Church; for instance, Easter was celebrated on different days. Oswiu, the king of Northumbria, followed the Celtic Church but his wife followed the Roman Church. He called all the leaders of the Celtic and Roman churches to a meeting at Whitby in AD 664, where they decided to follow the Roman traditions after King Oswiu heard that St Peter had the keys to Heaven; the King did not want to risk being turned away from Heaven. Now the whole of the country followed the same religious practices and the Christians in Britain were united.

Monks and monasteries

Lots of new churches and monasteries were built. One young boy who entered a monastery was called Bede. He later moved to the monastery at Jarrow and spent much of his time writing books. His writings provide us with an insight into Anglo-Saxon life. Monks and nuns were taught to read and write in Latin as well as Anglo-Saxon, and many served as teachers and writers. This was before the invention of the printing press, so books were all written and illustrated by hand, a slow and laborious process.

Key words

Pagan: Paganism covers a group of religions that place high importance on nature, often with many gods.
Woden: The Anglo-Saxon god that corresponded to the Norse god Odin.
Monk: A member of a religious community usually living under strict religious rules such as obedience, chastity and poverty.
Monastery: A house or residence that monks lived in.
Pope: The head of the Roman Catholic Church. Also known as the Bishop of Rome.
Roman Catholic: A person that follows the Roman Catholic Church, a branch of Christianity governed by the Pope.
Archbishop of Canterbury: The senior bishop and spiritual leader of the Church in England. Up until the English Reformation in the sixteenth century, the Archbishop of Canterbury followed the authority of the Pope.

Important dates

AD 432: The British monk Patrick travels to Ireland to spread Christianity and convert the Irish.
AD 563: The Irish monk Columba sails from Ireland to Iona and builds a monastery.
AD 597: Pope Gregory sends missionaries from Rome to Britain.
AD 602: St Augustine establishes the first archbishopric at Canterbury.
AD 635: Oswald, the king of Northumbria, sends the monk Aidan to start a monastery on the island of Lindisfarne.
AD 664: The Synod of Whitby takes place, where it is decided to follow the ways of Rome.

Important people

Patrick: British monk.
Columba: Irish monk.
Pope Gregory: Pope from 590–604.
Augustine: Benedictine monk who became the first Archbishop of Canterbury.
Bertha: The wife of Ethelbert; she was a Christian.
Ethelbert: Saxon king of Kent, also known as Aethelberht.
Oswiu: Saxon king who called the Synod of Whitby.
Bede: English monk and historian.

Interesting fact

Some pagan names live on, with the days Tuesday, Wednesday, Thursday and Friday named after the Anglo-Saxon pagans' gods – Tiw's day, Woden's day, Thor's day and Frig's day – and the Christian festival of Easter is named after Eostre, a pagan goddess.

Useful links

www.123ict.co.uk/invaders-settlers-history-web-links/

Lesson 1 Pagan gods

Getting started
Write the word *pagan* on the board and ask the class to say what they understand by the term. Write their ideas in spider-diagram format around the key word.

Class activities
- Explain that although the Romans had introduced Christianity to Britain, the Anglo-Saxons were pagans. Define the word and then look back at the pupils' ideas in the starter activity.
- In pairs or small groups, pupils research some of the Anglo-Saxon gods.
- Explain that we get the days of the week from pagan gods: hand out a sheet with the days of the week on one side and their origin on the other side. Pupils match the correct pagan god and definition with the right day of the week.
- Pupils illustrate their sheet with one or more of the gods, adding definitions.

Plenary material
Pupils feed back to the rest of the class which their favourite pagan god is and why.

Lesson 2 The spread of Christianity

Getting started

Recap the days of the week named after pagan gods: in pairs or small groups, pupils match the gods with the days of the week.

Class activities

- Pose the question: how would you go about changing the beliefs of the pagan worshippers? What sort of person would you have to be to do so? Write the pupils' ideas on the board.
- Tell the pupils about Patrick and Columba. Pupils create a short fact file about the monks.
- Show pupils what the monastery at Iona would have looked like: ask them to describe the area and what it would be like to live there.
- Pupils write a short story, as either Patrick or Columba, on spreading the word of Christianity to the Anglo-Saxons.

Plenary material

Play a Hangman-style game on some key words from the session: *Patrick*; *Iona*; *Christianity*; *Columba*; etc.

Lesson 3 Augustine

Getting started

Recap the work of Patrick and Columba: pupils can get into pairs and tell each other about one of the monks, then swap.

Class activities

- Tell pupils the story of Pope Gregory and the Angles he saw in Rome. According to the tale, why did he want to convert the Anglo-Saxons to Christianity? Do pupils think it is a true story? Elicit reasons for and against.
- Pupils research the story of Augustine; they plot the main events on a timeline.
- Show a painting of Augustine and Ethelbert. Ask pupils to explain what is happening: look at the imagery; posture; clothes; reaction. What can they interpret from the painting?
- Pupils imagine they are Ethelbert, Bertha or Augustine and write an account of the meeting between them.

Plenary material

Pupils read their accounts to the rest of the class, or in small groups.

Further activities for pupils

- Investigate daily life in a monastery; research the jobs monks did.
- Look at what happened at the Synod of Whitby. Why was it so important what was decided there?
- Research Lindisfarne and design your own monastery. Where would you build it and why?

Further research for pupils

Iona: **www.welcometoiona.com**
Lindisfarne: **https://www.lindisfarne.org.uk**

Cross-curricular links

Art and design: Pupils draw their own picture of Ethelbert meeting Augustine.
English: Write a series of diary entries as one of the monks spreading the word of Christianity to the Anglo-Saxons.
Religious studies: Investigate how much pagan culture is still with us today. On a timeline, plot the spread of early Christianity in Anglo-Saxon times.
Computing: Create a poster to encourage the Anglo-Saxons to convert to Christianity.
Geography: Research the places where monasteries were built.
Drama: Act out the meeting between Ethelbert and Augustine. In small groups, one pupil is a monk trying to convince the rest of the group, who are Anglo-Saxons, to convert to Christianity and abandon their pagan beliefs.

Progression

1. Pupils understand that the Anglo-Saxons were pagans.
2. Pupils can explain what a pagan is.
3. Pupils understand that monks spread Christianity.
4. Pupils can identify where monasteries were built.
5. Pupils can explain the origins of the Archbishop of Canterbury.

8 The Viking and Anglo-Saxon struggle for the kingdom of England to the time of Edward the Confessor

What does the curriculum say?

- *Non-statutory examples include: Viking raids and invasion; resistance by Alfred the Great and Athelstan, first king of England; further Viking invasions and Danegeld; Anglo-Saxon laws and justice; Edward the Confessor and his death in 1066.*

Viking raids and invasions

In 30 seconds...

The Vikings came from Scandinavia (Norway, Sweden and Denmark) and, as well as being excellent sailors, they were ferocious fighters. They sailed over to Britain in their longboats and plundered the rich and defenceless monasteries that were built in coastal areas before heading inland to raid. Eventually, the Vikings started to settle, finding the land more suited to farming than the forests and mountainous regions of their home. The Vikings spread terror wherever they went, destroying or driving away any that stood before them until only the kingdom of Wessex stood against them.

What do I need to know?

Who were the Vikings?

The Vikings did not come from one country, but from the region of Scandinavia, made up of Norway, Sweden and Denmark. As well as being fighters, they were farmers, traders and excellent sailors.

Why did the Vikings raid?

Much of the land back in Scandinavia was made up of forest and mountains, making farming difficult. This was in stark contrast to the lush and fertile farmland that could be found in Britain. Younger sons of Viking farmers would not inherit their father's land, so they went looking for fortunes elsewhere. Roaming the waters in strong wooden boats, they explored in all directions; they colonised Iceland, Greenland and Russia, raided Constantinople and landed in America 500 years before Columbus.

Smash-and-grab raids

The monasteries were an easy target for a number of reasons: they were full of valuables and treasure, they were often built in remote coastal locations and they were 'guarded' by monks. The first Viking ship landed in Dorset in AD 787 and the local reeve went to greet them, asking if they wanted to see the king. Instead, they killed him and sailed away. This was a sign of things to come. Lindisfarne was the first monastery to be raided: in AD 793 the Vikings stole anything of value from the monastery before burning it and killing any monks that got in the way. The Vikings returned in AD 794 and raided the monastery at Jarrow, but the monks were ready this time and fought back. They managed to kill some of the Vikings, including their leader, who they threw into a snake pit of adders! The Vikings returned again the next year in AD 795, attacking the monastery at Iona. There were more Viking raids in the 830s in the south of England, with the invaders mostly coming from Denmark.

Settlers

Vikings from Norway sailed to Scotland and settled there after driving out the Picts. From AD 795, they also settled in parts of Ireland. Then in AD 851, a huge fleet of around 350 Viking ships from Denmark arrived at the mouth of the River Thames. There was no navy to stop them and London was plundered, as was Canterbury. Whereas previously the Danish Vikings would plunder all they could and then sail back home before winter came, this time, some of them stayed on for the winter in the Isle of Thanet in Kent. An even bigger fleet came in AD 865. The Viking invaders were now looking for land to settle on, not just to grab treasure and disappear. The Anglo-Saxons could not stop them, as kingdom after kingdom fell: East Anglia, Mercia and Northumbria were conquered, leaving only one major kingdom standing. That was the kingdom of Wessex, which in AD 871 lost its king, Ethelred, to be replaced by his brother. His name was Alfred.

Key words

Vikings: People from Norway, Sweden and Denmark.
Reeve: Royal official.
Plunder: Stealing things, taking them by force.

Important dates

AD 787: Three Viking ships arrive from Denmark and land in Dorset.
AD 793: The Vikings plunder Lindisfarne monastery.
AD 794: The Vikings raid Jarrow monastery.
AD 795: The Vikings plunder Iona monastery.
AD 851: A huge fleet of 350 Viking ships attack the south and London.
AD 851: Vikings start to settle in Britain.
AD 865: The biggest Viking army yet lands in Britain.
AD 871: Wessex is the only Anglo-Saxon kingdom left to resist the Vikings.

Important people

King Edmund: The Saxon king of East Anglia, killed by the Vikings for refusing to give up his Christian faith. Allegedly, he was tied to a tree and used for archery practice.
Ethelred: King of Wessex.
Alfred: Brother of Ethelred and soon to be Alfred the Great.

Interesting fact 1

Contrary to popular myth, Vikings did not wear horned helmets.

Interesting fact 2

The Vikings collected a fungus called touchwood (from the bark of trees) and boiled it in urine for several days. It was then pounded into a felt-like substance and the sodium nitrate found in the urine would cause it to smoulder slowly (rather than burn), meaning the Vikings could take fire with them wherever they went!

Useful links

www.bbc.co.uk/schools/primaryhistory/vikings/
www.pbs.org/wgbh/nova/ancient/viking-ships.html All about Viking ships.
There are many companies that will visit your school, such as **http://vikingschoolvisits.com** and **www.longship.co.uk**. For a site visit, there is none better than **http://jorvik-viking-centre.co.uk** in York.

Lesson 1 Viking warrior

Getting started

Tell a short story about the Vikings: every time you mention the word *Vikings*, pupils have to all do their best Viking impression! Add other actions or phrases to make it more fun.

Class activities

- Write the word *Viking* on the board and ask pupils to say what they think of when they hear the word.
- Using the descriptions on the board, pupils draw and label their own Viking warrior.
- Pupils invent a name for their Viking warrior and explain what it means.
- Ask pupils where they think the Vikings came from; then show the regions on a map of Europe. Where else do pupils think the Vikings went apart from Britain? Pupils then colour in a photocopied map, showing where Vikings came from and the places they went. Ask pupils what this tells us about the sailing capabilities of the Vikings.

Plenary material

Pupils complete short written task, filling in blanks about where the Vikings came from and where they settled.

Lesson 2 Why did the Vikings invade?

Getting started

In pairs or small groups, pupils recap where the Vikings came from and the countries they sailed to.

Class activities

- On the board, show a picture of a monastery: what sorts of treasures or valuable items would be in a monastery? Why would a monastery be an easy target?
- Explain that, initially, the Vikings would raid and then sail home before the winter. Pupils write a short report under the title 'Why did the Vikings raid Britain?'
- Explain that, eventually, the Vikings started to stay and not sail home in the winter. Pose the question to the class: why would the Vikings settle in Britain? Show a picture of the landscape of where the invaders came from (showing forest, mountains, etc.). Ask pupils to identify features and difficulties of living there. Give them a hint: farming.
- Contrast it with a picture of fertile farmland of Britain. What differences can the pupils see?
- Pupils write a short report under the title 'Why did the Vikings settle in Britain?'

Plenary material

In groups of four or five, pupils act out a short sketch (singing short verses, if they like), explaining why the Vikings first raided and then settled in Britain. They can be as creative as they like! Give them five minutes to rehearse and 30 seconds to perform their sketch.

Lesson 3 Experiencing a Viking raid

Getting started

Read out a number of true/false statements to do with why Vikings first raided and then settled in Britain. Pupils have to stand up and salute if they think a statement is true, or sit down and fold their arms if they think it is false.

Class activities

- Show a picture of a Viking raid on the board. Pupils describe what they see and how it would have felt to experience such a raid. Record their descriptions on the board.
- Ask pupils to identify the sorts of places that Vikings first raided: recap why monasteries were an easy target.
- Pupils could act this out: three-quarters of the class are monks, and their pencil cases represent valuable items. The rest of the class are Vikings. (Perhaps the teacher acts as the Viking leader to ensure it doesn't get out of hand!) How much resistance would monks pose to Vikings?
- Describe the raids on Dorset and the monasteries at Lindisfarne and Iona. Pupils write an eyewitness report as either a bystander in Dorset or a monk at the one of the monasteries.
- Explain that the Vikings did not always have it their own way: tell pupils the story of what happened at Jarrow.

Plenary material

Pupils write a dramatic headline for a newspaper front page, describing a Viking raid on one of the monasteries. This can then be completed in a future lesson.

Further activities for pupils

- Design a newspaper front page describing a Viking raid on one of the monasteries: it can be either a raid that plundered and destroyed, or one where the Vikings got a nasty surprise.
- In small groups, make up a Viking song that they can sing on their way to plunder new lands.
- Investigate how the Vikings lived when they settled in Britain.
- Research which areas stayed under Viking influence as the Middle Ages arrived.
- Go to www.bbc.co.uk/history/ancient/vikings/launch_gms_viking_quest.shtml for an interactive game where you can try your luck as a Viking.

Further research for pupils

TV: Most of the recent offerings with Vikings are not suitable for young pupils, but an older film worth a look is *Prince Valiant* (1954), directed by Henry Hathaway starring Robert Wagner and James Mason. Pupils will probably already be familiar with the *How to Train Your Dragon* animated films: though slightly off-topic, they are still an enjoyable watch involving Vikings.
The Vikings (1958), directed by Richard Fleischer an epic film with Kirk Douglas.
Viking Blood: A Viking Warrior AD 1008 by Andrew Donkin; an exciting book about a teenage Viking.
iPad: *Viking Saga: The Cursed Ring* (Realore, JSC). Highly rated Viking strategy game.

Cross-curricular links

Art and design: Make your own Viking helmet, shield or weapons.
English: Write a series of diary entries as a monk, an Anglo-Saxon farmer or a Viking raider.
Religious studies: Research the religious beliefs of the Vikings.
Computing: Create a presentation on Vikings: their raids; settlements; beliefs; etc.
Geography: Shade in on a map of Britain to show where Vikings raided and settled.
Science: Look at the design of a Viking ship; design your own Viking boat.
Drama: Act out Viking raids in the playground. Record a series of news reports chronicling Viking raids.
Music: Record a poem, verse or short song about Vikings.

Progression

1. Pupils can recall some features about Vikings.
2. Pupils can recall areas that Vikings originally came from.
3. Pupils can identify areas that Vikings sailed to.
4. Pupils recognise why Vikings first raided Britain.
5. Pupils can explain why Vikings came to settle in Britain.
6. Pupils can explain how Vikings lived in Britain.

Resistance by Alfred the Great and Athelstan

In 30 seconds...

After fighting against the Vikings before he was king, Alfred, with the Anglo-Saxons, lost a number of battles that saw him making a deal with the Vikings and their leader, Guthrum. However, the Vikings did not keep their word and invaded Wessex in the depths of winter, forcing Alfred to flee. From the marshes in Somerset, Alfred planned his revenge while building up an army. He came back to defeat the Vikings before forcing them into another treaty. Alfred strengthened the forts, navy and army. Eventually, after his death, his grandson Athelstan took over the rest of the Danelaw to be recognised as King of Britain.

What do I need to know?

Last kingdom standing

One by one, the Anglo-Saxon kingdoms had fallen to the Vikings, until only Wessex remained. Then the Vikings started to attack Wessex. Aethelred, the king of Wessex, along with his brother, Alfred, fought back against the invaders. In AD 871 the Anglo-Saxons won a battle at Ashdown, but the Vikings eventually proved too strong. After Aethelred died later that year, the 22-year-old Alfred succeeded him as king but was defeated by the Vikings in a series of battles. However, Alfred managed to buy off the Danes in return for leaving Wessex alone. The Viking leader Guthrum signed the treaty and headed back to Mercia.

Betrayal and setback

At Christmas in AD 877, Alfred sent his nobles home and he went back to Chippenham. This meant that they were not ready when the Vikings broke the agreement and attacked early in AD 878, with Guthrum's army joining another Viking army from Wales. This came as a huge surprise, as they would not have been expected to attack in winter. Many Saxons were killed but Alfred managed to escape, hiding in the marshes in the Isle of Athelney in Somerset. It was while in he was exile that the story of Alfred burning the cakes originates, although this is unlikely to be true! While the Vikings ransacked Wessex, Alfred plotted how to win his kingdom back and got word to people that he was alive. More and more men joined his ranks until he was ready to make his move, in May 878.

A key victory

Alfred led his new army to Salisbury Plain to meet Guthrum, who marched with the Vikings up from Chippenham. Utilising shield-wall tactics, Alfred defeated the Vikings at the Battle of Edington in May 878. The Vikings fled back to Chippenham, chased by the Saxons. The Vikings were beaten and at the mercy of Alfred; however, Alfred knew it was unrealistic to expect all the Vikings to leave, so instead he offered them peace terms. This agreement, known as the Peace of Wedmore, saw Alfred rule Wessex and much of Mercia, with a boundary line from Chester to London along the old Roman road of Watling Street separating the two kingdoms, and the Vikings in the other half. The area that the Vikings lived in was known as the Danelaw, as they were from Denmark and the people therefore had to follow Danish law. Alfred also demanded that Guthrum be baptised into Christianity and that Alfred be made Guthrum's godfather; this made it harder for the Viking to betray his new family loyalty.

How did Alfred protect Wessex?

Alfred knew that the Viking threat was far from over and planned accordingly. He built forts, or buhrs, that grew into fortified towns and built up the navy with ships twice the size of the Viking longboats. He also built up the army, made up of fyrds, who were part-time soldiers. Half the year they worked on the farms and the other half they were stationed in forts. This meant that there was always a ready force on standby, and the Vikings were beaten again in 885, before Alfred marched to London and took it over. Alfred restored the monasteries and churches, educated people and had books written in Anglo-Saxon and Latin. He also instructed the monks to begin the *Anglo-Saxon Chronicle*, recording what had happened in the country from the time of Jesus. Alfred made good laws and was known as Alfred the Great.

Athelstan

When Alfred died in 899, he was succeeded by his son, Edward. Edward continued to have military success against the Vikings and gained control of most of the Danelaw. He was succeeded by his son Athelstan in 924. Athelstan, grandson to Alfred, would become the first Anglo-Saxon king to rule over Britain; his coronation was in 925. He took over the Viking stronghold of York in AD 927 before marching up and conquering Northumbria, which at that time stretched into parts of Scotland. In AD 937 at the Battle of Brunanburh, he fought and beat a mixture of Irish, Vikings, Scots, Northumbrians and Strathclyde Britons; Athelstan was recognised as king by all of Britain. Like his grandfather Alfred, Athelstan was a good ruler, using one coinage throughout the land and securing treaties by marrying his sisters to foreign rulers.

Key words

Wessex: Anglo-Saxon kingdom in what is now Hampshire, Dorset, Wiltshire and Somerset.
Mercia: Powerful Anglo-Saxon kingdom in what is now the Midlands.
Chippenham: A town in what is now Wiltshire, where it is thought that Alfred had a hunting palace. Chippenham was seized by the Vikings but Alfred managed to escape.
Shield wall: A military tactic where soldiers would stand next to each other, shield to shield, thus protecting the person next to them.
Peace of Wedmore: Agreement reached between Alfred and Guthrum that established a clear frontier between the Anglo-Saxons and Vikings.
Danelaw: The area of England controlled by the Vikings, under Danish law.
Buhrs: Fortified towns.

Important dates

AD 870: The Vikings attack Wessex.
AD 871: Alfred becomes King of Wessex.
AD 876: Alfred signs a treaty with Guthrum and the Vikings.
AD 877: Alfred sends his nobles home at Christmas.
AD 878: The Vikings break the treaty and invade Wessex, defeating Alfred (January).
AD 878: Alfred beats the Vikings at the Battle of Edington (May).
AD 925: Athelstan, Alfred's grandson, becomes king.
AD 927: Athelstan takes the Viking stronghold of York.
AD 937: The Battle of Brunanburh: Athelstan wins and is recognised as King of Britain.
AD 939: Athelstan dies.

Important people

Aethelred: King of Wessex from 865–871, before being succeeded by his brother Alfred.
King Alfred (849–899): Legendary King of Wessex who fought back against the Vikings and prevented England falling.
Guthrum: Leader of a Danish invasion who later made himself King of East Anglia. He fought against Alfred but was later baptised by him after being beaten at the Battle of Edington.
Edward: Son of Alfred the Great who became king in 899 when Alfred died.
Athelstan: Alfred's grandson who became king in 925 and became a great ruler.

Useful links

www.bbc.co.uk/schools/primaryhistory/anglo_saxons/alfred_the_great/
www.historytoday.com/barbara-yorke/alfred-great-most-perfect-man-history Detailed article.
www.theschoolrun.com/homework-help/alfred-the-great
www.ducksters.com/history/middle_ages/alfred_the_great.php Biography and facts; accessible for pupils too.
www.regia.org They do many historical enactments; check to see if they're doing one near you.

Lesson 1 We need a saviour!

Getting started
To refresh earlier learning on the Vikings, pupils get into pairs: one pupil starts to tell their partner about the Vikings; after 20 seconds, they swap and the second pupil continues where the first left off. This can continue back and forth until they run out of things to say. If they get stuck, their partner can prompt them with a key word or a hint. They keep track of how many hints or long pauses they have; the one with the fewest is the winner for each pair.

Class activities
- Ask the class what the situation looked like around AD 860. The Vikings seemed unbeatable. Record on the board any ideas that show how tough the Vikings were.
- Write the word *saviour* on the board. Ask the class what it means, and then record their ideas on the qualities a saviour would need in order to be successful against the Vikings.
- Pupils design and illustrate a 'Wanted' poster, advertising for a saviour against the Vikings. Ensure that pupils list the qualities needed to be successful against the dominant Vikings.
- In their exercise books, pupils write a short passage on what sort of person would be a saviour. *In order to beat the Vikings, they would have to be. . .* They can use bullet points to list their attributes.

Plenary material
In pairs, pupils make up a short rap about the saviour needed to beat the Vikings. They then perform it to the rest of the class.

Lesson 2 Who burnt the cakes?

Getting started
Assemble the class in a long line or circle. Very quietly, tell a short message to the first pupil, such as 'Send reinforcements as the ice-cream van has run out of choc-ices and the queue of angry seven-year-olds are starting to look like they mean business!'. Each pupil has to pass the message on so only the person next to them can hear it. When the last person is told the message, they repeat it out loud. Has it changed?

Class activities
- Recap from the last lesson: what qualities would a saviour need to be successful against the Vikings? A saviour would not only need to be a good warrior, but clever as well.
- Ask pupils if they know what a *myth* is; can they give any examples?
- Using a timeline, go over the early life of Alfred, and when he was betrayed by Guthrum.
- Decision time: after being betrayed, should Alfred fight back immediately or flee in order to fight another day? Should a great leader ever run away? Debate both sides to the argument.
- Read class the story about Alfred burning the cakes: take a class poll on whether they think it is a myth or not. What does the episode say about Alfred?
- Pupils write either a short script on the exchange between Alfred and the woman whose cakes he burnt, or an alternative myth. They act some of them out to the rest of the class.
- Tell the class what happened next, with Alfred getting word to his people. Pupils complete a writing task, beginning: *Alfred showed that he was a good leader after he was betrayed because. . .*

Plenary material
Write a number of events in Alfred's early life in a jumbled order; pupils put them in order.

Lesson 3 Alfred the Great

Getting started
Split the class into four groups. Each has to give a reason why things looked bad for Alfred.

Class activities
- Find some pictures of the Battle of Edington: where it is on the map; a Saxon shield wall; the two armies fighting; and what happened after the battle, when Alfred surrounded the Vikings.
- Arrange pupils into groups of three or four. Using only the pictures, pupils use the pictorial evidence to piece together what happened at the Battle of Edington.
- When they have finished, each group feeds back to the rest of the class.
- Hand out a worksheet on the Battle of Edington: pupils arrange the events into correct chronological order. **(Bloomsbury Online Resource 8A)**

Plenary material
Pupils imagine they are King Alfred. What would they have done with the Vikings after the Battle of Edington?

Further activities for pupils

- Create a comic strip of the life of Alfred the Great. **(Bloomsbury Online Resource 8B)**
- Class debate: does Alfred deserve the title 'Great'?
- Look at the ways Alfred protected Wessex.
- Look at the achievements of Athelstan: was he as 'great' as Alfred?
- Class debate: who was the greater ruler – Alfred or Athelstan?

Further research for pupils

Alfred the Great (1969), directed by Clive Donner.
King Alfred the Great: Adventures from History by L. Du Garde Peach and John Kenney.

Cross-curricular links

Art and design: Paint a famous scene from the life of Alfred the Great.
English: Write a series of diary entries from the time Alfred was betrayed to when he was victorious at the Battle of Edington.
Religious studies: Read the account of the Battle of Edington at www.viking.no/e/england/guttorm/ethandun.htm. Discuss the references to Odin.
Computing: In groups, create a presentation on Alfred the Great – either his whole life or a particular part – for presentation to the rest of the class.
Geography: On a map of England, mark in the boundary as agreed in the Peace of Wedmore. Colour it in and illustrate each side, showing the Vikings and Anglo-Saxons.
Drama: Act out some key moments in Alfred's life. Write a short radio play and record it using GarageBand or a similar program.
Music: Write a series of short songs/sonnets about the life of Alfred the Great.

Progression

1. Pupils recognise that Alfred was a great king who beat the Vikings.
2. Pupils can recall some of the early life of Alfred and the problems he faced.
3. Pupils can explain how Alfred managed to beat the Vikings.
4. Pupils can explain Alfred's victory and how he maintained control.
5. Pupils can assess how great Alfred and Athelstan were.

Edward the Confessor and his death in 1066

In 30 seconds. . .

After the Viking king Harthacanute (also known as Harthacnut) died without an heir, Edward the Confessor was chosen by the Witan to be king of England. Edward, the son of a previous king, Ethelred the Unready, was very religious and soon upset the powerful nobles due to his reliance on Norman advisors. Although he oversaw the building of Westminster Abbey, he died in 1066 without an heir, and Harold Godwinson, the most powerful English noble, was named king. The problem was that there were other rulers in Norway and Normandy who had their eye on the throne of England.

What do I need to know?

The link

After Athelstan died in 939, a succession of Anglo-Saxon kings managed to keep the Vikings at bay for a while, until Eric Haraldsson (with the wonderful nickname of Eric Bloodaxe!) sailed over from Norway and rallied the Vikings, eventually being defeated. Ethelred the Unready became king and, as his name suggests, he was not up to the task. He paid the Vikings Danegeld (taxes to keep the Danes away) not to invade, but they understandably kept coming back for more. Ethelred eventually stood up to them but not in a battle; he ordered every Scandinavian in the country to be murdered on the same day in the St Brice's Day massacre of 1002. Rather than solving the problem, this made it much worse. Many of the murdered Danes were farmers and had been living peacefully in the country for generations, as opposed to the warriors who had recently sailed over from Norway. The King of Denmark's sister was killed and so the king, Sweyn, sailed over to exact bloody revenge. This he duly did, and when Ethelred fled to Normandy, Sweyn became king of England. When Sweyn died in 1014, his son Canute (also known as Cnut) invaded. When Ethelred died in 1016, some nobles saw Canute as king but a few recognised Edmund Ironside, the son of Ethelred. Despite some early success, Edmund was eventually defeated later in 1016 and when he died soon after, Canute was the sole king of England. After Canute died in 1035, his sons Harold and then Harthacanute became king. They would not reign for long.

Early life

Edward was the son of Ethelred the Unready and Emma of Normandy and spent the first part of his life in Normandy. After his father Ethelred died, the Danish king Canute took the throne of England. (Canute's father Sweyn had ravaged England in revenge after Ethelred had massacred many Danes in response to Danegeld. When Sweyn died, his son Canute was named king.) Edward's mother Emma then married Canute, which made them friendly with the powerful Duke of Normandy, Robert the Magnificent.

A complicated line. . .

Canute died in 1035 and had three sons to succeed him: Harthacanute, by his wife Emma; and then Sweyn and Harold, sons from another wife. After Sweyn and Harold died, Harthacanute became king of England and invited Edward back from Normandy. When Harthacanute died in 1042, there were no more Danish kings to take over so the nobles decided on Edward, the son of Ethelred, to become king. Edward the Confessor was crowned in 1042.

A very religious king

Edward married Edith, the daughter of the most powerful noble in the land, Godwin of Wessex. Edward was very religious, and earned the 'Confessor' part of his name as he spent so much time confessing his sins to God. Edward collected many religious relics and oversaw the planning and building of Westminster Abbey, started in 1052 and finished in 1065, built in a Norman style.

The struggle for power

It came as no surprise that Edward, having spent so much of his early life in Normandy, should have Norman influences and advisors at court. This did not go down well with the powerful Saxon nobles, such as Godwin of Wessex, who raised an army against the King: Godwin had been sent to deal with the people of Dover after some Normans had been killed, but Godwin refused. However, Edward was supported by the earls of Mercia and Northumbria and Godwin was forced to move to Flanders. Edward continued to give Normans land, jobs and positions in the court, which angered the Witan. Sensing an opportunity, Godwin returned from Flanders with an army led by his two sons, Harold and Tostig. Edward was forced to send many of his Norman advisors back to France and return all lands to Godwin. When Godwin died in 1053, his son Harold Godwinson succeeded him as Earl of Wessex. Although Edward was married, he was celibate and had no children, so when he died in 1066, a number of people got ready to seize the throne of England.

Four contenders

When Edward the Confessor died in January 1066, there were four people with a claim to the throne.

Harold Godwinson

The most powerful noble in England and a skilled warrior, Harold Godwinson, Earl of Wessex, was the popular choice with the people of England and the Witan. Edward named him as successor on his deathbed.

William of Normandy

A powerful French noble, William was related to Edward and said that Edward had also promised the throne to him. Not only that, Harold Godwinson had supposedly sworn an oath on some relics that he would help William become king when William rescued him from Guy of Ponthieu after Harold had been captured in France some years earlier.

Harald Hardrada

A powerful Viking king of Norway, Hardrada claimed that he should be king of England. Previous Viking kings Magnus and Harthacanute had agreed that when one of them died, the other would inherit their kingdom; Harthacanute died heirless, so Magnus assumed his kingdom of Norway and made plans to invade England. Magnus died before he could put this plan into action, so when his uncle Harald took over as king of Norway, Harald wanted to reclaim the throne of England as it had been part of Harthacanute's kingdom.

Edgar Atheling

Edgar was around 14 in January 1066 when Edward the Confessor died, and was too young to have an effective claim to the throne. However, he would go on to present a challenge to William of Normandy in years to come. He was a grandson of Edmund Ironside and a great-grandson of Ethelred the Unready.

Two major battles

The scene was set for two major battles that would decide the throne of England: the Battle of Stamford Bridge and the Battle of Hastings. Godwinson beat Hardrada and his own brother Tostig at Stamford Bridge, eliminating one of the threats to his throne. However, instead of resting and gathering his army, he then raced south to meet William and the Norman army that had arrived on the south coast and was laying waste to parts of Wessex. The Battle of Hastings, where William triumphed, would bring an end to the reign of Saxon kings, while introducing Norman rule to the country.

Key words

Danegeld: Huge sums of money paid by Ethelred the Unready to the Danes to prevent the Vikings from invading. It didn't work, and they kept coming back for more.

Important dates

c.1003: Edward is born.
1016: Canute becomes king.
1035: Canute dies. He is succeeded by his sons Harold and Harthacanute.
1040: Harold dies and Harthcanute becomes king.
1040: Edward is recalled to England from Normandy.
1042: Harthacanute dies and Edward becomes king.
1045: Edward marries Edith, daughter of Earl Godwin.
1051: Earl Godwin of Wessex is banished to Flanders.
1052: Godwin returns to England, with his two sons, Harold and Tostig.
1052: Building starts on Westminster Abbey.
1066: Edward dies.

Important people

Ethelred the Unready: Father of Edward. (Unready means 'evil advice'.)
Sweyn: Also known as Sweyn Forkbeard; Danish king.
Canute: Also known as Cnut; Danish king of England.
Edmund Ironside: Son of Ethelred, by his first wife, Aelfgifu.
Emma of Normandy: Mother of Edward; wife of Ethelred; later married to Canute.
Robert the Magnificent: Duke of Normandy, father of future William the Conqueror.
Edward the Confessor: King of England.
William of Normandy: Son of Robert the Magnificent; one of the claimants to the throne of England when Edward died.

Godwin of Wessex: Powerful noble; father of Harold and Tostig.
Edith: Daughter of Godwin; wife of Edward the Confessor.
Harold Godwinson: Son of Godwin; future king of England.
Tostig: Son of Godwin.
Harald Hardrada: One of the claimants to the throne of England when Edward died.

Interesting fact

Edward the Confessor appears in the Bayeux Tapestry.

Useful links

www.theschoolrun.com/homework-help/edward-the-confessor Contains facts and a timeline.

Lesson 1 Was Edward the rightful king?

Getting started
Write the phrase *Edward the Confessor* on the board. In groups of three or four, pupils discuss what they think this name means.

Class activities
- Take feedback from the class, gathering their ideas what the name means; use a spider diagram.
- Explain how Edward the Confessor got his name. Ask the class what this tells us about the sort of person he was.
- Using a timeline and family tree, explain that Canute was king of England and Edward fled to Normandy: why would he do this? (Look at what Edward's father had done to upset the Danes.) In groups, pupils discuss ideas.
- Look at what happened after Edward's father died: was it the right decision to flee to Normandy when the Danes invaded or should he have fought for his rightful throne? Pupils discuss as a class and then write a short report looking at both sides of the argument. *Edward was right to go to Normandy because. . .and Edward should have stayed because. . .*
- Take a class vote on whether Edward was right to go to Normandy instead of staking his claim to the throne of England.

Plenary material
Split the class into groups of four. The first person in each group starts to tell the rest of their group what they have learnt in the lesson. After ten seconds, the teacher signals for the next in the group to continue.

Lesson 2 Powerful nobles

Getting started

In small groups, one pupil acts as teacher for their group and answers questions on what was learnt in the previous lesson. If they cannot answer, the questioner takes over.

Class activities

- Piece together the early life of Edward, and his upbringing in Normandy; remind pupils that his early life and the people he depended on in Normandy are going to play a big part in what happens when he is king. Is it any surprise that he relied on Normans for advice?
- Explain that when Edward was king, there were powerful Saxon nobles: Godwin of Wessex, Leofric of Mercia and Siward of Northumbria. Leofric and Siward were loyal to Edward.
- Tell pupils what happened at Dover: was Edward right to banish Godwin, or was Godwin right to be upset with Edward for relying on the Normans? Pupils discuss ideas in groups.
- Pupils complete a writing activity as Edward, titled 'How dare Godwin defy me!' As king, they explain why they are so upset with the powerful noble.
- Pupils complete a writing activity as Godwin, titled 'The King favours the Normans!' As Earl Godwin, they explain why they are not happy with how Edward is behaving.

Plenary material

The class votes on who was right: Edward or Godwin.

Lesson 3 What did Edward achieve?

Getting started

In groups of four, pupils assign themselves characters: Edward, Leofric, Siward and Godwin. Give them a couple of minutes to act out in their groups what they learnt last lesson.

Class activities

- On the board, write *What makes a king worth remembering?* Ask the class to feed back ideas on what makes a monarch memorable. Many ideas will be to do with military might.
- Ask the class what other duties a monarch has. Is a king that reigns over a peaceful nation better or worse than one who wages war? Pupils discuss and feed back.
- Explain that much of Edward's reign was peaceful: trade was good; financial and court systems were working well. He also built Westminster Abbey.
- As a counter-argument, explain that Edward introduced more and more Normans to court, which upset the Witan and the powerful nobles.
- Pupils write up the two sides, using a pair of scales. Once they have done so, they tip the scales in favour of the direction they think is more convincing.

Plenary material

In pairs, pupils take turns presenting a case for and against Edward being a good king.

Further activities for pupils

- Research the building of Westminster Abbey.
- Look at Godwin's return from Flanders and his growing power and influence.
- Edward left no legitimate heir as he had no children: was this his biggest failure as king, especially considering what happened after he died? (The Normans took over, ending Saxon rule.)
- Investigate the four contenders for the throne in 1066: who should be king?

Further research for pupils

www.bayeuxtapestry.org.uk Lots of information and activities on the Bayeux Tapestry.

Cross-curricular links

Art and design: Make a model of Westminster Abbey as it looked in Edward's time.
English: Write a speech from the point of view of one of the four contenders in 1066, saying why you should be king and the others should not.
Religious studies: Research the legacy of Edward the Confessor and his role as a saint.
Computing: Design a poster on who should be king in 1066.
Drama: Write a short script on Edward's reign and death: include the Danish invasion, the powerful Saxon nobles and the argument about who should be king in 1066. Perform it to the class or write and record smaller parts of it as a news project using GarageBand or a similar program.

Progression

1. Pupils understand who Edward the Confessor was and how he got his name.
2. Pupils can place his reign on a timeline and recall his achievements.
3. Pupils can name the contenders for the throne in 1066.
4. Pupils can explain why Edward went to Normandy and how he upset the Saxon nobles.
5. Pupils can make a case for and against Edward being a successful king.
6. Pupils can make a case for each contender to the throne in 1066.

Part 3:
Upper Key Stage 2

9 A local history study

What does the curriculum say?

- **Non-statutory examples include: a depth study linked to one of the British areas of study covered previously; a study over time tracing how several aspects of national history are reflected in the locality (this can go beyond 1066); a study of an aspect of history or a site dating from a period beyond 1066 that is significant in the locality.**

What do I need to know?

Due to the nature of this chapter and the choice of material being dependent on the locality of the school, these are more generic ideas to prompt further investigation.

The local history study is a wonderful opportunity for pupils to get their teeth into a topic, incorporating cross-curricular links and activities to explore what is on their doorstep. Look at what is around you with fresh eyes. I have in the past been guilty of overlooking the magnificent Hampton Court that is barely one mile from the school – for an adult, the same place can become rather old hat and familiar but there is no mistaking the joy that pupils display when they roam its awesome grounds and buildings. There is also the opportunity to use a truly cross-curricular approach in the activities you do, and pupils readily embrace the chance to flaunt their skills in other subjects; all this is great in bringing history alive for them.

Depending on how old your school is, this might be an interesting start point. For instance, the school where I work was an old people's home before it was a school, but after investigating further back to Victorian times, we found that it was a private residence! Getting hold of a census report from the 1800s or early 1900s revealed a huge amount about not only the building that would become the school, but the area around it. The census also listed the occupations of the people who lived in the building, so we did some research into the jobs that they did, with pupils presenting their work in a number of ways: written in their book; written up using a computer, often with images; some did a PowerPoint presentation and a few even made a movie. They all presented their work to the class which, although it might take a little time, gave them a huge sense of achievement and it was great fun having them play teacher.

Find old maps of the area around your school and compare them with a modern one: the changes between, for instance, 1500, 1850 and 2015 should be striking and provide plenty of interesting opportunities for a depth study. The arrival of the railways should make most maps from the 1800s drastically different from those of the rural 1500s, and with the train came the exodus from the countryside to the towns, which grew accordingly. Even in our lifetime, the local area tends to grow and change, with boundaries constantly pushed out as far as they can go, especially in more rural areas.

Have a look at how buildings have changed in the locality; are they all new or is there a mix of older buildings? If so, in what era were they built? What was their purpose? Who lived/worked there? Explore any famous or successful people who lived in the locality. One way to start would be walking around the local graveyard at the nearest church. The local library should have information on any famous (or infamous!) former residents of the area. Are there any local sports clubs that have been established for a long time? Tracing their history and any successful former members would be an interesting project for pupils. Whatever you do, let the children loose with their research and investigation: their imagination, curiosity and natural inclination to ask questions and seek answers should be the driving force behind the study.

A depth study linked to a British area of study

Ideas

1. Study one of the topics mentioned above in more detail.
2. Star Carr: Neolithic site.
3. Skara Brae: New Stone Age site.
4. Stonehenge: ancient monument.
5. Sutton Hoo: Anglo-Saxon treasure ship.
6. Jorvik: a Viking City.

A study of an aspect of history or a site dating from a period beyond 1066 that is significant in the locality – e.g. Victorian or Tudor site

Ideas

1. Victorian buildings or monuments in the area.
2. Older buildings from Tudor times in the locality.
3. Life on the Home Front in the locality during the Second World War – air raid shelters, pupils speak to grandparents, etc.

A study over time tracing how several aspects of national history are reflected in the locality (this can go beyond 1066)

Ideas

1. A study of architecture from Victorian times in the locality.
2. The impact of Victorian inventions and technology on the area.

10 A study of an aspect or theme in British history that extends pupils' chronological knowledge beyond 1066

What does the curriculum say?

- *Non-statutory examples include: the changing power of monarchs using case studies such as John, Anne and Victoria; changes in an aspect of social history, such as crime and punishment from the Anglo-Saxons to the present or leisure and entertainment in the twentieth century; the legacy of Greek or Roman culture (art, architecture or literature) on later periods in British history, including the present day; a significant turning point in British history, for example, the first railways or the Battle of Britain.*

The changing power of monarchs, using case studies of John, Anne and Victoria

In 30 seconds. . .

Kings and queens used to rule as absolute monarchs, with complete control over how the country was run. However, King John's barons forced him to sign Magna Carta in 1215, which stated that the powers of the monarch would be limited. In the 1600s, the Stuart kings believed in Divine Right, saying they were answerable only to God, which led to problems with Parliament. After the Civil War, the monarch's power was reduced and when William III was invited to replace the Catholic James II in the Glorious Revolution, the king saw his power limited further. Anne was chosen by Parliament to be queen; she had no surviving heirs to pass the crown on to, so Parliament offered it to the Hanover family. With the new king speaking no English and spending time in Hanover, Britain needed someone to run the country – the first unofficial prime minister, Robert Walpole. By the time Victoria was queen, the monarch's influence had lessened over political matters.

What do I need to know?

The traditional power of a monarch

Monarchs used to have absolute power, but today most monarchies are constitutional, with a more limited political power or none at all. Most monarchies are still hereditary.

Why did John's power change?

King John was not a popular king for a number of reasons: he had succeeded his powerful and popular brother, Richard I (also known as Richard the Lionheart), and was not a successful warrior like Richard. Richard had bankrupted the country fighting in the Crusades and left John in a difficult position, as the barons were tired of paying high taxes. John also lost land in France and launched unsuccessful military campaigns to get it back, which all cost a lot of money, again funded by high taxation. This failure to win battles and reclaim land resulted in John being labelled Lackland and Softsword, which were uncomplimentary nicknames for a king. John had also fallen out with the Pope, Innocent III, over who should be appointed Archbishop of Canterbury and, in retaliation, the Pope had closed all the churches in England for five years, from 1208 to 1213. This posed a serious problem to the people of England, as there could be no church services, baptisms, marriages or burials; for a deeply religious population, this was terrifying and they blamed John. After John failed to take back land lost in France against the French king Philip II in 1214, the barons had finally had enough. After their demand to meet the King was refused, they formed an army and marched to London, forcing John to meet them at Runnymede, near Windsor. It was here that they presented Magna Carta to John in 1215 and forced him to sign it.

The result of this change

Magna Carta (Latin for 'Great Charter'), contained 63 statements rectifying what the barons were unhappy about. Most of these statements concerned the current problems with the monarch, but some of them had a significant impact on future rights. Magna Carta said that no man could be punished or imprisoned without a fair trial; that the Church had to be left alone; that John could not raise taxes without the agreement of the barons. Forced into signing Magna Carta, John had no intention of sticking to it and backed out as soon as he could. Nevertheless, the ideas in Magna Carta would go on to be an important milestone in the rights of people and would later influence the constitution of America.

Why did Anne's power change?

The absolute power that monarchs before Anne, such as James I and Charles I, had enjoyed was at an end. Parliament was determined to rein in their power so that no monarch could wield power in the way that the early Stuart kings had, with their unflinching belief in Divine Right. Parliament had already started limiting the monarch's power with Anne's predecessors, William III and Mary II, who ruled jointly. In 1701, the year before Anne became queen, Parliament had controversially declared that it should decide the succession, as William and Mary had no children. The throne was passed to Anne, who was Mary's sister, and the Act of Settlement in 1701 declared that the descendants of James II and Mary of Modena (the former Catholic king, who had fled England when William arrived in the Glorious Revolution) would forever be barred from the throne of England. It meant that nobody who was a Catholic, became a Catholic or married a Catholic could become a sovereign. Effectively, Parliament would decide who the next monarch would be.

The result of this change

The Act of Union in 1707 saw the English and Scottish Parliaments unite, with a new flag and name: Great Britain. Although Queen Anne had given birth many times (13!), her last surviving child died after she was too old to have any more and so Parliament decided to pass the crown from the House of Stuart to that of Hanover. Sophia of Hanover had been named as Anne's heir but died before Anne, so the crown passed to Sophia's son, George. With the new king spending more time in Hanover, the country needed someone to run it on a daily basis; Robert Walpole was the leading cabinet minister and is viewed as Britain's first prime minister. Britain was now a constitutional monarchy and would never return to being an absolute monarchy. With Parliament now having more of a say in how the country was run, it gave the opportunity for talented individuals from any upbringing to make their mark, no longer constrained by their lack of noble blood. It also meant that Parliament initiated an efficient tax system that collected a lot of money, thus funding military campaigns and providing the springboard for Britain to become more of a world power.

Why did Victoria's power change?

Victoria reigned for almost 64 years and oversaw the British Empire at its greatest; it was said that the sun never set on the empire, as it was always daylight somewhere due to the vast expanse of the worldwide colonies. Although Victoria is regarded as one of the country's greatest monarchs, there had been a gradual reduction in the influence of the ruler over the running of the country and, under Victoria, it had truly become a constitutional monarchy. Victoria relied closely on advice early on from her husband, Albert, and her first prime minister, Lord Melbourne, but when Albert died aged 42 from typhoid, she was devastated. Dressed in black, a mourning Victoria retreated to residences such as Windsor and Balmoral and was rarely seen in public until she gradually started to reappear in the 1870s. A couple of failed assassination attempts helped to reignite her popularity and a republican movement which had been gathering pace then dwindled after a victorious parade through London after her son Edward recovered from typhoid. Although Victoria did not have the powers of earlier monarchs, she still had influence over domestic affairs. Things did not always go her way, however.

The result of this change

The old idea of an absolute monarchy, with the king or queen being in charge of all things to do with the state, and military, economic, foreign and domestic policy, regardless of whether or not they were up to the job, had gone for ever. In its place were talented, driven and hardworking individuals who were there on merit at a time when the country was making huge industrial, economic and imperial strides. Britain became the industrial centre of the world and its empire spread, importing raw materials from its colonies across the globe to the factories, before exporting goods worldwide. Prime ministers such as Lord Melbourne, Robert Peel and Benjamin Disraeli had a good relationship with Victoria and she still exerted some influence. Reigning for so long at a time when Britain was at its strongest helped secure her legacy, so even though she did not have the power of earlier monarchs, Victoria became the symbol of the British Empire at its absolute peak.

Key words

Magna Carta: Document the barons forced King John to sign in 1215, meaning 'Great Charter', listing all their grievances with the king. It set limits on the power of the king, as well as setting out rights to freemen and protecting Church rights. Some of the points survive to this day (for example, no man may be imprisoned without a fair trial), and the Magna Carta influenced the American constitution.

Divine Right: Belief that the monarch is answerable for their actions only to God and holds absolute power over their subjects, who should obey them without question.

Act of Settlement: An Act that stated that nobody who was Catholic, or married to a Catholic, could be a monarch. This ensured a Protestant succession.

Important dates

1199: John becomes king.
1208–1213: The Pope, Innocent III, closes churches in England.
1214: King John fails to win land back from Philip II in France.
1215: The angry barons force King John to sign Magna Carta.
1216: John dies.
1701: The Act of Settlement is passed: the descendants of James II and Mary of Modena are forever barred from the throne.
1702: Anne becomes queen.
1707: The Act of Union: English and Scottish Parliaments are united and Great Britain is formed.
1714: Anne dies and the throne passes to the Hanover family in Germany.
1837: Victoria becomes queen.
1840: Victoria marries Albert, her cousin.
1861: Albert dies of typhoid fever.
1876: Victoria becomes Empress of India.
1887: Victoria celebrates her Golden Jubilee.
1897: Victoria celebrates her Diamond Jubilee.
1901: Victoria dies.

Important people

Richard I (1157–1199): Son of Henry II and king from 1189 until his death; also known as Richard the Lionheart. Richard spent only six months ruling in England, and the rest fighting in the Third Crusade.
John (1166–1216): Brother of Richard, John ruled from 1199–1216. He was very unpopular with the barons after years of heavy taxation and military failures in France. John also upset the Church, and the result of all this was the *Magna Carta*. However, it could be argued that he was put in this tricky position by his brother bankrupting the country during the Third Crusade; now the barons were taking their revenge.
Innocent III: Pope from 1198–1216. He clashed with King John over the appointment of the Archbishop of Canterbury (the Pope wanted Stephen Langton appointed but John did not); in the end, Innocent III excommunicated King John and closed churches in England for five years. Eventually, John accepted Langton and the Pope's authority, and the ban was lifted.
James I (1566–1625): Son of Mary, Queen of Scots who reigned from 1603–1625. James believed in the Divine Right of kings and was the focus of the unsuccessful Gunpowder Plot.
Charles I (1600–1649): Son of James I, Charles also inherited his father's belief in Divine Right. Charles quarrelled with Parliament over many issues, resulting eventually in the Civil War. After losing the war against Parliament, Charles was executed in 1649.
Charles II (1630–1685): Son of Charles I, who was invited to restore the monarchy in 1660. His reign came as a welcome relief to many after the puritanical Oliver Cromwell, and Charles was nicknamed 'the Merry Monarch' due to his love of music, theatre, partying and leading an extravagant lifestyle. His reign oversaw two monumental events: the Great Plague in 1665 and the Great Fire of London in 1666.
William III (1650–1702): Invited by a group of leading English landowners to become king after they had grown disillusioned with the current monarch, James II. William, the Protestant ruler of the Netherlands, duly accepted and became king in the 'Glorious Revolution' of 1688.
Mary II (1662–1694): Daughter of James II, Mary was the joint ruler with her husband, William III.

Anne (1665–1714): Daughter of James II, Anne's reign oversaw the Act of Union, uniting England with Scotland in 1707.

George I (1660–1727): The Act of Succession meant that when Queen Anne died, the throne passed to the Hanoverian George, whose mother Sophia was a granddaughter of James I. He arrived in England aged 54 and spoke little English and spent little time in England, with most of his time spent in Hanover.

Robert Walpole (1676–1745): As a result of King George I spending more time in Hanover, Walpole became the first prime minister, ruling from 1721–1745.

Queen Victoria (1819–1901): Ruled from 1837–1901. Her reign saw Britain's empire at its peak, with huge industrial and economic progress made.

Lord Melbourne: William Lamb, prime minister. He was a big influence early on in Victoria's reign.

Prince Albert (1819–1861): Husband of Queen Victoria. Albert was appointed Prince Consort in 1857 and was an influential figure before dying aged 42 from typhoid.

Benjamin Disraeli (1804–1881): Served twice as Prime Minister under Queen Victoria.

Useful links

http://magnacarta800th.com All things Magna Carta.
www.bbc.co.uk/schools/primaryhistory/british_history/magna_carta/
www.theschoolrun.com/homework-help/the-magna-carta
www.historylearningsite.co.uk/queen_anne.htm Information on Anne.
www.ducksters.com/biography/women_leaders/queen_victoria.php Biography of Victoria, also suitable for pupils.
www.primaryhomeworkhelp.co.uk/victorians/victoria.htm Lots of questions and answers on Victoria.

Lesson 1 Control the king!

Getting started
In groups, pupils discuss whether they have ever challenged something that they have seen as unfair. They feed ideas back to the class.

Class activities
- Explain that King John was forced to sign Magna Carta in 1215 by the barons, who were upset with him. Briefly go through the reasons they were upset. Were all the problems John's fault, or should Richard shoulder some of the blame?
- Pupils split into small groups: within these groups, half argue for the barons, the remainder argue for the king.
- Using their ideas discussed in groups, pupils write a paragraph as King John, titled 'How dare the barons make demands of me!'
- Using the other half of their ideas discussed in groups, pupils write a paragraph as the barons, titled 'How dare the King treat us like this!'

Plenary material
Pupils vote on whether the barons were right to force John to sign Magna Carta.

Lesson 2 The rise of Parliament

Getting started
Should the monarch of England be English? Pupils discuss in small groups.

Class activities
- Explain that the power of Parliament had grown through history: from Elizabethan times, through the Civil War, Charles II, James II and with William and Mary – by the time Anne took over, Parliament was powerful. Pupils plot changes on a timeline.
- Pose the question that the pupils will answer at the end: was Parliament right to limit the power of the monarch? Read them a quote from James I about Parliament: 'I am surprised that my ancestors should have permitted such an institution to come into existence.' How would an MP feel, having read this? Pupils write a short speech as an MP.
- Then explain that there was a Civil War between Charles I and Parliament, with Parliament victorious and Charles being executed: the monarchy was eventually restored but Parliament made sure that the monarch would no longer have absolute power.
- Explain that in 1701 Parliament declared that it would decide the succession of the monarchy. Pupils discuss whether this was fair or not, assuming the roles of both royalists and parliamentarians.

Plenary material
Class vote: was Parliament right to limit the power of the monarch?

Lesson 3 Just look at the empire!

Getting started
On the board, write *The empire on which the sun never sets.* Ask pupils to discuss in groups and then feed back what they think it means.

Class activities
- Explain that under Queen Victoria, Britain had the largest empire the world has ever seen. Ask pupils if they think Victoria had more or less power than previous monarchs.
- On a map, show pupils the extent of the British Empire. Then hand out a photocopied blank map for them to colour in, showing the British Empire at its peak.
- Ask the class what the benefits were of having such a large empire.
- On the map, pupils write in what was imported from and/or exported to some of the countries.
- Explain that in adding a new colony, Britain would impose language, religion and customs on the new country. In small groups, pupils discuss why this is a good and a bad thing.
- Pupils complete a written piece from the point of view of an unhappy native of a colonised country.
- Pupils then write from the opposing view, outlining the benefits that British rule will have for the country.

Plenary material
Take a class vote on whether colonising other countries is right or wrong.

Further activities for pupils

- Investigate what might have happened had John not signed Magna Carta.
- King John tends to have a bad reputation: investigate in depth whether or not this is a fair appraisal.
- Pupils write their own Magna Carta, with things they would like changed about their school.
- Discuss whether Anne would be upset about Parliament deciding who should be monarch – after all, it was Parliament that decided that she should be queen in the first place.
- Research the Act of Union: who did it benefit more?
- Investigate the life and work of Robert Walpole.
- Investigate the life of Queen Victoria.
- Research Prince Albert and his work.
- Do a project on the Great Exhibition of 1851.
- Do a project on Victorian inventions.

Further research for pupils

iPad: *Runnymede Explored* (Lewis Chun), interactive app for those who can't visit Runnymede in person.
Visit: **www.nationaltrust.org.uk/runnymede/** Runnymede, where Magna Carta was signed.
www.vam.ac.uk Victoria and Albert Museum.

Cross-curricular links

Art and design: Paint a picture of a Victorian invention.
English: Create a newspaper front page reporting on Magna Carta.
Religious studies: Research the impact Christianity had across the British Empire.
Computing: Create a presentation on Magna Carta or an aspect of Queen Victoria's reign.
Geography: Use a world map to trace the rise of the British Empire. When did it reach its peak?
Science: Investigate some of the inventions during the Victorian era.
Drama: Act out the moment the barons tell King John they want him to sign Magna Carta.
Music: Make up a rap about Magna Carta.

Progression

1. Pupils understand that the monarch today has less power than they did many years ago.
2. Pupils can name an example of a monarch whose power changed.
3. Pupils can describe how a monarch's power changed, using a specific example.
4. Pupils can chart the rise in power and influence of Parliament.
5. Pupils can compare and contrast the changing power of monarchs, using examples.

Changes in crime and punishment from the Anglo-Saxons to the present

In 30 seconds. . .

For many years, committing a relatively minor crime could result in mutilation or even death. There were ordeals that the accused had to go through to determine guilt, the outcome of which relied on chance more than anything else. This changed after Magna Carta, but punishments were still brutal, with public floggings, hangings, burnings and other more grisly ways of dispatching those labelled as guilty. The organised police force did not arrive until Victorian times, although earlier times did have constables and watchmen on the streets. The death penalty was abolished, as was hard labour in prison, but the march of technology has resulted in cybercrimes as well as more traditional ones, and terrorism.

What do I need to know?

Anglo-Saxons

There was no police force in the Anglo-Saxon era. If somebody was accused of committing a crime, they would attend a village meeting. If they admitted to the crime, they would be punished. If they said they had not done it, then the accused would need to find 12 people who would swear an oath that they were innocent. If they could do that, the accused would go free. However, if they could not, then they could be fined a sum of money or go through an ordeal. There were a number of different ordeals, and none of them were pleasant. They included being tied up and thrown into a pool blessed by a priest – if they sank more than a certain depth, they were innocent, but if they floated, they were guilty. Another ordeal was to reach into boiling water and pick up a stone and carry it a certain distance; after three days, if the hand had started to heal, the person was innocent but if it hadn't, they were guilty. A 'wergild' was a fine that had to be paid, sometimes to the family of the wronged person. If they could not pay it, the accused could become the slave to the family. Parts of the body were amputated for the smallest crimes, like stealing, and slaves could be stoned or burnt to death.

Middle Ages

Things had not changed that much by the early Middle Ages. Punishments were harsh in order to deter potential criminals, and mutilation, public shaming, fines and being put to death were commonplace. The pillory, for more serious offences, fastened around the miscreant's legs and head. This kept them in place, to be shamed in public, and the stocks followed a similar design but locked both arms and legs in place. A jury of 12 people would hear some cases, with each manor providing the jury and the Lord's steward hearing the case. More serious crimes could be heard by the King's court, and the accused were subjected to a trial by ordeal. These were similar to those in Saxon times: trial by fire involved carrying a red-hot bar and walking a few paces – if, after three days, the hand was healing, the person was innocent. The ordeal by water again involved being tied up and thrown into the river – if the person floated, they were guilty but if they sank, they were innocent. (Of course, this would result in death too.) For nobles, a matter of honour would be settled by a duel, often to the death. After 1215 and Magna Carta, the trial by ordeal was replaced with a trial by jury.

Tudors

Punishments were harsh in Tudor times and were often a public spectacle, with hangings, burnings and beheadings for more serious crimes. Committing treason resulted in the guilty being hanged, drawn and quartered before their body parts were displayed as reminders to others. Nobles who committed treason tended to be beheaded. After Henry VIII made himself Head of the Church in England, those who did not follow the religious beliefs of the monarch could be burnt for being a heretic. As the religious pendulum swung between each Tudor monarch, it resulted in many people from all sections of society falling foul of the brutal heresy laws. For more minor crimes, there were still the stocks and pillory, and torture was also used to extract confessions from unwilling prisoners. There were a lot of beggars in Tudor times and Elizabeth I passed Poor Laws in 1597 and 1601, which remained in place for almost 300 years. These laws tried to distinguish between different types of poor people – deserving poor and undeserving poor. Those who were judged to be deserving were given aid. Those who were judged to be undeserving were whipped and made to work. If they did not do so, they could be sent to a House of Correction, like a prison, or even killed.

Victorians

As the population of the towns and cities grew due to the Industrial Revolution, with people flocking to work in the factories, so crime increased. These areas would be overcrowded, with many living in awful conditions and in poverty. This resulted in high levels of crime, from the young to the old; gangs of children would roam the streets, looking to steal from the unwary. Walking the streets at night was risky, with criminals looking to entice their prey into darkened alleys before mugging, garrotting, beating or even killing them. In 1829, Sir Robert Peel founded the Metropolitan Police Force. They were armed with a truncheon, handcuffs and a rattle, which later became a whistle, to attract attention. Punishments were harsh in Victorian times, with scant regard for age: children were punished alongside adults. However, in 1854, an Act of Parliament saw Reformatory Schools being built to house young criminals, aiming to rehabilitate them as opposed to punishing them so harshly, although these reform schools were still tough places. Some criminals had been transported to faraway colonies like Australia, although this practice had ended by 1868. There were public hangings, often attended by huge crowds, but these happened less under Queen Victoria. Conditions in Victorian prisons were very poor and prisoners were treated badly; they could be in solitary confinement, work in silence or be made to do hard labour. In times of war, men could be forced to enlist in the armed forces, especially the navy, and could even earn a pardon at the end of their service. Victorian times gave us two enduring crime-related characters, one fictional and the other very real: Jack the Ripper and Sherlock Holmes.

Present day

Punishments have changed in modern times, and public executions and floggings no longer happen in Britain. These days, many of the crimes that were committed in the other time periods are still being committed, as well as more modern crimes. Criminals have embraced technology, resulting in cybercriminals, credit card and Internet fraud, hacking, etc., but this same technology, in the form of CCTV, computerised records and modern surveillance equipment has also aided those hunting the criminals down. Instead of physically punishing criminals when they are locked up, there is more of a rehabilitation programme in place, looking to understand why the crime was committed in the first place. There are secure hospitals for those with mental health issues, something that was not recognised earlier. There are open prisons for offenders who are not seen to be a risk to society and, although there are still correctional facilities for juvenile offenders, their identity is now kept secret. Terrorism has brought unwanted headlines to many countries, with members of the public suddenly finding themselves in the firing line.

Key words

Wergild: A fine paid in Anglo-Saxon times.

Pillory: Used for punishing someone in public; a wooden frame with holes for head and hands to be secured.

Stocks: Similar to the pillory but for lesser offences; the stocks also secured the feet of the accused.

Magna Carta: Document that the barons forced King John to sign in 1215; one of the points stated that no freeman could suffer punishment without a trial by jury.

Treason: Betraying one's own country.

Hanged, drawn and quartered: Partially hanged, then taken down and the entrails drawn out while still alive, before being chopped into four pieces. A traitor's death.

Separate system: Form of imprisonment where prisoners were kept in solitary confinement.

Silent system: Prisoners were not allowed to speak to other prisoners.

Important dates

c. 5th century: Hanging is first introduced in Anglo-Saxon times.

1351: The Treason Act defines high treason and petty treason in law.

1542: Witchcraft is punishable by hanging.

1649: Charles I is executed for treason; the only king in England to be killed this way.

1718: The Transportation Act enables prisoners to be transported to America, but this is interrupted by the American War of Independence.

1788: Transportations to Australia begin.

1814: 'Disembowelling and quartering' is removed from the High Treason Act.

1868: Last public hanging of a woman.

1875: Last fully public hanging in the British Isles.

1908: Execution of those under the age of 16 is outlawed.

1933: Execution of those under the age of 18 at the time of the crime is prohibited.

1965: Last person to be sentenced to death penalty in England. (He was reprieved and sentenced to life in prison.)

1969: Abolition of capital punishment for murder.

1999: The British government formally abolishes the death penalty.

Important people

King John (1166–1216): Brother of Richard, John ruled from 1199–1216. He was very unpopular with the barons after years of heavy taxation and military failures in France. John also upset the Church. The result of all this was the Magna Carta.

Queen Elizabeth I (1533–1603): Became queen after her half-sister Mary I died in 1558. Considered one of the greatest monarchs Britain has had, Elizabeth's reign saw the Spanish Armada of 1588 repelled. Also known as 'The Virgin Queen', Elizabeth did not marry, and when she died the Tudor reign came to an end.

Jack the Ripper: Nickname given to the unidentified serial killer who committed a number of murders around the Whitechapel area in 1888.

Sherlock Holmes: Fictional detective, aided by Dr Watson, in a series of stories written by Sir Arthur Conan Doyle.

Interesting fact

It costs about £37,500 to keep a person in prison for a year.

Useful links

www.britainexpress.com/History/Anglo-Saxon-Legal-System.htm
http://vcp.e2bn.org Victorian crime and punishment.
www.sherlockian.net/canon/ List of stories and links about Sherlock Holmes.
www.localhistories.org/pun.html A glossary of many punishments.
www.elizabethan-era.org.uk/elizabethan-crime-and-punishment.htm Elizabethan crime and punishment.

Lesson 1 Punishment fits the crime

Getting started
Ask pupils to discuss the school sanction/punishment system. Do they think it is fair? Groups feed back ideas to the class.

Class activities
- Explain that for every action, there are consequences: give some examples.
- Ask pupils what methods of punishment there are today: are these reasonable punishments?
- Hand out the resource on crimes and ask pupils to fill in what they think would be an appropriate punishment for each crime. **(Bloomsbury Online Resource 10A)** Pupils can either discuss and fill in as a group, or work individually.
- Pupils feed back ideas to the class. Vote on what pupils think punishments should be for various modern crimes.
- Compare the voted punishments with the actual punishments. Are there any differences?
- Pupils make their own list of sanctions for the school: what would they change and what would they keep the same?

Plenary material
In groups, pupils discuss their new school rules.

Lesson 2 Trial by ordeal

Getting started
On the board, write *What would happen if you were caught stealing in Anglo-Saxon times?* Either put options on the board for pupils to choose from, or let them discuss in groups.

Class activities
- Explain that the punishment system was very different in Anglo-Saxon times.
- Look at the types of crimes that were committed in Anglo-Saxon times and discuss the punishments: what do pupils think about the fairness of some of the punishments?
- Investigate an example of Anglo-Saxon justice: create a scenario involving an Anglo-Saxon who has been accused of a crime. Pupils read through the case study and make a list of questions they would need answering to work out if the accused was guilty or not.

Plenary material
In groups, pupils pick a card with an Anglo-Saxon punishment on it and tell the rest of the group about it.

Lesson 3 Tudor troubles

Getting started
Ask pupils to think what religion they are. Take feedback, noting answers: for instance, Church of England; Catholic; Baptist; Muslim; Sikh; Buddhist. Explain that there is religious tolerance today but that was not always the case.

Class activities
- Explain that in Tudor times you would be accused of being a heretic if you did not follow the established faith: to believe something different to the monarch at the time could result in death. Many people were burnt at the stake for their religious beliefs.
- Look at the woodcut of Thomas Cranmer being burnt, where he is lifting his hand to the flames (it is suitable). Explain that he had previously signed a confession to change from Protestant to Catholic but then changed his mind; he said that when he faced the fire, 'his unworthy right hand' would be the first to feel the flames.
- Look at other Tudor punishments: hanging; hanging, drawing and quartering; hanging in chains; beheading; flogging; stocks etc. Pose the question: why did large crowds watch public executions?
- Devise a worksheet showing a list of people in Tudor times who have committed various crimes: pupils have to state what the punishment should be. Alternatively, use the example prepared. **(Bloomsbury Online Resource 10B)**

Plenary material
Should any of the punishments from Tudor times stand now? Pupils discuss in groups and feed back to the class.

Further activities for pupils

- Pupils design their own board game about crime and punishment through the ages: work in pairs or individually to make a game about trying to survive a trip from Anglo-Saxon times to the present day. One idea is to make it a simple game, trying not to land on certain spaces; or have 'chance' cards to pick up, or questions to answer, in order not to get caught or punished.
- Pupils plot on a timeline the changes in punishments from Anglo-Saxon times to the present day.
- Pupils investigate the 'trial by ordeal' method of punishment used in the Middle Ages.
- Explain that in Victorian times, the punishment would be far worse: they could be transported across to the other side of the world to serve their sentence. Go to **http://vcp.e2bn.org** and watch the case study of Henry Catlin, aged 14. Investigate transportation and do written exercises.
- Research and do a project on Sir Robert Peel and the start of the Metropolitan Police Force.
- Look at Victorian cases studies to see what crimes could be punished and how, even for children.
- Research cybercrime today: downloading games, movies and music without paying for it is illegal and can lead to prosecution.
- Look at the spread of terrorism today: how should it be dealt with?
- Debate whether punishments are too lenient these days.
- Pupils create a comic strip that charts punishments from Anglo-Saxon times to the present.

Further research for pupils

www.hyperstaffs.info/work/history/klamar/ Interactive site on Anglo-Saxon punishments.
Read some of the Sherlock Holmes stories by Sir Arthur Conan Doyle. See if you can solve any of them before Holmes reveals what happens!
iPad: *Crime and Punishment in the Middle Ages* (Jack Solomon), free, contains information and a quiz.
Visit: **http://vcp.e2bn.org/teachers/11468-places-to-visit.html** List of places to visit.

Cross-curricular links

Art and design: Paint a trial by ordeal in the Middle Ages – the gorier, the better!
English: Write a short story about a young boy or girl caught stealing in Victorian times: what happens?
Religious studies: Investigate some of the people who were burnt as heretics in Tudor times.
Computing: Create a presentation chronicling crime and punishment through the ages.
Geography: Investigate where convicts were shipped to in Victorian times and research their treatment.
Science: Investigate some of the instruments of torture and execution over the ages.
Drama: Act out a trial in one of the time periods.

Progression

1. Pupils recognise that punishments have changed over the years.
2. Pupils can give examples of crime and punishment from a specific era.
3. Pupils can place punishments on a timeline, chronicling how they have changed over the years.
4. Pupils recognise how different crimes were punished in more than one era.
5. Pupils can make comparisons between crimes and punishments from Anglo-Saxon times to the present day.

Significant turning points in British History: Magna Carta

In 30 seconds...

King John succeeded his brother Richard the Lionheart but, as well as inheriting his debts from the Crusades, he made more problems for his people. John had fallen out with the Pope, who had then banned church services in England, making the people worry for their souls. As well as being blamed for that, the King had lost land in France again, and had then asked the barons for more taxes to fund another military excursion that would no doubt fail too. So the barons, by now prepared to make a stand, got together and forced John to sign the Magna Carta, which placed limits on his kingly power.

What do I need to know?

Upsetting the barons

John's older brother, Richard, was the king. Popular, brave and good at fighting, he had the nickname Richard the Lionheart, and spent a huge amount of money fighting in the Crusades. John finally became king in 1199 and, at this time, the king of England also had quite a lot of land in France. He would ask the barons for money and men to defend these territories. That was fine as long as he was winning, but when he started to lose, he needed more money and men. He did this by raising taxes and asking for more men. The barons were not happy. By 1204, John had lost his land in northern France. In order to try to get it back, he raised taxes and demanded more men without asking the barons. *This was against the law.* Normally, the king had to ask the barons first when he wanted to raise taxes, as the barons would be the ones collecting the money and it would be the barons who would provide men for the king's army.

Upsetting the Church

As well as the barons, John upset the Church. The new Pope, Innocent III, wanted to appoint Stephen Langton as the next Archbishop of Canterbury but John argued that he, as king, should choose the new man, as his father Henry II had done. The Pope decided to punish John by first banning all church services in 1208, which meant there could be no christenings, funerals or marriages, and then by excommunicating John in 1209. The Church was a very important part of people's daily lives and people worried for their souls. They were naturally very upset with this and blamed King John. John eventually apologised to the Pope, who then lifted the ban, but the Pope still didn't like John. The following year, in 1214, John lost his last remaining territory in France. Desperate for funds, he demanded more money from the barons, who were thoroughly fed up by now. They got together and decided to take action.

Where was it signed and what was in it?

Magna Carta was signed in Runnymede, in Surrey, not far from Windsor Castle. Magna Carta was a list of 63 promises and clauses made between the king and his subjects. It meant that the king had to rule

England and govern the country within the law, and not just do as he wanted. Here are some of the key points:

- The Church shall be free from interference.
- No more than the normal amounts of money can be collected to run the government, unless the king's feudal tenants give their consent.
- No free man shall be seized or imprisoned, or stripped of his rights or possessions…except by the lawful judgement of his peers.

What happened next?

King John signed Magna Carta and put the royal seal on it. However, he felt he was forced into signing it and had no intention of keeping to all the promises he had made. He signed it merely to bide his time and keep the barons from bothering him. But when John did not keep his promises, the barons asked the French to invade and kick him off the throne. Before they could successfully do so, John died and left the throne to his son, Henry III.

Did it work?

At first it did, but John had no intention of keeping his promise; he said he had been forced into signing the charter and had not done so of his own free will, therefore he was not bound by the promise. However, two important parts of it lived on and were referred to under later kings: that no man could be unfairly imprisoned without a trial by jury, and that the king was not above the law and could not raise taxes without the consent of the people. Magna Carta influenced Bills of Rights in both the UK and the USA and it is still said that 'even the sovereign is subject to God and the law'.

What if. . . John had not signed Magna Carta?

If John had refused to sign Magna Carta, it is most likely that the barons would have rebelled against John and had a civil war. As it was, this happened when John started to go back on his word in 1216 and the barons asked Louis of France to invade to seize the crown. However, he didn't get the chance to take the crown of England by force, as John died in 1216. When John died, his son Henry III became king. With John now dead, the barons united behind the new king and forced the French out of the country. So if John had not signed Magna Carta, things would have turned out pretty much as they did regarding the monarchy. Having said that, if future kings after John had continued to abuse their power, it is likely they would have been forced to sign a similar document under threat of civil war. In fact, when the early Stuart kings started to abuse their power, it resulted in the English Civil War.

Key words

Excommunicated: Thrown out of the Catholic Church. This meant that John's subjects were no longer bound to obey him and could overthrow him legally.

Important dates

1166: The future king John is born.
1199: Prince John becomes King John after his brother Richard the Lionheart dies.
1204: John's army is defeated in northern France and he earns the nickname Softsword.
1208: After John falls out with the Pope, the Pope bans all church services. People fear they will go to Hell and blame John.
1209: The Pope excommunicates John.
1213: John apologises to the Pope.
1214: John loses his last land in France. The nobles are very angry and start to rebel.
1215: John signs Magna Carta at Runnymede (15 June).
1216: King John dies.

Important people

Richard II: Also known as Richard the Lionheart; fought in the Crusades; brother of John.
John: Prince John, brother of Richard; became king in 1199.
Innocent III: The Pope who fell out with John and banned church services.
Philip II: King of France, who was threatening to invade England.
Louis: Son of Philip II of France, eventually sent to invade England.
Henry III: Son of John; the barons rallied behind Henry and beat Louis.

Interesting fact

King John is often seen as a cruel man, especially in fictional accounts such as the Robin Hood stories. However, his brother Richard the Lionheart had bankrupted the country fighting in the Crusades and left John in a very difficult position when he assumed the throne. Was it all John's fault? When John fell out with the Pope, who banned all church services in the country, many contemporary accounts were written by the monks who would have blamed John for this; it is these accounts that provide much of what we know from the time, so is it any wonder they speak against him? It could be argued that John was unlucky rather than evil.

Useful links

http://notesinhistory.blogspot.it/2012/01/good-king-john.html A balanced view of King John.
www.bbc.co.uk/history/british/middle_ages/lusig_01.shtml Comprehensive account of King John.

Lesson 1 He's not his big brother!

Getting started
Pupils discuss in groups whether they have ever waited a really long time for something: was it worth it when it finally arrived?

Class activities
- Ask pupils if they have heard of King John before (or when he was Prince John). Many will have got their ideas from Robin Hood stories. How has he been portrayed? Write ideas on the board.
- On the other side of the board, write *Richard the Lionheart*. Tell pupils Richard was John's big brother and king before him, and that he fought in the Crusades. What would people have thought of Richard? Write ideas on the board.
- There should now be two contrasting characters: pupils write a short description of each in their book.
- How would John have felt now he was king? Pupils write a speech saying what John hoped to do now he was in charge.
- Explain that the Crusades had cost the barons a huge amount of money and men: what would they be expecting now that there was a new king? Pupils write a short speech on behalf of the barons.

Plenary material
In pairs, pupils decide which of them is John; the other represents a baron. To start with, the baron states their expectation of the new king; then John replies saying what he expects to happen now that he is king. Can the two agree?

Lesson 2 Evil or unlucky?

Getting started
Hand the class a primary source about King John:

> 'After arguing with the Pope, John ordered the. . .monks who remained at Canterbury, including the blind and crippled, out of the country. . .The whole of England was taxed heavily. He imprisoned many and only released them in return for money.'
>
> *Gervase, a monk from Canterbury in Kent*

Ask the pupils to read and discuss it in small groups.

Class activities

- Pupils feed back ideas from Gervase's source: what impression does it give about John? Show a clip of how John is portrayed in films, looking suitably evil. (See Errol Flynn's version of Robin Hood.)
- Explain John's falling out with the Pope – on one side, the people of England blamed John for the churches being closed but, on the other hand, John was only trying to stop the Pope meddling in business that he should not have been involved in. Find a source about John and the Church to read out. Pupils write the heading 'Problems with the Church', then write a few bullet points stating why John was evil and then stating why he was unlucky.
- Explain about the high taxes that John charged the barons. On one hand, say that the barons were fed up with high taxes and losing land in France. On the other hand, say that Richard had been taxing them for years. Under the heading 'Taxing the nobles', pupils write a few bullet points saying why John was evil and then a few stating why he was unlucky.
- Explain that pupils should now have a balanced account of John. Now they write their own conclusion, from the evidence in front of them. Was King John evil or unlucky?

Plenary material

Take the hot seat as King John, taking questions from the pupils, who can be monks and barons. Can the teacher convince them he has been dealt a harsh historical hand?

Lesson 3 Time for a change!

Getting started

Pupils think of three ground rules enforced at home that they disagree with, and change them in their favour. Poll them on the board to see what the majority want changing.

Class activities

- Explain that the barons decided to take matters into their own hands and forced John to sign Magna Carta at Runnymede. Explain that it means 'great charter'.
- Ask pupils to recap why the barons were upset with John. Then ask them what they think was in Magna Carta. Record their ideas on the board.
- Go through some of the famous points in Magna Carta and ask pupils to write them down.
- Class debate: as John was forced to sign the charter against his will, should he have been bound by his signature? After pupils have discussed it and voted, explain that John went back on it as soon as he could.
- Tell pupils that they are going to write their own Magna Carta – what would they like to see changed at their school? After pupils have written their points in rough, check them to ensure they are not too fanciful. They can either be copied up and illustrated in books or done on paper for a display.

Plenary material

Run a short *true or false* quiz on Magna Carta, with pupils working individually.

Further activities for pupils

- Investigate how Magna Carta has influenced laws, and the American constitution today.
- What would have happened if King John had not signed Magna Carta?
- If the prime minister could be forced to sign a Magna Carta today, what would be in it?
- Research more about Magna Carta: where it was signed, what was in it, etc.
- Investigate sources about King John; comment on their reliability.

Further research for pupils

www.bbc.co.uk/schools/primaryhistory/british_history/magna_carta/ Easy-to-understand facts, pictures and a quiz.
The Adventures of Robin Hood (1938), directed by Michael Curtiz and William Keighley.
The Adventures of Robin Hood by Roger Lancelyn Green
iPad: *Magna Carta – The Definitive Guide* (Daniel Dickinson)
Visit: Runnymede, the National Trust site in Surrey where Magna Carta was signed. Find it at TW20 0AE. There is a visitor centre and other fascinating attractions, including a 2,500-year-old yew tree. From there, why not combine it with a trip to Windsor Castle? It's only 3.5 miles away, a 15-minute drive. Find it at SL4 1NJ.

Cross-curricular links

Art and design: Create an authentic-looking Magna Carta and decorate it.
English: Write a series of diary entries as a baron, monk and commoner, explaining why you are all so unhappy with King John.
Religious studies: Investigate the impact it had when the Pope banned church services for five years.
Computing: Design a booklet on Magna Carta, either written at the time, or from the present.
Geography: Investigate why Magna Carta was signed at Runnymede.
Drama: Act out the barons confronting King John; or record a series of news reports, either using GarageBand (or a similar program) or on screen.
Music: Make up a rap about Magna Carta.

Progression

1. Pupils can recall who signed Magna Carta and when.
2. Pupils can say what sort of person John was from interpreting and understanding sources.
3. Pupils can give a reason why King John was forced to sign Magna Carta.
4. Pupils can assess its importance at the time for different people.
5. Pupils can explain the importance of Magna Carta today.
6. Pupils have a balanced view of John from interpreting different sources and assessing their reliability.

Significant turning points in British History: The Spanish Armada

In 30 seconds. . .

Tension between Elizabeth I and Philip II, the rulers of England and Spain respectively, had been building for years. After ignoring his hand in marriage, stealing his treasure from the New World, helping Dutch rebels fight against him, refusing to change religion and executing a Catholic queen, Elizabeth had finally upset Philip enough. He assembled the mighty Armada to teach Elizabeth's heretic island a lesson. However, a combination of poor tactics, luck and bad weather resulted in defeat for the Armada, with many Spanish sailors dying on the journey home. England was safe.

What do I need to know?

Why was the Armada sent?

Marriage

Philip II of Spain had previously been married to Mary Tudor, who was Elizabeth's half-sister. That marriage had been very unpopular with the English people, resulting in Wyatt's Rebellion. Philip was interested in marrying Elizabeth but she refused. This hurt Philip's pride.

Religion

Before Elizabeth, England had been a Catholic country for a very long time. Elizabeth's father, Henry VIII, had played about with religion, breaking away from the Pope and Rome more for his own private goals of securing a divorce and getting his hands on the Church's vast fortune rather than anything to do with religion; he still died a Catholic. But his son, Edward VI, changed the country from Catholic to Protestant before dying only six years later. Then Mary earned the slightly unflattering nickname of Bloody Mary, as she introduced her infamous 'turn or burn' approach to converting people back to Catholicism. She burnt almost 300 Protestants, turning the country from Protestant back to Catholic before she died in 1558, leaving Elizabeth to take over a rather confused country. The religious roller-coaster had been going this way and that and Elizabeth saw no reason to change this approach, as she promptly turned the country from Catholic back again to Protestant. While this was going on, Philip II of Spain, in charge of the most powerful Catholic country in Europe, was keen to turn England back to Catholicism again, as it had been for hundreds of years previously.

Helping the Dutch

Spain was ruling much of the Netherlands but was meeting some stiff resistance from some Dutch rebels. The Netherlands was a Protestant country, as was England at this time, and Elizabeth lent her support to the Dutch in 1572. A few years later, in 1585, she sent an army over to help them fight. Religion may have been one reason for sending it but she may have been worried about how close Spain was getting to England; a Spanish-ruled Netherlands would have been a convenient base from which to launch an invasion of England in the future if the Spanish could wipe out any rebel resistance.

Pirate or privateer?

The Spanish had control of the New World, what is now Central and South America. Francis Drake and other sailors took delight in raiding the slow and cumbersome Spanish treasure ships and relieving them of their cargo. Philip saw Drake as a pirate under orders from Elizabeth to rob him of his treasure. Elizabeth denied this, saying that Drake was not a pirate but a privateer. However, Elizabeth knighted Drake in 1581, making him Sir Francis Drake, and seemingly rewarding him for his escapades.

Mary, Queen of Scots

Mary, Queen of Scots, had fled Scotland, hoping for sanctuary in England, only for Elizabeth to put her under house arrest for 19 years. Mary was a Catholic and many people thought she should be queen instead of Elizabeth. Elizabeth and her advisors were worried by this and Elizabeth was urged by her ministers to execute Mary for her own protection; as long as Mary was alive, plots against Elizabeth would continue. However, Elizabeth refused to do so, as Mary was an anointed queen and also her cousin. Elizabeth was also worried about the reaction of powerful Catholic countries such as France and Spain should Mary be executed. But after Mary was supposedly involved in the Babington Plot of 1586, another attempt to overthrow the Queen, Elizabeth was left with little choice; she signed the death warrant but didn't send it. Lord Burghley, her chief advisor, grabbed it and sent it to Fotheringhay, where Mary was put on trial and beheaded before Elizabeth could change her mind again. This was the final straw and Philip II of Spain started to prepare a mighty Armada to remove this annoying thorn in his side!

The Armada prepares

With the Armada preparations under way, Sir Francis Drake led a daring raid into the Spanish port of Cadiz and set fire to the ships there. This was known as the 'Singeing of the King of Spain's beard' and delayed the Armada for another year. Philip had originally wanted Santa Cruz to lead the Armada, a very experienced and brilliant sailor who died before the Armada could sail. In his place went Medina Sidonia, who was put in change as he was from a noble family; however, he was no sailor, and got seasick!

What was the plan?

The aim of the Spanish Armada was to sail to the Netherlands to pick up the Duke of Parma and his army of 30,000 experienced soldiers. From there, they would cross the short distance to England and take London. If this happened, it is likely that Elizabeth would not have been able to stop them, as she did not have a strong or big enough army. The Spanish also hoped English Catholics would rise up in support of them. The Armada was spotted off the coast of Plymouth and beacons were lit to pass the message on. As legend has it, Drake was playing a game of bowls and refused to leave until he had finished his game. Either he was remarkably cool under pressure or the wind meant he couldn't sail yet anyway. Finally, the wind changed and the English navy set out after the Armada. Lord Howard of Effingham was in charge of the English navy. He was a very experienced and able sailor, backed up by Drake and others such as Frobisher and Hawkins. The Armada sailed in a crescent formation, with the cargo ships in the middle protected by massive galleons on the ends of the formation. The English ships were smaller and faster, and had cannons that could fire further. Although there were a few attacks, however, little damage was done to either side. The Spanish ships were full of soldiers and they tried to get close to the English ships to use huge grappling hooks to board them, but the agile English smartly stayed well away. The English still had to stop the Armada from meeting up with the Duke of Parma, though, otherwise it would be game over.

Fireships

Unfortunately for the Spanish, the Duke of Parma had no idea when the Armada would show up. Besides, he was busy fighting the Dutch and it would take at least two weeks to gather his army to board the vessels. Running out of chances to land to pick him and the army up, the Armada decided to moor just off what is now Calais in France and wait. However, Calais was not a good place to stop: it provided little shelter from storms and the current was very strong. Nevertheless, the English still had to stop the Armada from picking up Parma. If he and his land army managed to reach the Armada and they set sail for England, there would be nothing the English navy could do. The English had already seen how little damage their cannons did: they had so far failed to sink a single ship. They needed a plan. With some of the English sailors going down with disease, Lord Howard of Effingham had to take action. Drake had an idea. They got eight ships and filled them with flammable material, set them on fire, and let them drift towards the anchored Spanish fleet. The Spanish were terrified, thinking they were 'hellburners' and, in their panic to get away, cut their anchors. They were now at the mercy of the wind and drifted out into the open sea just off Calais. The stage was now set for the major battle, the Battle of Gravelines.

The Battle of Gravelines

With the Spanish ships scattered and no longer in formation, the English closed in to do battle. Medina Sidonia bravely turned his flagship to delay the English, to give the Spanish time to reform their crescent formation. Sidonia's ship, the *San Martin*, was hit around 200 times but did not sink. The Spanish managed to get back into their crescent formation but, with the English blocking their way to the Duke of Parma and the wind against them, Medina Sidonia had little choice but to sail his fleet around Britain to get home to Spain. Many were shipwrecked off the coasts of Scotland and Ireland. Those sailors who staggered ashore in Ireland were either killed or held for ransom. Only 90 of the Spanish ships returned to Spain, with 60 in total lost at sea. Twenty-five were wrecked off the coast of Ireland, and only four were captured or sunk. Men had to resort to eating rope on the way home, and many were sick or wounded. Out of the 30,000 Spanish soldiers and sailors who set out, around 11,000 died. But it was not all good news for the English. Unsure if the Spanish would return, the English fleet was kept in harbour in readiness, with many dying of illness and disease. They also did not get paid; not the reward they expected.

Why did the Armada fail?

There are many reasons why the Armada failed: the Spanish said it was down to bad luck; the English said they had better sailors and God was on their side. However, it is important to have a fair and balanced view of why it actually failed. Consider the following reasons:

- Poor leadership of the Spanish
- Talented English leaders
- Big and slow Spanish ships full of soldiers
- Fast and agile English ships
- Superior English cannons that fired faster and further
- The Spanish having more priests than gunners on board ships
- The Spanish failure to pick up the Duke of Parma
- English fireships and the Spanish cutting their anchors
- The wind blowing the Armada away
- Storms wrecking Spanish ships
- The Spanish not attacking when the English were stuck in port in Plymouth

What would have happened if the Spanish Armada had succeeded?

It could be argued the Spanish had two chances of success. If they had sailed into Plymouth harbour and destroyed the English fleet when the wind prevented the English from sailing, then things would have been very different: they would have had no opposition when they went to pick up the Duke of Parma. Also, if they had managed to get the message to the Duke of Parma and picked him up with his army of 30,000 men, it is unlikely the English could have stopped them crossing and landing in England. Remember, the English had not managed to sink any ships through cannon fire and would have been powerless to stop the bigger ships sailing through them and then landing. Had they landed, the Spanish army would have met little resistance as they marched up to take London. If they had done *that*, Elizabeth would have been overthrown and England would have returned to being a Catholic country.

Key words

Armada: Spanish word for 'naval fleet'.
Hellburners: Ships filled with gunpowder and shrapnel; used by the Dutch against the Spanish at the Siege of Antwerp to terrifying and great effect.
Fireships: Ships deliberately set on fire and steered into an enemy fleet.

Important dates

1558: Elizabeth becomes queen.
1559: Philip proposes to Elizabeth. She says no.
1568: Mary, Queen of Scots flees Scotland and arrives in England, where she is imprisoned for the next 19 years.
1569: Francis Drake seizes Spanish treasure ships.
1585: Elizabeth sends an army to help the Dutch rebels fight the Spanish.
1587: Mary, Queen of Scots is executed, proving the final straw and leading to Philip's attempted invasion.
1587: Sir Francis Drake sails into Cadiz and sets fire to the moored Spanish ships there, setting invasion plans back a year; known as the 'Singeing of the King of Spain's Beard'.
1588: The mighty Armada finally sets sail.

Important people

Elizabeth I: Queen of England.
Philip II: King of Spain.
Mary, Queen of Scots: Catholic queen and Elizabeth's cousin, executed in 1587.
Mary I: Catholic half-sister of Mary, queen before her and married to Philip.
Santa Cruz: Original leader of the Armada, who died before it sailed.
Medina Sidonia: Leader of the Spanish Armada.
Sir Howard of Effingham: Leader of the English navy.
Sir Francis Drake: Vice-admiral of the English fleet.
Martin Frobisher: English sailor.
John Hawkins: English sailor.
Juan Martinez de Recalde: Spanish admiral and second-in-command of the Spanish fleet.

Useful links

www.historylearningsite.co.uk/spanish_armada.htm A helpful summary.
Visit: The Golden Hinde II, a full-size replica of the ship Sir Francis Drake used to circumnavigate the globe. Find it at SE1 9DG. Lots of exciting interactive tours and programmes. From there, why not combine it with a trip to the Globe Theatre? It's only a short walk away. Find it at SE1 9DT. Also The Golden Hind, a full-size replica in Brixham, Devon. Find it at TQ5 8AW.

Lesson 1 Recipe for disaster

Getting started

Have the class discuss the phrase 'the straw that broke the camel's back'. Can they think of any examples or scenarios? (Perhaps tell a story where lots of little things go wrong during the day until one more little thing causes someone to burst into tears. Although it might seem that one single event caused the meltdown, it was actually due to a build-up of many little things.)

Class activities

- Similar to the starter activity, explain that the Armada was not something that was sent because of one reason. List the five main headings on the board: *Marriage*; *Religion*; *Stealing Spanish treasure*; *Helping the Dutch rebels*; *Mary, Queen of Scots*. Tell pupils they are going to side with Elizabeth or Philip for each one.
- Explain the reasons one by one, starting with *marriage*. Remind pupils that Philip had previously been married to Elizabeth's half-sister, Mary. Make the points that Spain was a traditional enemy of England at the time and that a marriage may have reduced England to a Spanish colony. Pupils write who they would have sided with and why.
- The next point is *religion*. England had been Catholic for years, but Elizabeth had watched Mary burn Protestants and Elizabeth was a Protestant. She changed the country to Protestantism but let Catholics worship privately as long as they still went to church. Explain that Philip wanted to turn England back to Catholicism. Pupils write who they would have sided with and why.
- The next point is *stealing Spanish treasure*. The Spanish were bringing back riches from the New World and privateers like Francis Drake were raiding their lumbering ships and stealing the treasure. Elizabeth then knighted Drake. Pupils write who they would have sided with and why.

- The next issue is *helping the Dutch rebels*. On one hand, Philip was annoyed that Elizabeth was helping the Dutch fight in a war against the Spanish; on the other hand, the Netherlands was Protestant and if Spain defeated the rebels, they would have a launch pad very close to England. Pupils write who they would have sided with and why.
- The last issue is *Mary, Queen of Scots*. From Philip's point of view, Mary was a Catholic queen who had been murdered by Elizabeth. From Elizabeth's point of view, Mary had been involved in plots against her and it was perhaps only a matter of time before one of them was successful. Pupils write who they would have sided with and why.
- Pupils look over their answers and write a conclusion: Was Philip right to send the Armada?

Plenary material

Pupils sort the reasons for sending the Armada into order of importance, with 1 being the most important and 5 being the least important. Poll class results.

Lesson 2 Prepare the Armada!

Getting started

Go over the reasons why the Armada was sent. In pairs, pupils take turns explaining each reason.

Class activities

- Look at the preparations for sending the Armada; tell pupils about the 'Singeing of the King of Spain's Beard', where Drake sailed into the port of Cadiz and set fire to the ships there, thus delaying the Armada. How would Philip have felt about this?
- Who should be in charge of the Armada? Ask pupils to describe the qualities the leader of the Armada would have.
- Explain that the original leader, Santa Cruz, died and was replaced with Medina Sidonia, who was not an experienced sailor but a noble. Ask pupils why he would have been chosen for the task.
- On a map, show the planned route of the Armada; explain that the plan was to pick up the Duke of Parma and 30,000 men from the Netherlands for the invasion of England.
- Pupils write about whether Philip had a good plan or not; if not, what should he have changed at this point before it sailed?

Plenary material

Have a game of Hangman on the board, using key words from the lesson.

Lesson 3 We shall be victorious!

Getting started
Split the class into pairs. Write out the names *Elizabeth I*, *Philip II*, *Sir Francis Drake*, *Mary I*, *Santa Cruz* and *Medina Sidonia* on pieces of paper, so that every pupil has one name. In their pairs, they show the name they have to their partner without seeing it themselves. Each pupil gets to ask three questions, answerable with *yes* or *no*, to try to guess whose nametag they have.

Class activities
- Explain that, at the time of the Armada, Spain was a very powerful nation and confident of success. With the addition of the troops in the Netherlands under the Duke of Parma, it is unlikely the English would have been able to stop the invasion.
- Show the class a picture of the Armada in crescent formation. Encourage the pupils to imagine what it would have been like to view it from the south coast of England, and ask them to write a description.
- Explain that the English ships were stuck in Plymouth harbour because of the tide. What could the Armada have done at that moment? Pupils write a script between Medina Sidonia and his admirals, debating what to do. Remind them that Philip's orders were to sail to pick up Parma, and Sidonia was hoping to find a temporary harbour off the Isle of Wight to wait for word from Parma.
- Explain that the English sailed out and managed to get the Spanish to head out to open sea, eventually mooring at Calais as they waited for Parma. So far, no ships had been sunk by cannon fire. Pupils discuss what the English could do to stop the Spanish at this point.
- Explain about the fireships; remember, the Spanish thought they were hellburners, and cut their anchors so they were now at the mercy of the wind. Pupils imagine they are a Spanish sailor and write a description of seeing the fireships heading towards them.

Plenary material
Pupils debate who was winning at this point: the Spanish or the English.

Further activities for pupils

- Look at the reasons why the Armada failed and rank them.
- Research some of the men involved on both sides for a project.
- Read Elizabeth's famous speech delivered at Tilbury. What is so great about it?
- Draw an alternative timeline and describe what would have happened if the Armada had succeeded.
- Analyse what Elizabeth and Philip said after the Armada. Was either of them correct?
- Imagine you were in charge of the Spanish Armada. If you could change one decision, which would it be and why?
- Imagine you are an English sailor. Write a series of diary entries from when you are stuck in port and see the Armada arriving, to just after the Battle of Gravelines.
- Split into groups of four or five. Write a radio script about the Armada.

- Debate the following statement: 'The Spanish Armada failed more due to bad luck than anything the English did.' Try to argue both for and against this statement and have a vote at the end to see if you agree or disagree as a class.
- Research what happened to the English sailors after the Armada.
- Study the Armada portrait by George Gower. What can you identify in it?

Further research for pupils

Battlefield Britain (documentary), presented by Peter and Dan Snow
The Story of Elizabeth I and the Spanish Armada by Colin Hynson: a gripping novel set in Elizabeth's reign.
Avoid Sailing in the Spanish Armada! by John Malam, David Antram et al. A fun, accessible book that will hook children.
iPad: *Spanish Armada*, Vanaple Technology: A Battleships-type game.

Cross-curricular links

Art and design: Pupils design a recruitment poster for Spain, encouraging men to sign up to join the Armada. Illustrate it and include reasons why it is being sent. Or, design a recruitment poster for England, urging men to join the navy, including reasons why the Spanish must be repelled.
English: Pupils imagine they are an English or Spanish sailor and write a series of diary entries, detailing the Spanish Armada and its aftermath.
Religious studies: Investigate the religious problems during Elizabeth I's reign.
Computing: Create a presentation (e.g. in PowerPoint) detailing the Spanish Armada and why it failed.
Geography: Plot the course and main events of the Spanish Armada on a map.
Science: Research how effective cannons were on ships.
Drama: In small groups or pairs, write a short playscript about why the Armada was sent. It can be set in England and in the Spanish court, or just one of them. Some ideas:

- Elizabeth telling Drake to annoy Philip
- Mary being executed and Elizabeth getting angry
- Philip asking Elizabeth to marry him
- Philip's advisors reporting the bad news to him about each reason and Philip's reaction
- A phone call between Philip and Elizabeth

Music: Make up a song about why the Spanish Armada was sent.

Progression

1. Pupils can place events on a timeline and give a reason why the Spanish Armada failed.
2. Pupils can identify some of the reasons why the Armada was sent.
3. Pupils can recall the main events of the Armada.
4. Pupils can explain the reasons behind the Armada and why it failed.
5. Pupils can make a logical argument why the Armada failed and why it was an important turning point in British history.

Significant turning points in British History: The Battle of Britain

In 30 seconds. . .

After France surrendered to Germany, Britain stood alone against the might of the German war machine. Before Hitler could invade Britain with his land army, he had to get control of the skies; this meant destroying the RAF (Royal Air Force). He sent over the Luftwaffe, but despite outnumbering the RAF, they did not manage to gain control of the skies. In September 1940, Hitler changed his plans and started bombing the cities, known as the Blitz. The Battle of Britain was over and Germany did not manage to launch its invasion.

What do I need to know?

Britain had come very close to losing the Second World War early on, as the British Expeditionary Force (BEF) was nearly wiped out at Dunkirk in May 1940, only for an incredible rescue mission to bring back the majority of these professional soldiers. But with France surrendering to Germany in June 1940, Britain now found itself standing alone against the powerful German war machine that had so far swept all before it. Hitler's planned invasion of Britain, codenamed Operation Sea Lion, could only take place if the skies were cleared of the RAF. If not, the RAF would be able to target and destroy the German land army as it made its way across the Channel to the English coast. Also, the Royal Navy would provide stern resistance to any attempted hostile crossing, so the Luftwaffe needed total control of the skies to use its bombers against the British fleet.

First targets

The Germans had over twice the number of planes of the RAF but had a big problem to overcome – radar. There were many radar stations over the south coast of England, and the Stuka dive bombers were sent to destroy these vital military targets – if the radar stations were destroyed, then Britain would not know when the German planes were heading over and the RAF would not be able to scramble in time to meet them as effectively. The Stuka bombers (or Junkers Ju 87s), had been devastating in attacking and defeating ground targets in Poland, but they were no match for the faster RAF fighters, the Spitfires and Hurricanes. German losses were high and, as a result, the radar stations were not destroyed.

A big advantage

Despite being heavily outnumbered by the Luftwaffe, the RAF pilots had one big advantage: they were fighting over their own land. This meant that they were very close to their own airfields, so could fly for longer before having to land, refuel and rearm. In contrast, the Luftwaffe had to take off from airfields in France and so the German fighters could only be fighting over English skies for a limited time before having to head back across the Channel. Also, dogfighting, with fighter planes diving, turning and accelerating during battle, burnt up fuel quickly. The German bombers could fly much further with their bigger fuel tanks, but they would be more vulnerable without their fighter escort, who would have to turn back long before them, thus leaving the slow bombers exposed to the faster and more agile RAF fighters.

What happened next?

As the Stukas had not managed to destroy the radar stations, the task of destroying Fighter Command proved harder for the Luftwaffe. There were big losses on both sides and no doubt a lot of propaganda too, but the fact remained that the RAF was very close to being overwhelmed. Some historians think the RAF was just a week away from losing when Hitler changed his plans and started bombing the cities, hoping to destroy public morale, thus forcing Britain to surrender. This was the Blitz, and it provided another stern test for Churchill and his people; however, the Battle of Britain was over and Germany had lost for the first time.

What if Germany had succeeded?

Even if the Luftwaffe had destroyed the airfields and the RAF, it is not certain that the Germans could have invaded successfully. The Royal Navy was very strong and would have provided strong protection, and some historians think Operation Sea Lion would still not have been successful.

Why did Germany lose?

- The German fighter planes could not stay in the air for very long over Britain and had to head back to refuel and rearm.
- The Luftwaffe failed to destroy the radar stations, which gave the RAF advance warning of incoming attacks.
- The RAF fighters could land, refuel and rearm more easily and could stay in the air much longer than their German counterparts, with their bases being much nearer.
- The RAF had excellent planes in the Spitfire and Hurricane.
- Hitler stopped attacking the airfields and switched tactics, targeting and bombing the cities. This gave Fighter Command vital breathing space when it most needed it.

Key words

RAF: Royal Air Force.
Luftwaffe: German Air Force.
Radar: New technology that allowed Britain to see when German aircraft were approaching (**ra**dio **d**etection **a**nd **ra**nging).
Operation Sea Lion: The planned land invasion of Britain by Germany.
BEF: British Expeditionary Force, the professional soldiers who were rescued at Dunkirk.
Blitzkrieg: 'Lightning war', the method of fighting Germany had used to such devastating effect in the early part of the Second World War as they swept through Europe. First they sent in paratroopers to destroy enemy communications, bridges, etc., then Stuka bombers bombed key targets. Next were the Panzer tanks blasting through defences, followed by lighter tanks and armoured vehicles. Finally, the rest of the army on foot would mop up anyone left. This was all done at breathtaking speed, hitting key strategic positions hard and fast. No country had yet been able to withstand the mighty Blitzkrieg.
British fighter planes: Spitfire, Hurricane.
German fighter plane: Messerschmitt Bf 109.
German bomber planes: Messerschmitt Bf 110 (fighter-bomber); Junkers Ju 87 'Stuka' dive bomber; Junkers Ju 88; Heinkel He 111; Dornier Do 17.

Important dates

26 May 1940: The BEF starts to be evacuated from the beaches of Dunkirk.
22 June 1940: France surrenders to Germany.
10 July 1940: The first day of the Battle of Britain.
15 September 1940: The last day of the Battle of Britain.

Important people

Sir Winston Churchill: British prime minister.
Sir Hugh Dowding: Leader of Fighter Command, part of the RAF.
Adolf Hitler: Leader of the Nazi party.
Herman Goering: Commander-in-chief of the Luftwaffe.

Useful links

www.winstonchurchill.org Contains all his famous speeches made during the war.
www.historylearningsite.co.uk Great site full of detailed information.
www.eyewitnesstohistory.com First-hand accounts by pilots who fought in the Battle of Britain.
www.britishpathe.com Contains vintage newsreels from the time.

Lesson 1 Why was the Battle of Britain important?

Getting started
Show a short clip of the German Blitzkrieg in action; pupils make notes on key features that made it so effective.

Class activities
- Briefly go through the main stages of the Blitzkrieg, emphasising the important factor of speed. Pupils make a note of the different stages, including pictures if necessary.
- Explain that these tactics had swept all before it and, on a map, show how the BEF and French were trapped at Dunkirk. Ask pupils how they could escape from the beaches.
- Pupils should now have a better understanding of not only the power of the German forces, but the dire situation Britain was in. Pupils write *Britain was in such a perilous situation in May 1940 because. . .* They can write bullet points or a paragraph.

Plenary material
Create a short presentation that shows a picture of key elements of the lesson: a picture of each stage of the Blitzkrieg and Dunkirk. As each picture comes up, pupils discuss in pairs or small groups what it means.

Lesson 2 Defeat the RAF!

Getting started
Recap with the class the stages of the Blitzkrieg, acting them out with noises, or using contents of pencil case for props.

Class activities
- Explain that the Germans had a name for the planned invasion of Britain: Operation Sea Lion. Ask pupils what this plan might be. If they need a hint, tell them that the RAF and British Navy stood in the way of Hitler's plan: which would need to be dealt with first, and why? Pupils discuss in groups and then take a class vote.
- Using a map that shows England and France, mark where the German planes would be taking off from. Can pupils see any advantages that the RAF pilots would have?
- Show pictures of some of the main planes involved in the Battle of Britain. Tell pupils to write a couple of facts about the Spitfire, Hurricane and Messerschmitt 109 – what were their good and bad points?
- Ask pupils how the RAF would know when the Luftwaffe would be heading over. Explain how radar worked and its importance. Draw a diagram to show radar, with a German plane in the sky.

Plenary material
In pairs, pupils devise their own variation of Rock, Paper, Scissors, instead using the calls of Stuka, Radar and Fighter. Stuka beats Radar but loses to Fighter. Radar beats Fighter but loses to Stuka. Fighter beats Stuka but loses to Radar. They invent their own gestures to represent each option. This should ensure a noisy and fun end to the lesson.

Lesson 3 Dogfight over Dover

Getting started

Pupils work in pairs. The first pupil has ten seconds to say what they have learnt so far; cue lots of fast talking and noise! Then they swap over. The best gets to say it to the rest of the class.

Class activities

- Ask the class what the Luftwaffe would need to do about the radar stations. Which planes would they use to attack them?
- Explain that although the Stuka had been very effective in other countries, it was no match for the RAF fighters that found it easy prey. Therefore, the radar stations were not destroyed. Pupils complete two speech bubbles: one is from a German pilot, saying: *We must destroy the radar stations because. . .* The second is from a British pilot, saying: *We must protect the radar stations because. . .*
- Show a clip of a dogfight; either from Pathé news or from a film such as *Battle of Britain* (1969). Also, print out a few eyewitness accounts of pilots from www.eyewitnesstohistory. com/airbattle.htm. Pupils write a short story as either a German or RAF pilot.

Plenary material

Gradually reveal something from the Battle of Britain (radar, a type of plane, one of the leaders, etc.), starting with a vague clue. Each clue gradually reveals more details, with a maximum of five clues. Pupils write their answers at the back of their books; award five points if they get it correct after the first clue; four points after the second etc. They should have five answers, and their highest scoring correct answer gets them the points.

Further activities for pupils

- Create a table showing the numbers of pilots who fought in the Battle of Britain, planes lost and nationalities.
- Explore the reasons why Germany lost the Battle of Britain.
- In groups, discuss what would have happened if the RAF were beaten. Investigate a number of scenarios.
- What was the single most important reason why Germany lost the Battle of Britain? Explain carefully.
- What could Germany have done differently in the Battle of Britain?
- If the RAF had lost, do you think Operation Sea Lion would have been a success? Explain your answer carefully.
- Research some of the pilots involved in the Battle of Britain.
- Research the leader of either Fighter Command or the Luftwaffe.
- Investigate some quotes from Winston Churchill.
- Design a newspaper front page from before, during or after the Battle of Britain.
- In groups, write a series of news reports about the Battle of Britain. They could contain quotes from Hitler, Churchill, Dowding and Goering, plus live reports as the planes fight it out in the skies. If a program such as GarageBand is used, there are many excellent sound effects available.

- Think about what would have happened if Germany had won the Battle of Britain. Design a newspaper front page the day after their crushing victory. What would the future hold for Britain?
- Look at what Germany did next. Was bombing the cities a good plan?

Further research for pupils

Battle of Britain (1969), directed by Guy Hamilton.
Forgotten Voices of the Blitz and the Battle for Britain by Joshua Levine; incredible eyewitness accounts by those who took part in the conflict.
iPad: *Battle of Britain Aircraft*: a detailed app listing all the aircraft that fought in the Battle of Britain.

Cross-curricular links

Art and design: Draw/paint a dogfight. Make it as exciting as possible!
English: Write a series of diary entries as a pilot from the RAF or Luftwaffe during the Battle of Britain.
Computing: Create a presentation telling the story of the Battle of Britain.
Geography: Plot on a map where the airfields were for both the RAF and Luftwaffe.
Science: Investigate what happens in a dogfight: fuel, type of guns, etc.
Drama: Write a short playscript set in either a German or a British airfield.
PE: Re-enact the problems German fighter planes faced with radar and having to return to France to refuel and rearm. Split the class into groups, assigning pupils as RAF, Luftwaffe and radar stations.

Progression

1. Pupils know what the Battle of Britain is and when it happened.
2. Pupils understand the aims of the Luftwaffe.
3. Pupils recognise the different planes used by each side.
4. Pupils understand the advantages and disadvantages of each side.
5. Pupils understand why the Germans lost the Battle of Britain and what they did next.
6. Pupils acknowledge that there are different opinions on what may have happened had the Luftwaffe beaten the RAF.

11 The achievements of the earliest civilisations

What does the curriculum say?

- *Pupils should learn an overview of where and when the first civilizations appeared, and a depth study of one of the following: Ancient Sumer; The Indus Valley; Ancient Egypt; The Shang Dynasty of Ancient China.*

Ancient Egypt

In 30 seconds...

Egypt was home to a very developed civilisation 3,000 years before the birth of Christ. We know so much about the Ancient Egyptians because of all the artefacts we have found that tell us about their daily life. They worshipped many gods and goddesses, fought with nations around them and lived on the banks of the Nile. Their empire came to an end when the Romans arrived, but their influence lived on in Greek, Roman and even modern times.

What do I need to know?

When and where were the Ancient Egyptians around?

Egypt, situated in North Africa, was home to a very developed civilisation more than 3,000 years before the birth of Christ. The Ancient Egyptians were united under one ruler, Menes, and this empire lasted until 30 BC, when the Romans conquered Egypt. Their civilisation depended on the River Nile, the longest river in the world (4,187 miles or 6,738 km), providing them with water and fertile land for farming in a hot and humid landscape. Ancient Egypt survived the rule of several foreign rulers, including Ethiopians (Nubians), Greeks and Romans, until the death of Egyptian queen Cleopatra in 30 BC, when Egypt became part of the vast Roman Empire.

How do we know about the Ancient Egyptians?

Archaeologists have found many artefacts from Ancient Egypt, mostly from rich people and kings (pharaohs), who had objects buried with them when they died. These were discovered in the tombs inside the pyramids and later in some of the tombs that were hidden underground. There are also written accounts of life in Ancient Egypt, from Roman and Greek writers and references in the Bible. The well-preserved bodies of dead Egyptians have been discovered in the tombs, complete with objects from daily life that tell us how they lived – jewellery, pottery, furniture and tools.

How they lived

The richer Egyptians lived in stone houses, whereas the poorer folk had homes built of mud that had been baked solid in the sun. Nobles had servants, furniture and banquets where they would eat the finest foods including different meats, cakes, figs, dates and so on, washed down with beer and wine. Poorer families tended to make do with a more basic diet, which included fruit, bread, vegetables, beer and occasionally meat. Children would enjoy playing with toys such as spinning tops, carved animals and balls, and adults would enjoy listening to and playing music, and dancing.

How they worked

Living in a hot and dry country, the Egyptians depended on the Nile, which runs through the middle of Egypt. Each year, heavy rains between July and October would raise the level of the Nile and flood the ground around it, depositing a layer of silt that was very fertile. The farmers would scatter seeds by hand and oxen would drag ploughs. The Egyptians grew mostly wheat and barley and also hunted animals that lived along the river banks, as well as picking papyrus reeds to use as scrolls. They also dug channels to irrigate the fields, although there was a danger of flooding. There were three main seasons for the Ancient Egyptians: Akhet (when the Nile would flood); Peret (when the crops were planted into the fertile soil); and Shemu (the harvest season). As well as farming or working on the land, there were also craftsmen and scribes. Scribes could read and write and belonged to a very well-regarded profession. Scribes wrote in hieroglyphs on tombs and temples. Craftsmen included metal-workers, carpenters, jewellers and barbers; boys from an early age were expected to learn a craft from their father or an artisan, and only the rich children went to school. Girls would stay at home and learn from their mother how to look after the household; women were held in high regard in Egyptian society.

How they fought

During the Old Kingdom, Ancient Egypt was generally a peaceful kingdom and it did not have a standing army. However, after being invaded by the Hyksos, who conquered Lower Egypt, the Egyptians developed their own army; they built powerful chariots and fought with archers, footsoldiers and charioteers. During the Middle and New Kingdoms, some of the pharaohs, such as Rameses II and III, would lead the army into battle. The most famous battle was the Battle of Kadesh in 1285 BC, fought between the pharaoh Rameses II and the Hittites. After being ambushed by the Hittites, Rameses was saved by the arrival of reinforcements and the pharaoh claimed a famous victory, although it was more of a draw. At various times, the Egyptians were conquered by the Greeks, Romans and Persians.

What they believed

The Ancient Egyptians had many gods and goddesses. Many had the body of a human mixed with the head of an animal, as the Egyptians believed that gods and goddesses could appear as a human or an animal. Some of the most important deities included: Ra, Shu, Tefnut, Geb, Nut, Osiris, Isis, Set and Nephthys.

Mummies and tombs

Egyptians believed that when they died, they went to another world and so needed to be equipped for this eventuality. That is why the rich people and the pharaohs were buried with jewellery, tools, chariots, weapons and so on, and their tombs became targets for grave robbers. The pharaohs were originally buried in the pyramids before their tombs were moved to underground sites. They were buried in the Valley of the Kings, near Luxor, and that is where the tomb of Tutankhamun was discovered in 1922 by Howard Carter. Ancient Egyptians mummified the dead bodies of the rich nobles and kings, preserving them as much as they could for use in the afterlife in the company of Osiris, the King of the Dead. To get there, their heart would be weighed against the Feather of Truth by the god Anubis; if they passed, they would enter the afterlife with Osiris, but if they failed, they would be eaten by the monster Ammit. Egyptians believed that the spirit may die if the body was not preserved, which is why they made mummies.

Why we remember them

There are many reasons why we remember the Ancient Egyptians. First of all, we have discovered so many artefacts from their daily life which have given us valuable information on how they lived, although there are not many items from the poorer sections of society. Nevertheless, we know more about Ancient Egypt than any other ancient civilisation. The pyramids, still so impressive, are even more incredible when you realise they were built without modern machines: just thousands of people, not slaves, working together to move mountains of stone, thus creating a structure that is now synonymous with the name Egypt. Their medical skills in mummifying bodies spread to Greek and Roman doctors. There were also a huge number of inventions that the Ancient Egyptians were credited with, such as mosaic glass, the sailing boat, paper (papyrus), beer and many other things.

Key words

Nubians: The people of southern Egypt and northern Sudan.
Pharaoh: The name the Ancient Egyptians gave to their kings.
Pyramids: The giant tombs built for dead pharaohs.
Hieroglyphs: Writing system that uses pictures rather than words.
Papyrus: Reeds that were pressed together, dried, pressed again and written on. They could also be used to make small fishing boats.
Ammit: The Devourer of the Dead; if the dead person's heart was weighed against the Feather of Truth and was found to be too heavy (because of their evil deeds) to enter the afterlife, this goddess would devour their heart.
Akhet: The first season.
Peret: The second season.
Shemu: The third season.

Important dates

Old Kingdom: 2649–2150 BC
Middle Kingdom: 2134–1783 BC
New Kingdom: 1550–1070 BC

Important people

Menes: Ancient Egyptian Pharaoh who reigned between c.3000 BC and c.3100 BC. It is thought by many scholars that King Menes united Upper and Lower Egypt, making him the first pharaoh of both kingdoms.
Cleopatra: Ancient Egyptian queen who had romantic liaisons with Julius Caesar and Marc Anthony. Marc Anthony was falsely informed that Cleopatra had died, so he committed suicide. When Cleopatra heard the news about Anthony's death, she famously ended her own life too and they were buried together.
Rameses II: Also known as Rameses the Great, often thought to be the greatest and most powerful pharaoh of Ancient Egypt.
Rameses III: Often considered the last great pharaoh; it is thought that Rameses III was assassinated.

Useful links

www.ancientegypt.co.uk/menu.html Excellent site from the British Museum.
www.childrensuniversity.manchester.ac.uk/interactives/history/egypt/
www.bbc.co.uk/education/topics/zg87xnb
www.ancientegyptonline.co.uk/index.html
www.pbs.org/wgbh/nova/ancient/explore-ancient-egypt.html Explore Ancient Egypt.
www.neok12.com/Ancient-Egypt.htm Videos on Ancient Egypt.
www.eyewitnesstohistory.com/tut.htm Primary sources from Howard Carter.

Lesson 1 Where is Egypt?

Getting started
In pairs, pupils write down one word or phrase that they first think of when they hear the phrase 'Ancient Egypt'. Poll their answers and see what the most popular answer is.

Class activities
- Show the class a map of Africa. Can they identify where Egypt is? Can they name any of the surrounding countries?
- Provide pupils with a photocopied map of Egypt. Can they find the Nile? Ask pupils how they would describe the climate and landscape in Egypt. Why would the Nile be so important to Ancient Egyptians? Pupils write/draw in key features such as Mediterranean Sea, Red Sea, Nile, major cities. When they have finished, ask them up to the front to fill in details on the board.
- Explain the three main seasons: Akhet, Peret and Shema. Pupils create a table to write and illustrate what happens in each season. Less-able pupils can make a wheel-type diagram.
- Pose the question: what would happen if the Nile did not flood enough, or flooded too much?

Plenary material
Pupils form pairs. The teacher calls out one of the key words from the lesson (Nile; Akhet; Peret; Shema) and the first pupil tells their partner about it. They swap for each key word.

Lesson 2 How were the pyramids built?

Getting started
Ask pupils to write down in the backs of their books who they think built the pyramids.

Class activities
- Make a list of answers from pupils; some of them probably said the pyramids were built by slaves or foreigners. Ask them where they got this impression from – a film or cartoon?
- Explain that the pyramids were built by native Egyptians, many of whom would have been agricultural workers; during the season when the Nile flooded, they would have looked for other work. Show some pictures of the pyramids and give the class some facts about their size: how would they be built? Pupils discuss ideas.
- Go to www.hyperstaffs.info/work/history/nixon/versions/flashindex.html. Pupils make brief notes on key points as they go through the slides.
- Show pupils five short clips on building the pyramids: **www.bbc.co.uk/education/clips/ z849wmn**.
- Pupils imagine they are working on the pyramids; ask them to write a series of short diary entries.

Plenary material
Pupils choose the most descriptive sentence from their diary as a pyramid builder and read it out to the rest of the class.

Lesson 3 Inside a tomb

Getting started
Pupils recap who built the pyramids: the teacher asks a number of key questions that pupils answer in small groups or pairs.

Class activities
- Ask pupils if they know why the pyramids were built. After fielding their ideas, explain why the pyramids were built: to bury the Egyptians' pharaohs and queens. Scenes from their life were painted on the tomb walls. As they believed in an afterlife, they would be buried with belongings and riches that they would need in the next life.
- Show pupils a picture of paintings found inside a tomb or go to www.britishmuseum.org/explore/galleries.aspx and explore Room 61: the tomb chapel of Nebamun. He was not a pharaoh but, as were other rich Egyptians, he was buried with possessions and paintings of his life. Pupils imagine they will be buried Ancient-Egypt style: what would their painting show? They illustrate this and annotate it; it should show things they enjoy doing and objects that are important to them today.
- Pose the question: with riches and treasures buried in the tombs, what might happen? Explain that many of the tombs were raided by grave robbers who stole the treasures within.
- Ask pupils how this could be avoided. After fielding their answers, explain that the Ancient Egyptians stopped building pyramids for their pharaohs and started burying them underground in the hope they would not be discovered by tomb raiders. (But they still found almost all of them!)
- Show pupils the Valley of the Kings on a map. Explain who was buried there.

Plenary material
In pairs, one pupil pretends to be an Ancient Egyptian; the other is a modern-day reporter. The reporter gets to ask three questions for the Ancient Egyptian to answer about how they were buried.

Further activities for pupils

- Investigate Howard Carter discovering the tomb of Tutankhamun. What might the archaeologist have been feeling as he discovered it in 1922?
- Look at how the Ancient Egyptians preserved the dead: mummification.
- Investigate the gods and goddesses of Ancient Egypt.
- Look at daily life in Ancient Egypt and what jobs people had.
- Research food and drink in Ancient Egypt.
- Look at what archaeologists have found. What does it tell us about life in Ancient Egypt?
- Compare modern Egypt with Ancient Egypt. Is there anything that has stayed the same? How is it different?
- Investigate how the Ancient Egyptians fought, focusing on the Battle of Kadesh.
- As each topic is covered, plot events on a timeline.

Further research for pupils

www.britishmuseum.org
www.museum.manchester.ac.uk
www.hyperstaffs.info/work/history/nixon/versions/flashindex.html Interactive site with activities on gods and goddesses; mummies; hieroglyphs; River Nile and pyramids.
www.bbc.co.uk/history/ancient/egyptians/launch_gms_pyramid_builder.shtml Pupils can be a pyramid builder! Have they got what it takes?
The Prince of Egypt (1998), directed by Brenda Chapman, Steve Hickner and Simon Wells.
Cleopatra (1963), directed by Joseph E. Manciewicz.
The Kane Chronicles by Rick Riordan: An entertaining series of fictional books with plenty of Ancient Egyptian content.
A Place in the Sun by Jill Rubalcaba.
iPad: *Gods of Egypt* (Francisco Pageo); *Pocket History Ancient Egypt* (MAD Learning); *Pharaoh's Escape* (Mobest Media Ou), *The Timebuilders: Pyramid Rising 2* (BlooBuzz Studios).

Cross-curricular links

Art and design: Make or paint a death mask for a pharaoh.
English: Write a story based on a character from Ancient Egypt, such as a scribe or a farmer.
Religious studies: Investigate the religious beliefs of the Ancient Egyptians and create a fact file of some of their most famous gods and goddesses.
Computing: Design a poster all about the pyramids.
Geography: Investigate the climate and terrain in Egypt and how this influenced how the Ancient Egyptians lived and worked.
Science: Investigate Ancient Egyptian inventions.
Drama: Write a short script and act out Howard Carter discovering the tomb – or a similar discovery of an undiscovered, undisturbed tomb in the Valley of Kings.
Music: Make up a song about the Ancient Egyptians; either focus on one particular aspect or make it a general summary.

Progression

1. Pupils can locate Egypt on a map and describe its landscape and physical features.
2. Pupils can explain who the pyramids were built for, and their purpose.
3. Pupils can recall the three different seasons and what happened in each of them.
4. Pupils can explain how the pyramids were built and why the Ancient Egyptians stopped building them.
5. Pupils understand what was buried with Ancient Egyptians and why.

The Indus Valley

In 30 seconds. . .

Built around the fertile valley of the Indus river, the Indus Valley civilisation flourished at around the same time as the Egyptians built the pyramids. Although we have so far been unable to decipher their ancient writing, archaeologists have managed to piece together what life in their cities would have been like through careful examination of ruins, pottery, seals and other objects.

What do I need to know?

Where and when was the Indus Valley civilisation?

The Indus Valley is found in what is now Pakistan, near the border of India, in South Asia. It gets its name from the Indus river, which flows from the Himalayas to the Arabian Sea. As a civilisation, it lasted between 2500 BC and 1700 BC, with archaeological evidence suggesting there were hundreds of towns in the area.

What did archaeologists find?

Although the ruins of Harappa were initially discovered in the 1820s, it was not until 1921 that archaeologists started to excavate the site. They found lots of objects made of gold, silver, stone and clay, as well as statues, walls and the ruins of buildings.

Why did people live in the Indus Valley?

Being situated around the Indus river meant that the land was very fertile, and so excellent for crops. The river would have provided fresh water, which could also have been used to irrigate crops. Being near to the river also meant that people and goods could be transported easily, with Harappa perhaps being used as a place for trading.

How did people live in the Indus Valley?

The city of Mohenjo-Daro contained flat-roofed houses made from mud bricks that had been baked. Houses were large and square-shaped, and some had a courtyard in the middle. There were wells for fresh water and a few houses even had a toilet, known as a privy. The city had a drainage system, which took waste water away from the houses. The Great Bath at Mohenjo-Daro was 40 feet (12 metres) long and 23 feet (7 metres) wide, and it is regarded as the earliest-known public bath. To make it waterproof, the builders used tight-fitting bricks and sealed them with waterproof tar. It may have been used for religious ceremonies. Overlooking the city was a mound, with a citadel on top. Within the citadel were several large buildings, including a granary, which stored grain. Shops were also discovered, as well as large halls where people could have met and talked. The streets were straight and laid out in a grid pattern. The city had strong walls, towers and gateways and there was a bustling trade with people travelling to the cities, as well as local traders venturing as far as Mesopotamia. To the north of the city, there were forests, whose trees would have provided fuel. There was also good grassland in the area, providing lush grazing for cattle, sheep and goats.

Seals and symbols

Thousands of seals were found at Mohenjo-Daro, and although they have writing on them, we have not yet been able to work out what it means. Many of the seals have pictures of animals, such as tigers, water buffalo, antelopes and fish. As we have been unable to decipher what the writing means, we know less about the Indus Valley than other early civilisations, although archaeologists have pieced together what they can through studying the buildings, statues, seals and other objects they have found.

Key words

Mohenjo-Daro and Harappa: Two of the biggest cities found in the Indus Valley.
Citadel: Fortress.

Important dates

5000 BC: Religious practices take place in the Indus Valley.
3300 BC: Farmers build villages in the Indus Valley.
3000 BC: Small towns and settlements start to appear in the Indus Valley.
2600 BC: Farmers use ploughs in the Indus Valley.
2500 BC: The Indus civilisation flourishes.
1900 BC: The Indus Valley civilisation starts to decline.

Important people

Daya Ram Sahni: Archaeologist who excavated the ruins of Harappa.
R.D. Banerji: Archaeologist who discovered the ruins of Mohenjo-Daro.

Interesting fact

The first clothing buttons and measuring ruler were found in the Indus Valley. The people also invented the stepwell, a series of steps leading to a pool, pond or bath.

Useful links

www.harappa.com/teach/ Range of resources for teachers.
www.dkfindout.com/uk/history/indus-valley-civilization/
www.teachindiaproject.org/Indus_Valley_Civilization.htm
www.ancientindia.co.uk/indus/home_set.html Includes an activity for pupils.
www.teachinghistory100.org/objects/about_the_object/indus_valley_seals Focuses on seals found and what they might mean.

Lesson 1 Where was the Indus Valley?

Getting started
List some famous dates on the board and ask pupils to place them in chronological order, from earliest to latest. For example: *1066, 1918, 1588, 1215, 55 BC, 1485.*

Class activities
- Explain to the pupils that they are going to be looking at an ancient civilisation. Show a picture of the Indus Valley on the board. Identify key geographical features of the area. Why did people settle in the area?
- Show slides from www.harappa.com to identify the landscape of the Indus Valley. What difficulties would there be when living in such an area?
- Pupils complete a short written task: *People settled in the Indus Valley because. . .*
- On a timeline, plot when the Indus Valley civilisation existed; plot some other historical periods on the timeline that pupils have studied to put it into perspective.

Plenary material
In groups, pupils describe the region of the Indus Valley and why people settled there.

Lesson 2 How do we know about the Indus Valley?

Getting started
Look at what is in the bin in the classroom. On the board, write out the items that are in there. In small groups, pupils come up with a few statements about what the items say about the people they came from.

Class activities
- Explain that the process they went through in the starter activity was similar to how archaeologists work. Ask pupils if they know what an archaeologist is.
- Ask pupils what sorts of things archaeologists find: what questions would the archaeologists have wanted answers to when they started to discover the remains at Harappa? If pupils need help, ask them what a future civilisation, 5,000 years in the future, might want to find out about us today. (Education; housing; food; religious beliefs; war/army; fashion; farming; childhood; pastimes; language; writing, etc.)
- Using www.harappa.com show pupils some remains of objects found in the Indus Valley. What do these objects tell us about the people?

Plenary material
On a piece of paper, pupils write down three objects that would tell someone 5,000 years in the future the most information about them. What would they be and why? They then feed their ideas back to the class.

Lesson 3 How did people live in the Indus Valley?

Getting started

Think of three objects that say something about you, the teacher (or about someone you know). Write them on the board and ask pupils in groups to extract as much information about the person as they can from those three objects. What statements can they make?

Class activities

- Explain that the pupils are going to be exploring some of the remains found at Mohenjo-Daro. What would they expect to find as archaeologists?
- Using www.harappa.com/har/moen0.html, show a picture of the Great Bath: without telling the pupils what it is, ask them what they think it is. Before revealing the answer, ask what questions they would need answering about it to make a decision on what it is.
- Pupils draw and annotate the Great Bath at Mohenjo-Daro.
- Show pupils some other pictures from www.harappa.com. Can they think of a set of three questions to ask about each picture? (What is it? What is it used for? Do we still have it today?)

Plenary material

In groups, pupils feed back what they have learnt about Mohenjo-Daro from the lesson. Each pupil has to talk for ten seconds before the next person in their group continues.

Further activities for pupils

- Reconstruct a plan of Mohenjo-Daro.
- Look at the evidence found at Mohenjo-Daro. How does it compare to a city today?
- Research the artefacts found at Mohenjo-Daro. What do they tell us about the people who used them? Make a list of artefacts, recording facts about them.
- Look at the symbols inscribed on seals and pots. What do pupils think they mean? Pupils could invent their own language using symbols.

Further research for pupils

www.bbc.co.uk/schools/primaryhistory/indus_valley/

Indus Valley: Green Lessons from the Past by Benita Sen, Rupak Ghosh and Yatindra Kumar.
iPad: *The Route to the Roots Part 2 of 2 (An Indus Valley Archaeological Adventure)*, iRemedi Corp, ages 9+, a comic-book adventure.

Cross-curricular links

Art and design: Draw/paint an artefact from the Indus Valley.

English: Write about a day in the Indus Valley. What would it be like to live there?

Religious studies: Investigate the religious views and beliefs of the Indus Valley and compare them with Hinduism.

Computing: Create a poster or PPT showing some of the artefacts and remains found.

Geography: Explore the region of the Indus Valley and investigate how it supported the early civilisation.

Science: Investigate some Indus Valley inventions: the button, ruler and stepwell.

Drama: Write a short radio script where pupils discuss what Indus Valley symbols might mean.

Progression

1. Pupils can place the Indus Valley on a map and timeline.
2. Pupils can explain why people settled in the Indus Valley.
3. Pupils can explain what some objects tell us about a civilisation.
4. Pupils can identify artefacts and describe how people used to live in the Indus Valley.
5. Pupils can describe types of buildings and what they tell us about people in the Indus Valley.

12 Ancient Greece

What does the curriculum say?

- *Pupils should engage in a study of Greek life and achievements, and their influence on the Western world.*

Life and achievements in Ancient Greece

In 30 seconds...

Although the Olympics are probably the most recognisable legacy from the Ancient Greeks today, if you dig a little deeper, you will unearth a huge amount that they contributed to modern life, in terms of government, inventions, writing, mathematics, philosophy, theatre and warfare. The list is almost endless.

What do I need to know?

Who were the Ancient Greeks?

When we think of the typical Ancient Greek civilisation, it is around the fourth to the fifth centuries BC, a period known as the Classical period. However, it existed for a long time before that, as far back as the Neolithic period, which started around 6000 BC.

How do we know about the Ancient Greeks?

We can still see Ancient Greek architecture today, with the Parthenon and its elegant columns as a fine example. The work of archaeologists has revealed all sorts of artefacts, such as pottery, jewellery, tools and vases; as science gets ever more advanced, so we are learning more about these ancient sites. With their command of a fully developed alphabet, the Greeks left us many writings that reveal life at the time, although, as ever, caution should be exercised when dealing with their reliability. Ancient Greek philosophers, writers, poets, historians, traders and politicians passed down writings, as well as myths, legends and oral traditions.

Ancient city-states

Ancient Greece was slightly different to the Greece of today in that it was divided up into several city-states that were self-governed. This was because many places were isolated due to the mountainous terrain. The two largest and most powerful city-states in Ancient Greece were Athens and Sparta. These two states were very different: whereas Athens was a democracy, Sparta was ruled by military might. At times, these two great city-states (and other city-states) came into conflict with one another, but they also allied with each other when faced with an enemy that threatened them all, such as the Persians.

Culture and society

Greek families were traditionally not very large, with boys seen as more important than girls. Girls would help around the home, while most of the boys would be sent to school. They learnt reading, writing and arithmetic at the teacher's house and did physical education. This would involve wrestling, running and other exercises. Richer girls may have had a tutor at home, where they would learn to read, write, sing and play music. However, women were expected to stay at home and look after the family and wait on their husbands. In Athens, women were not allowed to vote, and neither were slaves or foreigners. The first democracy originated in Athens in 508 BC, with the Assembly debating issues. There had to be 6,000 citizens present for the Assembly debate to start, and people were dragged in from outside if there were not enough. There were 500 members elected to the Council, who drew up new policies and laws before debating them in the Assembly. Slaves were either Greeks or foreigners, often captured soldiers from barbarian armies or tribes. Slaves would do the most unpleasant and dangerous jobs, such as working in the silver mines. They could be granted freedom after a long period of outstanding service but they would never be able to be part of the Assembly.

Warfare

Ancient Greek foot soldiers were called hoplites, and they formed a phalanx formation in battle. This was between four and eight rows deep, with hoplites ready to step in to fill any gap caused by a falling comrade. Hoplites wore armour and were armed with a shield, spear and short sword. Spartans were particularly renowned for their fighting ability and were expected to return home from battle either holding their shield or with their body laid out on it if killed in battle, but never without it. Athens had a powerful fleet and Greek warships were called triremes, which were powered by oarsmen (and a sail when necessary) and had a battering ram at the front. These were important in defending Greece due to the geography of the country, with so much water surrounding the islands. The Persians invaded Greece under the command of their king, Xerxes, and were defeated at the Battle of Marathon by the Athenians. The Persians retreated and returned with an even bigger army, which was famously held up by a much smaller force of Spartans at Thermopylae. However, the Persians eventually prevailed and marched into Athens, whose citizens promptly fled the city. Although the city was destroyed, the Greek army and navy were still intact and when Xerxes decided that the best way to reach the rest of Greece was by sea, the two navies collided in a massive battle. The Greeks lured the larger Persian navy into a narrow channel between mainland Greece and the island of Salamis and the Greek triremes destroyed the Persian ships, winning the battle. Although the huge Persian army stayed as its navy retreated, it too was eventually beaten by the Greeks, who no longer feared the Persians.

Religion

The ancient Greeks had many gods, with Zeus as the king of the gods. Others included:
Apollo: God of sun, light and music.
Aphrodite: Goddess of love and beauty.
Ares: God of war.
Athena: Goddess of wisdom and war.
Dionysus: God of wine and the grape harvest.
Hades: God of the underworld.
Hermes: Messenger of the gods.
Poseidon: God of the sea and earthquakes.

The Greeks believed that there were 12 major deities, considered to be the most important of the gods, who lived on Mount Olympus. Although there were many gods, these twelve came from the same group, called the Olympians, of which Zeus was leader. Hades was not always considered to be part of this group, since he resided in the underworld and not on Olympus. Although the gods were immortal, they experienced the same emotions as humans; they would argue, fight, fall in love, be jealous, be sad, be angry. The Greeks believed that the gods directly influenced how their lives went, so they wanted to please them as much as possible, to gain their favour. Temples were built that contained statues of gods, and the people made offerings of food and drink outside the temple, not in it. Sacrifices of animals such as oxen and sheep were also made on shrines or altars outside the temple. The animal would be killed by a priest, part of it used as a burnt offering to the gods and the rest used for a feast. The Parthenon is the most famous temple; work started on it in 447 BC and it contains a huge statue for the goddess Athena, for whom it was built.

Legends and myths

There are many famous legends and myths from the times of the Ancient Greeks, and these stories are still told today. Examples of legends and myths include:

- Theseus and the Minotaur
- Perseus and Medusa
- The 12 Labours of Hercules
- Icarus and Daedalus
- Pandora's Box
- King Midas and the Golden Touch

Greek influence on the Western world

Democracy

The legacy of the Ancient Greeks lives on to this day, and their way of life has had a huge influence on civilisations that followed them. Any country whose government is a democracy stems from a form of ruling that was first used in Athens in 508 BC.

Theatre

Originating from the Greek word *theatron*, theatre started as songs and dances performed at a religious festival for the god Dionysus. Over time, these developed into the plays that we know today. Two of the most popular types of plays were tragedy and comedy, and the word comedy comes from the Greek word *komoidia*, meaning 'merry-making'. Theatres were traditionally horseshoe-shaped, a style that is still copied, and only men were allowed to become actors. To portray the emotions of the characters, they would wear masks with exaggerated faces that could be seen at the back of the theatre.

Greek words

Many English words have Greek origins; indeed, the word 'history' comes from the Greek word *historia*, meaning 'enquiry'. The English alphabet is based on a Roman version that was in turn taken from a Greek alphabet. Originally, the Greeks wrote from right to left, as they had based their alphabet on that of the Phoenicians, who were from the Middle East. However, after the Greeks added vowels (the Phoenicians used only consonants), they started writing from left to right. Although almost all of their original works were written on papyrus and have therefore rotted away, Greek writing was copied by Romans and thus preserved. Today, many word roots, prefixes and suffixes come from Greek.

Amazing minds and inventions

Ancient Greece certainly had its fair share of brilliant minds, with many of them household names over 2,000 years later and their ideas living on. These include Pythagoras, famous for his theory on calculating the sides of a right-angled triangle; Euclid, another mathematician whose theories and mathematical rules were used in a textbook 2,000 years on; the astronomers Eratosthenes, who calculated with remarkable accuracy the circumference of the Earth, and Anaxagoras, who said the Moon reflected light from the Sun. Archimedes, the famous inventor and mathematician, is known for Archimedes' Principle; this states that an object displaces its own volume of water, and he also invented a giant screw which can draw water up from a low level to higher level: a similar device is still used by some farmers in Egypt. The famous Greek doctor, Hippocrates, is still known today for the oath that doctors have to take, the Hippocratic oath, and Greek doctors would perform dissections on human bodies to understand more about how they worked.

Olympics

The first ever Olympic Games were held in 776 BC in Olympia, to honour Zeus. Only Greek free men could compete, and some of the events are still recognisable today: running, horse racing, boxing and the pentathlon (long jump, discus, running, javelin and wrestling). The athletes were highly trained and their honed bodies were depicted in paintings and statues. The marathon race gets its name from the Battle of Marathon, where a Greek runner called Pheidippides ran all the way from the battlefield at Marathon to Athens, to deliver the message of victory. The modern Olympic Games started in Athens in 1896, and the Olympic torch and lighting of the flame are inspired by the lighting of a flame at the altar of Zeus from ancient times.

Key words

Democracy: From the Greek words *demos* (people) and *kratos* (rule).
Hoplite: Greek footsoldier.
Trireme: Greek warship.
Myth: A traditional story about gods or heroes.

Important dates

c.1250 BC: The Trojan War.
700s BC: Greece is divided into city-states.
776 BC: The first Olympic Games are held at Olympia.
c. 500–336 BC: The Classical period.
490 BC: The Battle of Marathon.
480 BC: The Battle of Thermopylae.
431–404 BC: The Peloponnesian Wars between Athens and Sparta.
338 BC: Philip II of Macedonia unites Greece and declares war on the Persians.
336 BC: Alexander becomes king and builds a vast empire.
323 BC: Alexander dies.

Important people

Alexander the Great: Legendary King of Macedonia and a brilliant general, who famously never lost a battle.

Pericles: A general and politician, elected into office between 443 and 429 BC. He was an outstanding speaker, able to sway people to his line of thinking.

Socrates: One of the three great Greek philosophers, alongside Plato (one of his students) and Aristotle.

Plato: Famous Greek philosopher who was student of Socrates and a teacher to Aristotle. Plato wrote down some of the ideas of Socrates but also came up with many of his own, including his famous work *The Republic*.

Aristotle: Another famous philosopher. He tutored Alexander the Great when Alexander was young.

Eratosthenes: Famous Greek mathematician who also excelled in geography, astronomy and history.

Anaxagoras: Philosopher whose work involved cosmology and nature.

Archimedes: Famous mathematician and inventor.

Pheidippides: Greek messenger who ran 25 miles (40 km) from Marathon to Athens to deliver the message that the Greeks had won the battle.

Interesting fact

The city-states were often at war, but a truce would be called before the Olympics, so everyone could travel to Olympia safely.

Useful links

http://greece.mrdonn.org/myths.html Good list of myths and legends with other resources. Pupil-friendly.
www.theguardian.com/education/teacher-blog/2013/sep/24/how-to-teach-ancient-greece
www.besthistorysites.net/index.php/ancient-biblical-history/greece
www.historyforkids.net/ancient-greece.html
www.ducksters.com/history/ancient_greece.php

Lesson 1 What did the Greeks ever do for us?

Getting started

Tell pupils to imagine that they are transported 3,000 years in the future. What will we most remember in the future about the present day? Take feedback and gather ideas on the board.

Class activities

- Tell pupils they are going to be investigating the legacy of the Ancient Greeks by looking at images and artefacts, working in pairs/groups to explain what they reveal.
- To each group, hand out pictures showing the following: an ancient Olympic athlete; a Greek mask from the theatre; the words *auto, mega, mania*; a picture of the prime minister; a mathematics sum; a library; the Parthenon; space; a lighthouse; Theseus battling the Minotaur.
- In pairs or groups, pupils discuss and then record their ideas. What does the picture show? What does it tell us about Ancient Greece? They then draw their own picture.
- Ask pupils to feed back their ideas before *briefly* explaining: the Greeks invented the Olympics; they created the first theatres and plays; many everyday English words come from Greek words; Greeks created the first democracy; they had many great mathematicians; the first library was the library of Alexandria; we still use Greek-style architecture today, with pillars; they had many great minds and philosophers; they invented the lighthouse; they gave us many famous myths and legends.

Plenary material

Flash up the pictures that the pupils worked on, one at a time, showing each for about ten seconds. In pairs, pupils take turns to describe to their partner the picture's connections to Ancient Greece and today.

Lesson 2 Let's fight!

Getting started
Write the ten points discussed in the last lesson on the board. Put all the pupils' names into a hat and draw the first name out. This pupil comes to the front of the class and picks one aspect of Greek influence to tell the rest of the class about. They have 30 seconds to deliver their talk before they pick the next name from the hat. Continue until all points have been recapped.

Class activities
- Ask pupils what they have heard about Greek soldiers; some may mention Sparta or refer to a film. Tell them that they will be investigating how Ancient Greeks fought by looking at evidence.
- Split pupils into small groups. Give each group an evidence pack, comprising the following: a quote from the Greek Plutarch, from *Moralia* – '*Men wear their helmets and their breastplates for their own needs, but they carry shields for the men of the entire line*'; a picture of the Chigi vase showing hoplites; a picture of a Persian archer. Ask pupils to deduce what they can from the evidence in front of them, writing it down. (The shield was used not only to protect the soldier holding it, but was held in such a way as to protect the right side of the soldier on the left. The Chigi vase shows the equipment a hoplite had – spear, shield, helmet, etc. The Persian archer shows who the Greeks fought against, and that they had a different fighting style and weapons from the Greeks.)
- Take feedback on what pupils have found out, giving hints if necessary to encourage further debate and analysis.
- Go to www.britishmuseum.org/learning/schools_and_teachers/resources/all_resources/ resource_hoplites.aspx. Show pupils the PowerPoint presentation on Greek hoplites; there is also a mini lesson plan if needed. Focus on the importance of the shield. As legend has it, a Spartan mother said to her son as he left for battle, 'Come back with your shield or on it.' Ask pupils what they think this means.
- Explain how the hoplites fought, in the phalanx formation, and how effective this was.

Plenary material
Pupils list the equipment a hoplite had, in order of importance.

Lesson 3 Myths and legends

Getting started
Ask pupils to discuss in pairs what a myth is.

Class activities
- Take feedback from the pupils, writing their ideas of what a myth is on the board in a spider-diagram. Explain what a myth is and that the Greeks told mythical stories about their gods.
- Explain that they are going to be working on a Greek myth in the lesson. Can they name any?
- Find a version of Theseus and the Minotaur that is suitable for the class: one version (from halfway through the information about Theseus) is here: www.greekmythology.com/Myths/The_Myths/Theseus_Adventures/theseus_adventures.html. Photocopy the myth for pupils, enough for one each.
- Ask the pupils to read it and then discuss it in groups of three or four. Ask them to jot down the following: who the main characters are; what the problem is; how the problem is resolved. What questions do they have at the end?
- Tell them to look at it again, to assess the probability of events happening as told. It could be split into three main columns: *true*; *maybe true*; *not true*. Ask them to consider all parts of the story as they fill the columns in. This should lead to some entertaining discussions. Collate their ideas at the end on the board.
- Ask pupils if there is a moral to the story. Again, they may have several different ideas: they might focus on Perseus, or on his father Aegeus.

Plenary material
Pupils act out Theseus and the Minotaur in groups of four: Theseus, Aegeus, the Minotaur and Ariadne. They have two minutes to plan/rehearse for a 30-second performance to the rest of the class.

Further activities for pupils

- Explain that we get many words from the Greeks. Can pupils think of any? Write some roots, prefixes and suffixes on the board that we get from the Greeks. (Roots: *chron, path*; prefix: *auto*; suffixes: *ism, ist, ize*). In small groups, pupils try to think of some words we use today.
- Focus on how the Greeks fought and some of their biggest battles.
- Look at Greek architecture and how it has influenced us today.
- Research the birth of democracy and how it worked in Ancient Greece.
- Explore myths and legends and have pupils write their own Greek myth.
- Research Greek theatre, plays and masks; pupils could write their own Greek tragedy or comedy.
- Look at some of the great Greek minds that have influenced us.
- Investigate the history of the Olympic Games and how they are similar/different to the Games today.
- Look at Greek gods and goddesses and what the Ancient Greeks believed.
- Research the city-states and the relationship between Greece and Sparta.

Further research for pupils

www.youtube.com/watch?v=DBNWZxlan8g Animation of hoplites.

www.bbc.co.uk/schools/primaryhistory/ancient_greeks/arts_and_theatre/ Clip on attending a Greek theatre.

TV: *Jason and the Argonauts* (1963). *The 300 Spartans* (1962), directed by Rudolph Maté: Film about the epic stand at Thermopylae.

Helen of Troy (1956), Directed by Robert Wise: Original 1950s movie – don't confuse it with later films of the same name.

Gods and Warriors series by Michelle Paver; a wonderful series of books set in Ancient Crete and Egypt.

iPad: *Ancient Greece* (Kids discover): Interactive reading experience.

Visit: **www.britishmuseum.org** British Museum; **www.fitzmuseum.cam.ac.uk/index.html** Fitzwilliam Museum, Cambridge; **www.liverpoolmuseums.org.uk** National Museums, Liverpool; **www.ashmolean.org/departments/antiquities/about/AGreece/** Ashmolean Museum, Oxford.

Cross-curricular links

Art and design: Make a Greek theatre mask and perform a short play.

English: Pupils imagine they are a Greek hoplite in a battle against the Persians.

Religious studies: Investigate Greek gods and goddesses and Mount Olympus.

Computing: Create a presentation (e.g. PowerPoint) on an aspect of Ancient Greece.

Geography: Look at the climate and terrain of Ancient Greece. How did it affect the Greeks' lifestyle?

Science: Investigate some of the inventions by the Ancient Greeks.

Drama: Act out a myth from Ancient Greece.

PE: Stage the Battle of Marathon or Thermopylae.

Progression

1. Pupils can identify when the Ancient Greeks were a powerful civilisation and plot where they lived on a map.
2. Pupils can identify aspects and features of Greek life that helped shape Greek society.
3. Pupils can list some of the achievements of the Greeks.
4. Pupils can identify ways in which the Greeks have influenced the western world.
5. Pupils can explain why the Greeks were such a powerful society.
6. Pupils can identify and explain ways in which the Greeks have influenced the western world.

13 Non-European civilisation

What does the curriculum say?

- *Pupils should learn about a non-European society that provides contrasts with British history – one study chosen from: early Islamic civilisation, including a study of Baghdad c. AD 900; Mayan civilisation c. AD 900; Benin (West Africa) c. AD 900–1300.*

Early Islamic civilisation c. AD 900

In 30 seconds. . .

Islamic civilisation, with the newly built city of Baghdad at its heart, led the way in science, literature, mathematics, astrology and many other fields. With the Silk Road enabling merchants, traders and travellers to travel from East to West, Baghdad became the centre of learning, trade, commerce and ideas. Great scholars translated ancient literature into Arabic in huge libraries in the House of Wisdom; pioneering scientists, mathematicians, doctors and astrologers penned their ideas that would pave the way for numerous inventions; and the bustling markets traded goods from Spain to China. Although Baghdad was destroyed by the Mongols in 1258, the Golden Age of Islam would influence civilisation for many years to come, and continues to do so today.

What do I need to know?

An ideal place

Due to its geographical location, the Middle East was an ideal place for travellers from Europe, Asia and Africa to exchange goods, ideas, knowledge and trade.

Building a great city

The Abbasid Caliphate started to build a new city from scratch; a city that would be the largest in the world and the centre for learning, as philosophers, mathematicians, astrologers, doctors, scientists and engineers all headed there to further their studies. The city was Baghdad; work started in 762 and was completed six years later. Also known as the Round City, Baghdad was soon the largest city in the world, with over a million inhabitants. Being situated on the banks of the River Tigris meant that Baghdad became a hub for new learning, inventions and ideas, as merchants from all over the world visited the city.

Centre of learning

The time from the mid-seventh century to the mid-thirteenth century is known as the Golden Age of Islam. The Muslim Empire was one of the largest in the world, and together with China, it led the way in scientific discovery and achievement. At the library in the House of Wisdom, scholars, both Muslim and non-Muslim, translated classical works into Arabic. This meant that works that may have otherwise been lost and forgotten were brought from all over the world; works from Ancient Egypt, Ancient Rome, China, India, North Africa and Ancient Greece were translated first into Arabic, and from there into other languages. The art of making paper had been learnt from Chinese prisoners in AD 751 and soon spread throughout the empire, before eventually heading to Europe in the thirteenth century. The libraries they set up were the first to show similarities with their modern equivalents: works were arranged by category; material could be loaned out; and the libraries became public places. Although the area was under Muslim control and displayed Islamic values, there was religious freedom and this encouraged great thinkers from Jewish, Christian and other faiths to visit and contribute to this great period of creativity. The Silk Road saw travellers, traders and merchants going from the Far East to Europe, and Baghdad became the centre for learning, new inventions, new ideas and goods travelling to and fro along the great road.

New ideas

It was during this Golden Age that many new ideas and concepts emerged. The first hospitals saw patients being treated free of charge and looked after until they had recovered. With so many great minds in the area, there were huge advances in the field of medicine that improved the health of the inhabitants. Art and design flourished, too, with beautiful ornamental floors, ceilings, gardens and pottery being produced.

Famous minds

During the Golden Age of Islam, there were many famous and brilliant minds who contributed a huge amount to the fields of science, astronomy, mathematics, medicine and other areas.

Al-Khwarizmi: He was a famous astronomer, scientist and mathematician, and it is from him that we get the words 'algorithm' and 'algebra', which were named after a book that he wrote.

Ziryab: A famous musician, stylist and mathematician, Ziryab introduced the lute to Europe, and his ideas revolutionised lifestyles. He introduced new social customs to other countries, which soon spread.

Abd Al-Rahman al-Sufi: He was a nobleman and astronomer, whose book *The Book of Fixed Stars*, published c. AD 964, catalogued over a thousand stars and also refers to the Andromeda galaxy.

Abbas ibn Firnas: The first person to make a successful human flight, he constructed a pair of wings made from wood, silk and feathers before jumping off a cliff and gliding down. However, he had been so obsessed with the dynamics of flying, that he had neglected to think about the landing and injured his back, putting an end to any further attempts of flight.

Ibn Al Haytham: A pioneering scientist, his *Book of Optics* influenced European thinkers in the Renaissance period. He reasoned that light reflected from objects enables us to see them, and his ideas would later lead to the invention of the camera.

Ibn Yunus: An astronomer, mathematician and poet, his books recorded eclipses and included astronomical tables that were remarkably accurate.

End of an era

Baghdad was overtaken by Cordoba as the world's largest city in around AD 930, and the influence of the Abbasid Caliphate started to recede. Then, in 1258, the invading Mongols attacked the city. They spent a week utterly destroying Baghdad, where it was said the Tigris ran black with all the ink from the books thrown in, and red from the blood of the scientists and philosophers killed. What had once been a hub of learning, philosophy, science, mathematics and great minds was now totally ruined, with perhaps up to a million inhabitants slaughtered, officially marking the end of the Golden Age of Islam.

Key words

Caliph: Political and religious leader.
House of Wisdom: Also known as the *Bayt al-Hikma*, a place of learning that had a huge library with knowledge from around the world.

Important dates

751: Arabs learn to make paper.
762: Caliph Al-Mansur founds the city of Baghdad, making the decision to build it.
c. 768: The Round City (Baghdad) is finished.
c. 800: Baghdad becomes the largest city in the world.
c. 810: Baghdad becomes the centre for learning, with great advancements in maths, science and other disciplines.
c. 950: The Abbasid Caliphate starts to decline.
1258: The invading Mongols destroy Baghdad.

Important people

Al-Khwarizmi: Famous astronomer, scientist and mathematician.
Ziryab: Musician and stylist from Baghdad.
Abd Al-Rahman al-Sufi: Famous astronomer.
Abbas ibn Firnas: Used the first hang-glider and made the first parachute jump.
Ibn Al Haytham: Famous scientist who recognised that light reflected from objects enables us to see things; known in the West as Alhazen.
Ibn Yunus: Famous astronomer.

Useful links

http://islamichistory.org/the-golden-age/ Detailed website that chronicles the Golden Age, plus much more.

Lesson 1 A new city

Getting started
Tell pupils that they will be studying a civilisation that was around during the Dark Ages; ask them to discuss what this term might mean.

Class activities
- Explain that the Dark Ages got their name because there are almost no written sources surviving from this period in Britain. However, at the same time, in AD 900, in another part of the world, Baghdad was a great city and a centre of learning.
- Pupils imagine that they are in charge of building a new city: what are the main requirements for a successful city from that period? Pupils discuss ideas in small groups/pairs and then as a class. (Types of buildings, design of streets, defence, geographical features, etc.)
- Pupils design their own city from scratch and give it a name.

Plenary material
Pupils each describe one feature about their city that makes it great.

Lesson 2 The Round City

Getting started
Recap the important features of a city; compare with modern examples.

Class activities
- Explain that Baghdad was a city built from scratch. Tell pupils who built it and when, illustrating on a timeline.
- Show a map of where Baghdad was built. What can pupils point out about its location? (Tigris and Euphrates rivers; Silk Road; location in comparison to other continents.) Why would Baghdad be well placed as a city?
- Show pupils a picture of what the Round City looked like and ask them to identify features. What are the advantages/disadvantages of a round city?
- Research some of the features of the Round City. (Size/thickness of walls; buildings; towers; ditches; Golden Palace; the Great Mosque; House of Wisdom; etc.)
- Pupils draw and annotate the Round City.

Plenary material
Pupils write five facts about the Round City.

Lesson 3 A centre of learning

Getting started
Ask pupils to discuss what 'The Golden Age of Islam' might mean.

Class activities
- Gather ideas from the class. Explain that 'The Golden Age of Islam' refers to the period from the mid-seventh to the mid-thirteenth century when Baghdad was the world's centre of learning.
- Either assemble some facts about some of the famous minds of the day (such as Al-Khwarizmi) or have pupils carry out independent research in pairs or individually, compiling a few bullet points about each.
- Show pupils the Silk Road. Ask how it would contribute to making Baghdad a centre for learning.
- Explain that the House of Wisdom attracted scholars from all over the world, who translated works into Arabic. If pupils were creating a new House of Wisdom, what are the most important books/topics that would need to be covered for future generations? Ask them to design their own library for the future.

Plenary material
In pairs, pupils take turns explaining key words from the lesson to each other. If they get stuck, they say 'pass' and their partner can help them out. The one who has said 'pass' the fewest times is the winner.

Further activities for pupils

- Investigate the importance of the Silk Road, who travelled along it and to where.
- Read some of the stories from *One Thousand and One Arabian Nights*. Pupils write their own stories in the same style.
- Research some of the famous minds and their influence/inventions.
- Investigate the Fall of Baghdad in 1258.

Further research for pupils

The Thief of Baghdad (1940), directed by Ludwig Berger.
Ali Baba and the Forty Thieves (1944), directed by Arthur Lubin.
Aladdin (1992), directed by Ron Clements and John Musker.
Illustrated Arabian Nights by Anna Milbourne and Alida Massari.
Sinbad the Sailor by Marcia Williams, told in comic-strip format.
iPad: *Sinbad the Sailor (Arabian Nights)* Mindshapes Limited; *Arabian Night Run 3D* (Thepparit Insa).

Cross-curricular links

Art and design: Paint a picture of how you think Baghdad would have looked at its peak.

English: Imagine you are a traveller along the Silk Road and you visit Baghdad in AD 900. Write a series of diary entries as you explore the city.

Religious studies: Research some of the key features of Islam.

Computing: Create a poster about the Golden Age of Islam.

Geography: Research the area around Baghdad, explaining why it was in such a good position to flourish.

Science: Investigate and create a display on some of the inventions that came out of the Golden Age of Islam.

Drama: Write a series of news reports that focus on the Golden Age of Islam, starting with the building of the Round City and finishing with the Mongols destroying it.

Progression

1. Pupils can place Baghdad on a map and the Golden Age of Islam on a timeline.
2. Pupils can name some key features of the city of Baghdad c. AD 900.
3. Pupils recognise and can describe how Baghdad became a centre of learning.
4. Pupils can describe some key features of Baghdad and their importance to contributing to the Golden Age of Islam.
5. Pupils can describe and name some of the key individuals and their work from this period.

Mayan civilisation c. AD 900

In 30 seconds. . .

The Maya were pioneers in many fields: they developed a form of writing, had a calendar of 365 days, were keen astrologers and mathematicians, and built great stone palaces and temples. Their great city-states were ruled by kings but, around AD 900, the Maya left the cities and never returned.

What do I need to know?

Where was it located?

The Mayan civilisation was an indigenous society from what was known as Mesoamerica, the area that is now Mexico and Central America. The Maya occupied a large part of what is now Guatemala, Belize and Western Honduras.

The early Maya

The early Maya lived in simple villages and were farmers, growing corn (maize) that was very important to their daily life; they even had a god of maize! They also inhabited a region that had cacao trees and, although the Olmec (an earlier civilisation) had probably harvested the trees for their beans, the Maya became the first to use chocolate on a widespread basis. However, they did not eat it as a solid delicacy, but as a drink; they would mix it with spices (such as chilli or vanilla) or honey, and it would generally be enjoyed by the richer section of society, although not exclusively. They would also mix the bean with corn and water to make a gruel-like substance to be eaten. Cacao beans were even used for currency!

The Classical period

By the time of the Classical period, the Maya were split into three main territories: the tropical rainforests of the lowlands; the highlands in Guatemala and the Pacific coast; and the northern Yucatan peninsula. The Mayan civilisation was made up of city-states, with each ruled independently by a king. The Maya believed that their kings were given this power by the gods, acting as mediators between the gods and men, and the government was made up of a council comprised of rich nobles. They had strict laws, with various punishments such as slavery, fines or death.

Religion

The Maya had many nature gods. Itzamna, who created the Earth, and ruled day, night and heaven, was the most important,. The priests performed sacrifices, including human sacrifice, which was the supreme way to appease the gods: they would sacrifice criminals, slaves, orphans and children, with four *chacs* holding the victim down by the arms and legs before the priest performed the sacrifice.

The Mayan calendar

The Maya priests had 20-day months and two main yearly calendars: the Sacred Round had 260 days and the Vague Year, incredibly, had 365 days! These two calendars would cross over every 52 years, known as a 'bundle'. The Vague Year, also known as the *haab*, consisted of 18 months of 20 days, a total of 360 days, with an additional five-day period at the end, which was considered unlucky. The Vague Year was a solar calendar and the Sacred Round, also called *tzolkin*, was a religious calendar.

Mayan writing

The Maya used a very advanced form of writing, similar to hieroglyphs. Although it looks similar to the writing used by the Ancient Egyptians, it is in fact different: the Maya used glyphs (symbols) that represented sounds, objects or words. By putting them together, the Maya could write sentences and tell stories, which they recorded on bark or leather. As in many early civilisations, only the priests could write and they made books called *codices*, most of which were destroyed by the Spanish when they conquered the Maya in the sixteenth century.

Numbers

The Maya had a base 20 system, as opposed to the base 10 system that we use. The number zero was represented by an oval shell-like shape, with dots for numbers. When they got to five, a bar was added.

Art and architecture

The Maya were very good at stone sculpture, which they decorated with writing and carvings. A tall stone sculpture was called a *stela*, with the largest over 34 feet (10.4 metres) and weighing in at 65 tonnes! The Maya also made a lot of pottery and murals, although few murals have survived to this day. They would portray scenes from everyday life, hunting expeditions, gods and religious ceremonies. They also built magnificent palaces and pyramids, with La Danta temple in El Mirador standing over 250 feet (76.2 metres) tall.

The decline of the Maya

Around AD 900, the Maya started to abandon their cities. There are a few theories as to why they did this: they may have used up all the resources in the area and could no longer support their cities; too much internal fighting between city states may have caused a breakdown in their cultural traditions; or there may have been a particularly devastating drought. All of these may have been factors that saw the great Maya stone cities deserted one by one.

Why should we remember them?

The Maya developed astronomy, a writing system, mathematics, the calendar and a hieroglyphic system. They were skilled pottery makers, wrote thousands of books, built temples and developed hundreds of cities with schools, libraries and even sports arenas.

Key words

Mesoamerica: The area of Mexico and Central America before the Spanish conquest in the sixteenth century.

Sacred Year: Yearly calendar of 260 days; also called the *tzolkin*.

Vague Year: Yearly calendar of 365 days; also called the *haab*.

Glyphs: Symbols used in Mayan hieroglyphs.

Codices: Books (*codex* for a single book).

Itzamna: The most important Mayan god, who created the Earth.

Chacs: Named after the Rain God *Chac*, these were men who assisted the priest in the sacrifice.

El Mirador: One of the first of the large city-states.

Important dates

c. 1800 BC: The first Mayan civilisation. This period is known as the Preclassic period.

700 BC: The Maya start to develop writing.

600 BC: The Maya start to farm.

400 BC: The first Mayan calendars are carved into stone.

100 BC: The first Mayan pyramids are built.

c. AD 250–900: The Classical period.

AD 400: Teotihuacan becomes the dominant city-state.

Interesting fact

The Maya people used saunas! They were also excellent medics, using painkillers, treating fractures and developing dental techniques.

Useful links

www.mexicolore.co.uk/maya Plenty of information, resources and also school visits (within two hours of London).

www.scholastic.com/teachers/lesson-plan/ancient-maya Lots of teaching activities and ideas.

www.touropia.com/ancient-mayan-temples/ Ten Mayan temples as they look today.

Lesson 1 What can we tell about the Maya?

Getting started
Ask pupils to discuss in groups what artefacts/remains we would need in order to study an ancient civilisation.

Class activities
- Gather ideas from pupils and put them on the board.
- Show some pictures of Maya objects/buildings. What can pupils deduce from these pictures? Tell them to list their ideas in pairs and then feed back to the class.
- Locate the area of Mesoamerica on a map. Ask pupils to identify the geographical features and the advantages/disadvantages of living in such an area.
- On a timeline, plot the Mayan civilisation and compare it to European ones. What do pupils notice? (The Maya had the longest-running civilisation in history.)

Plenary material
In pairs, one pupil asks the other a question about a key point learnt during the lesson. They then swap. If one cannot answer, they say 'pass' and the interviewer has to answer their own question.

Lesson 2 Why do we remember the Maya?

Getting started
Recap key points from last lesson, with pupils working in pairs with a blank map and timeline to fill in details.

Class activities
- Explain that pupils will be working in groups to investigate why we remember the Maya. By looking at various pictures, they should work collaboratively to come up with both statements and questions about the Mayan civilisation.
- After splitting pupils into groups of three or four, hand out pictures showing the following: a Mayan temple; some Mayan tools; a Mayan city; Mayan sacrifice (exercise caution with the picture!); a table showing Mayan numbers to base 20; a Mayan ballgame.
- Pupils make a table of their results, with three columns: the first column describes the picture, along with their own brief illustration; the second column shows what they can deduce from the evidence; the third column contains any further questions they have about the evidence. This should encourage them to discuss it as a group, make deductions and want to learn more about the Maya.
- Pupils feed back to the class what they have found out about the Mayas from their own investigative activity and what questions they would like answered to reveal more.

Plenary material
Each pupil stands up and makes one statement or asks one question about the Maya.

Lesson 3 Food and drink

Getting started
Look at a map of where the Maya lived and pose the question: what would they eat in such an environment?

Class activities
- Take feedback, recording the pupils' answers on the board. Are there any surprising answers?
- Explain that Mesoamerica did not have the sort of large grazing mammals that Europe had, such as sheep, cows or goats. Therefore, they ate a lot of vegetarian food but also turkey, venison, duck, fish and shellfish.
- Show some pictures of what the Maya ate and cultivated: tobacco, cacao (chocolate), vanilla, cotton, corn, beans, chilli, avocado, squash, tomatoes, pineapple.
- Take feedback from the class and fill in any gaps. Explain the importance of chocolate to the Maya; it was even used as currency!
- Research some of the Mayan recipes. Pupils design their own menu for a Mayan banquet. (You could even make some dishes for your Mayan banquet for an authentic experience: find some ideas at www.scholastic.com/browse/subarticle.jsp?id=3172.)

Plenary material
Pupils vote on what they would most like from the Mayan banquet and would least like!

Further activities for pupils

- Research the Mayan number system in base 20 (vigesimal). Pupils write their own maths problems for each other using this system. At the end, pupils could invent their own new number system.
- Investigate how the Maya travelled around in the jungle without beasts of burden. Also research their elevated structures, *sacbeob*.
- Investigate Mayan writing and calendar systems. Pupils write their own glyphs about an event in their life.
- Look at the Mayan city-states and the buildings within (pyramids, temples, palaces, etc.) and the relationship between the city-states.
- Investigate why the Maya carried out human sacrifice. (Proceed with caution!)
- Look into why the Mayan civilisation came to end; pupils debate the different theories.
- Research Mayan tool making and technology (sculpture, art, tools, crafts) and their feats of engineering.
- Investigate the reasons why the Mayan civilisation came to an end, and look at their continued influence today.

Further research for pupils

www.mayankids.com Accessible facts for pupils.
http://mayas.mrdonn.org/index.html A real treasure chest of information, plus lots of PowerPoints.
Kings of the Sun (1963), directed by J. Lee Thompson: Wonderful film starring Yul Brynner.
The Seven Serpents Trilogy by Scott O'Dell.
iPad: *Forgotten Riddles: The Mayan Princess HD* (Big Fish Games); *Mayan Mysteries* (Dig-It Games), ages 9–11; *Farm Tribe HD* (Big Fish Games).

Cross-curricular links

Art and design: Design your own Mayan mask.
English: Write a series of diary entries about living in one of the city-states at its peak. Describe what you do, eat and see around you.
Religious studies: Investigate the religious beliefs of the Maya, and design a poster showing some ideas.
Computing: Create a presentation on a particular area of Mayan civilisation.
Geography: Research the climate and terrain where the Maya lived. What problems would they have living in such an area? Research some of the archaeological sites that you can visit today.
Science: Research Mayan astronomy and science. How advanced were they?
PE: Investigate the Mayan ballgame and then invent your own along similar lines.

Progression

1. Pupils can place the Maya on a timeline and map.
2. Pupils understand some of the achievements of the Maya.
3. Pupils can explain some aspects of how the Maya lived.
4. Pupils can identify the achievements of the Maya.
5. Pupils can explain why the Mayan civilisation lasted so long and was so successful.

Appendix

General history websites

www.history.org.uk/resources/primary_resources_135.html Includes lesson plans.
www.mrdonn.org/index.html Lots on ancient civilisations and some presentations. Contains an area for teachers and one for pupils. Recommended.
www.tes.co.uk/teaching-resources/ Tons of resources shared by teachers across the world. Sign up and enjoy! Add your own, or just plunder. . . or both!
https://michaelt1979.wordpress.com/2014/04/23/possibly-useful-history-resource/ Excellent set of history sheets on the new curriculum.

Magazines

www.historyanswers.co.uk All About History. Outstanding magazine that my pupils read from cover to cover each month. Very highly recommended!

The national curriculum

The full National Curriculum for Key Stages 1-2 can be found here:

The National Curriculum in England: Key Stages 1 and 2 Framework Documents (September 2013)
www.gov.uk/government/publications/national-curriculum-in-england-primary-curriculum